Basic Moral Philosophy

FOURTH EDITION

Robert L. Holmes
University of Rochester

THOMSON

WADSWORTH

Australia • Brazil • Canada • Mexico • Singapore • Spain
United Kingdom • United States

For Veronica

Publisher: Holly J. Allen
Philosophy Editor: Steve Wainwright
Assistant Editors: Lee McCracken,
   Barbara Hillaker
Editorial Assistant: Gina Kessler
Technology Project Manager: Julie Aguilar
Marketing Manager: Worth Hawes
Marketing Assistant: Alexandra Tran
Marketing Communications Manager: Stacey
   Purviance
Creative Director: Rob Hugel

Executive Art Director: Maria Epes
Print Buyer: Linda Hsu
Permissions Editor: Roberta Broyer
Production Service: Interactive Composition
   Corporation
Copy Editor: Michelle Gaudreau
Cover Designer: Yvo Riezebos
Cover Image: Photodisc Green / Getty Images
Compositor: Interactive Composition
   Corporation
Cover and Text Printer: Webcom Limited

Thomson Higher Education
10 Davis Drive
Belmont, CA 94002-3098
USA

For more information about our products,
contact us at:
Thomson Learning Academic Resource Center
1-800-423-0563

For permission to use material from this
text or product, submit a request online at
http://www.thomsonrights.com.
Any additional questions about permissions
can be submitted by e-mail to
thomsonrights@thomson.com.

Library of Congress Control Number: 2005937464

ISBN 0495007978

Contents

PREFACE   X

PART I | THE CONCERNS OF MORAL PHILOSOPHY

CHAPTER 1
The Nature of Ethics   1

1.1   Why Study Moral Philosophy?   1
1.2   The Origins of Morality   2
1.3   The Activity of Evaluating   3
1.4   Guiding and Directing Conduct   4
1.5   Value Judgments and Prescriptive Judgments   4
1.6   Normative Judgments and Descriptive Statements   5
1.7   Moral and Nonmoral Judgments   6
1.8   Three Kinds of Moral Problems   7

Notes   10
Discussion Questions   11

CHAPTER 2
Theories of Moral Right and Wrong   12

2.1   Moral Legalism and Moral Particularism   12
2.2   Rights-Based Theories   15
2.3   The Relationship Between Goodness and Rightness   15
2.4   Axiological and Deontological Moral Theories   17
2.5   Strong and Weak Deontologism   17
2.6   Consequentialist and Nonconsequentialist Axiological Theories   18
2.7   The Balance of Good and Bad in Consequences   19
2.8   The Good of Self, Others, and Collectivities   20
2.9   Micro Ethics and Macro Ethics   21
2.10   Outline   22
2.11   Character and Conduct   22

Notes   23
Discussion Questions   24

PART II | THE ETHICS OF VIRTUE

CHAPTER 3

Virtue in Ancient Philosophy   25

3.1   Kinds of Virtue   25
3.2   Plato and the Virtuous Person   26
3.3   The Soul's Function   27
3.4   Virtue, Goodness, and Right Conduct   29
3.5   Some Parallels in Hindu Ethics   31
3.6   Aristotle and the Habits of Virtue   33
3.7   The Mean   35
3.8   Moral Perceptions   35
3.9   The Practical Syllogism   36
3.10 Aristotle's Deontologism   37
3.11 Moral Virtue and Right Conduct   39
3.12 The Priority of an Ethics of Conduct over an Ethics
      of Virtue   39

      Notes   41
      Discussion Questions   41

CHAPTER 4

Virtue and Happiness   43

4.1   Plato and Aristotle on the Necessity of Virtue
      for Happiness   43
4.2   Perfectionism and the Highest Good   45
4.3   Augustine and the Permanence of the Highest Good   46
4.4   Does Everyone Desire Happiness? Nietzsche on Master
      Morality and Slave Morality   48
4.5   Is Moral Virtue Desirable?   51
4.6   The Importance of an Account of Conduct for the Ethics
      of Virtue   53

      Notes   53
      Discussion Questions   54

PART III | THE ETHICS OF CONDUCT

CHAPTER 5

Ethical and Psychological Egoism   55

5.1   Should We Seek Only Our Own Good?   55
5.2   Three Objections to Ethical Egoism   56

5.3   The Paradoxical Nature of Ethical Egoism   59
5.4   Psychological Egoism in Human Motivation   60
5.5   A Critique of Psychological Egoism   61
5.6   Butler's Argument   62

Notes   65
Discussion Questions   65

CHAPTER 6

The Divine Command Theory   66

6.1   The Case of Abraham and Isaac   66
6.2   Greek and Christian Views of Human Nature   67
6.3   God's Commands According to Judaism, Christianity, and Islam   67
6.4   The Relationship Between God's Will and Moral Rightness   68
6.5   A Problem for the Divine Command Theory   70
6.6   Commands to Do What Seems Impossibly Idealistic   71
6.7   An Attempted Reconciliation of the Commandment to Love with Human Judgments of What Is Possible   72
6.8   Does God Ever Command Us to Do What Is Wrong?   73
6.9   An Attempted Reconciliation of God's Commands with Human Judgments   74
6.10 Would God's Commanding the Torture of a Child Make It Right?   75
6.11 What Does It Mean to Call God Good?   76
6.12 Is God Extrinsically Good Because He Is a Loving God?   78
6.13 Can "Right" Be Defined by Reference to God's Commands?   79
6.14 Conclusion   80

Notes   81
Discussion Questions   82

CHAPTER 7

Natural Law Ethics   84

7.1   Morality and Nature   84
7.2   What Does Natural Law Ethics Mean by "Nature"?   85
7.3   Stoic Natural Law Ethics   86
7.4   The Stoic Conception of Duty   89
7.5   Christian Natural Law Ethics   90
7.6   Saint Thomas Aquinas   91

7.7 Human and Theological Virtues   91
7.8 Problems for Natural Law Ethics: Homosexuality and
     Sexual Harassment   93
7.9 Natural Law as Social, Political, and Legal Philosophy   96
7.10 Is God Necessary for Ethics?   96

     Notes   98
     Discussion Questions   99

CHAPTER 8

Kantianism   100

8.1 Morality Is Not Founded on Happiness   100
8.2 The Good Will   101
8.3 The Concept of Duty   102
8.4 Objective Principles and Hypothetical
     Imperatives   103
8.5 Subjective Principles or Maxims   106
8.6 The Categorical Imperative   107
8.7 Applying the Categorical Imperative   108
8.8 Treating Persons as Ends   111
8.9 The Will as Universal Lawgiver   112
8.10 Kant Not a Consequentialist   113

     Notes   115
     Discussion Questions   116

CHAPTER 9

Consequentialism   117

9.1 The Attraction of Consequentialism   117
9.2 Deontological Consequentialism   118
9.3 Utilitarianism   119
9.4 Intrinsic and Extrinsic Value   119
9.5 Problems for Utilitarianism   121
9.6 Act Utilitarianism and Rule Utilitarianism   124
9.7 Actual Rule Utilitarianism and Ideal Rule
     Utilitarianism   125
9.8 Are AU and IRU Equivalent?   127
9.9 Can We Ever Know all of an Act's
     Consequences?   128
9.10 What Counts as a Consequence of an Act?   130
9.11 Conclusion   132

     Notes   132
     Discussion Questions   133

CHAPTER 10

Justice   135

10.1 The Idea of Justice   135
10.2 Distributive Justice   137
10.3 Justice, Consistency, and Rationality   138
10.4 Three Conceptions of Distributive Justice   139
10.5 Distributive Justice as Pure Procedural Justice   143
10.6 The Transition to Metaethics   145

Notes   146
Discussion Questions   147

PART IV | **METAETHICS**

CHAPTER 11

Ethical Relativism   149

11.1 Cultural Diversity   149
11.2 What Is Ethical Relativism?   150
11.3 Universalism and Absolutism   151
11.4 What Difference Does It Make Whether Relativism
    Is True?   153
11.5 Relativism and Moral Disagreements   154
11.6 Can There Even Be Genuine Moral Disagreements
    According to Relativism?   156
11.7 Is There Cultural Diversity in Basic Moral Beliefs?   157
11.8 Cultural Diversity in Basic Moral Beliefs Would Not
    Establish Relativism   158
11.9 Universalism and the Ground of Morality   160
11.10 Are Logic and Truth Themselves Relative?   161
11.11 Relativism and Moral Tolerance   162
11.12 Conclusion   163

Notes   163
Discussion Questions   166

CHAPTER 12

Can Moral Principles Be Justified?   167

12.1 Diversity at the Level of Principles   167
12.2 Moral Foundationalism: Intuitionism and Naturalism   168
12.3 Ethical Naturalism   170
12.4 Contractarianism   171

12.5 Rawls and the Original Position   171
12.6 Moral Coherentism   174
12.7 Problems in the Application of Rules and Principles   175

Notes   177
Discussion Questions   178

CHAPTER 13

The Nature of Moral Judgments   179

13.1   Ethical Language   179
13.2   Categories of Ethical Terms   180
13.3   Categorial and Cross-Categorial Definitions   181
13.4   Are Rights Reducible to Deontic and Value Terms?   183
13.5   Are Ethical Terms Definable by Non-Ethical
       Terms?   184
13.6   Is Ethics Autonomous?   185
13.7   Autonomy and Reductionism   186
13.8   Is "Good" Indefinable?   187
13.9   Moral Realism   188
13.10 Cognitivism   189
13.11 Ethical Naturalism and Intuitionism   190
13.12 The Naturalistic Fallacy   192
13.13 The Open-Question Argument   194
13.14 The Error Theory   196
13.15 Noncognitivism   197
13.16 From Meaning to Use   199
13.17 The Noncognitivist Objection to Cognitivism   200
13.18 Possible Cognitivist Replies   201

Notes   202
Discussion Questions   204

PART V | **NEW BEARINGS IN ETHICS**

CHAPTER 14

Feminist Ethics   206

14.1 Questioning Traditional Ethics   206
14.2 What Is Feminist Ethics?   207
14.3 Minimalist Feminist Ethics: Wollstonecraft's Rights-Based
      Theory   209
14.4 A Standard Feminist Ethics: The Ethics of Caring   212
14.5 Radical Feminist Ethics   215

14.6   Feminist Objections to Traditional Ethics   216
14.7   Interpreting Feminist Ethics   220

Notes   222
Discussion Questions   223

CHAPTER 15

Contextualism: An Ethics of Pragmatism   224

15.1   A Deweyan Approach to Ethics   224
15.2   Subjective, Actual, and Actionable Rightness   224
15.3   The Contextualist Alternative   226
15.4   Elements of the Moral Situation   227
15.5   Nurturing Goods   228
15.6   A Kantian Objection   230
15.7   The Importance of Personal Decision   230
15.8   Intuition or Emotion?   232
15.9   Conscience and Human Nature   233
15.10 Contextualism and Relativism   234
15.11 Universalism and a Moral Postulate   235

Notes   236
Discussion Questions   238

APPENDIX   239

INDEX   241

Preface

The principal aim of this book is to introduce those with no previous background in ethics to the main issues, concepts, and theories of Western moral philosophy. A secondary aim is to provide a handy supplementary text for more advanced undergraduates and others who want to review these topics.

Introductory ethics courses have changed dramatically in recent decades. There are traditional courses, dealing with the main historical writers; systematic courses, analyzing theoretical problems with little more than passing acknowledgment of their historical antecedents; and courses in applied ethics, dealing with practical problems, often after a brief introduction to theory.

No one textbook is equally well suited to all three of these approaches. What is most important in ethics, and how the whole subject is best approached, is in fact one of the more divisive issues in contemporary ethics. Most notably, perhaps, there are differences over whether a rational, systematic approach is even a useful way to try to understand morality.

It may not be. Some Eastern philosophies hold that enlightenment requires an altogether different approach, involving meditation, self-purification, and self-discipline. Conceptual thinking and rational argumentation are sometimes even considered an impediment. And some of feminist ethics views much of the Western tradition as representing a masculine concept of rationality that does not do justice to what is believed to be woman's different experience of morality.

Even if it should turn out that reason plays a limited role in the actual making of moral judgments, as even many writers in the Western tradition have maintained, to show that and to explain why it is so would require the systematic use of reason. And this would require placing alternative approaches in the broader context of competing traditional theories. It is these theories we examine in this book.

Although I believe that confronting the moral issues of how to live, and how best to deal with interpersonal and social moral problems, is ultimately of great importance, I also believe that no better grounding for this confrontation can be provided than by understanding the best of traditional theoretical work on moral philosophy. I therefore believe moral philosophy is best approached with at least one eye on the history of ethics. Moreover, I think an ethics course should also prepare students to do more advanced work in ethics if they should choose, and should enable them to understand recent (though not necessarily contemporary) philosophical literature on ethics. Thus it is important that they understand both the theory and the vocabulary of recent ethical theory (even if some of it is jargon). With this in view, this fourth edition contains a chapter on the metaethical issues in understanding the nature of moral judgments. The standard theories here—e.g., inuituitionism, naturalism, emotivism—have typically been the virtually exclusive concern of philosophers. But they can be understood by students, even at the introductory level, particularly, if they are enabled to see the ways in which the thinking about these theories grows out of the same concerns that many ordinary people have about ethics.

Finally, I believe it is important to do more than just present positions, concepts, and theories; it is also important to engage students in some philosophizing, to challenge them to think as well as to learn what others have thought.

In this book, students are exposed to some of the most important work in moral philosophy in the Western tradition—not in great depth, obviously, but enough to instill a sense of its importance and relevance to contemporary concerns. They also consider some of the problems twentieth-century philosophers have taken to be most important, which is essential to proceeding with more advanced ethical theory. Finally, by presenting my own assessments on a number of issues, I hope to involve students in *doing* moral philosophy as well as in learning about it. One problem with many ethics courses—is that students find themselves being convinced by each successive theory they study, or at least feeling that each theory is equally ingenious and irrefutable. So they often end up not knowing what to believe, or become convinced that every theory is as good as any other. In what follows, I do some philosophizing as well as explaining and analyzing what other philosophers have said. I do so in the conviction that becoming part of such an enterprise is a more constructive way of engaging philosophical issues than by being presented with a detached, neutral examination of one theory after another. The assessments I make, however, and the position I sketch in the final chapter, should, of course, be received in the same critical spirit as all the other theories we examine. They are certainly no less controversial, and I trust that instructors will take issue with these assessments where they see fit.

Students who do all this will, I believe, be well prepared to do more work in ethics, whether from a historical, theoretical, or practical approach. Those for whom this is their sole exposure to ethics should come away not only with an understanding of the primary issues in moral philosophy but also with some sense of how to deal with those issues philosophically.

I am especially indebted to Richard Werner of Hamilton College for thoughtful, perceptive, and invariably constructive comments on this book in its various incarnations. His contributions have been invaluable. I also wish to thank the following reviewers for careful and helpful suggestions: David W. Clowney, Rowan University; David Corner, California State University, Sacramento; Stephen Kershnar, SUNY–Fredonia; Mark Perlman, Western Oregon University; Jamie P. Ross, Portland State University; Barbara Swyhart, California University of Pennsylvania. Special thanks to reviewers for this edition: Barry Gan, Saint Bonaventure University; Patricia Murphy, Saint Johns University; and Phillip Long, Grace Bible College.

The good greets us initially in every experience and in every object. Remove from anything its share of excellence and you have made it utterly insignificant, irrelevant to human discourse, and unworthy of even theoretic consideration.[1]
George Santayana

The Nature of Ethics

1.1 WHY STUDY MORAL PHILOSOPHY?

Simply put, **ethics** is the study of morality. But there are many different approaches to studying morality, approaches reflecting different assumptions about its nature and about how best to understand it.

Moral philosophy is one such approach; it is unique in the scope and depth of the questions it raises and in the way it sets about answering them. Indeed, it is almost certain that one cannot understand morality fully without exploring the kinds of questions moral philosophy asks.

The ancients made a distinction between **knowledge** and wisdom: unlike wisdom, knowledge was understood to be something that can be taught. If you pay attention to a lecture on physics, chemistry, or history, you will probably come away with knowledge—facts and information—you didn't have before. Knowledge can be given, taught. Although possessing knowledge is important and an essential part of **wisdom**, it does not by itself ensure wisdom, whose elements are understanding, insight, good judgment, and the capacity to live and guide one's conduct well. Many educated people, in fact, are inept at making practical decisions, and they aren't noticeably better at living moral lives than other people are. They have *knowledge,* but they lack *wisdom.* And it is with wisdom that moral philosophy is most concerned, for **philosophy**, etymologically, is the love of wisdom (*philo-,* "love"; *sophos,* "wisdom"—from the Greek). *Moral philosophy,* therefore, is the love and pursuit of wisdom in moral matters.

Strictly speaking, then, moral philosophy cannot be taught because the love of wisdom cannot be imparted the same way that facts about the world are imparted. But the love of moral wisdom can be encouraged in everyone and nurtured in those who actively seek to understand morality and its place in human life. Although moral philosophy cannot promise to resolve your moral problems for you, it can help guide you in your efforts to resolve those problems and in your deliberations about what constitutes the wise conduct of life. And virtually nothing is of greater importance than the aim of conducting life wisely.

The study of moral philosophy is also exciting and challenging in its own right. Whatever the nature of reality, and however it came into being, morality is now part of it. Love, hate, values, thoughts, feelings, emotions, obligations, virtues, and principles—the elements of morality—are in their own way as real as atoms and electrons, and to understand our world fully we must be prepared to study them as seriously as we do the chemical and physical properties of things. These elements of morality are, of course, often dismissed as "subjective," "relative," or merely "matters of opinion." Even if this assumption should turn out to be true (which is far from inevitable), the elements of morality nevertheless exist in some way or can be explained in terms of things that exist. In any event, such dismissive claims simply reflect implicit theories about the nature of morality, and they are by no means the only such theories, nor necessarily the most plausible ones. These and other theories can be assessed adequately only through the study of moral philosophy.

Understanding ethics in any of its forms, as well as understanding moral philosophy in particular, presupposes at least a rudimentary understanding of the nature of morality. The problem is that we can only go so far in presenting such an understanding without beginning to presuppose answers to controversial issues contested by different ethical theories. Nevertheless, I believe we can tell a plausible story about the origins of morality—one that will highlight its main features as well as help us to understand the different approaches to studying it.

Let us begin with some relatively unproblematic observations, and then work our way into the more complex and controversial issues.

1.2 THE ORIGINS OF MORALITY

Humans have always needed food, warmth, shelter, and sex; the things that satisfy these basic needs have always had value for us. In this we are like other animals.

But at some point in our history we began to *think* of these things as valued. At that point, conceptualization began and the idea of goodness was born. This shift separated us from other animals. Animals need and want many things but (as far as we know) don't have a concept of **value** (or goodness) that helps them understand and think about such things and about the role such things play in their lives. This capacity for conceptualization makes moral philosophy possible.

As societies came into being, increased cooperation and a division of labor facilitated the satisfaction of needs. Human wants then began to outstrip needs, and interests extended beyond the things that merely make survival possible to the things that also enhance life. Societies began to value entertainment and leisure, artistic and musical expression, and, eventually, literature, science, and philosophy. People began to actively pursue learning for its own sake as well as for the sake of survival. Human aspirations grew, and with the development of human intelligence and its corresponding capacity for reflecting on life and the world, the idea of goodness expanded.

Anything society took an interest in eventually came to be invested with value, and the idea of goodness became pervasive.

1.3 THE ACTIVITY OF EVALUATING

The details of how this came about we do not know. We do know that in Western thought the philosophical significance of this phenomenon received its first full explication from Plato in the fourth century B.C. He pointed out that just as the sun is necessary for light, nutrition, and growth throughout the physical world, so the idea of goodness is essential to our understanding of people, conduct, institutions, and society.

This insight was one of the most profound in Western philosophy. Its importance cannot be underestimated. Let's consider what it means.

At this moment, you are, perhaps, reading this book for a specific purpose: to pass a course, to gather background for a term paper, or simply to learn about ethics. A full explanation of your behavior would require at least tacit reference to the *value* you attach to learning or passing a course or getting a college degree. Even a college or university itself presupposes the end of education. Education is a value served by the organization and operation of such institutions. In fact, you cannot fully explain what a college or university is apart from that value. Nor could you adequately explain what a library is apart from the purpose of making knowledge accessible and the assumption that to do so is deemed by some to be good; or what law is apart from the goal of regulating behavior and the idea that to do so serves a valued social purpose; or what a monetary system is apart from its role in making certain kinds of material transactions possible. This same concept applies to virtually all institutions.

Even simple, everyday choices typically reflect **value judgments.** That you chose to get up at 6 A.M. rather than at 9 A.M. today, or to wear your green sweater rather than the blue one, reflect judgments that (for whatever reason) it was *better* to do so. Of course, you didn't need to say to yourself, "It would be better to do this." The process of judging is more or less a self-conscious act and need not be verbalized. But we all do it, regularly. It isn't possible, in fact, to go through a single day of rational self-directed conduct without making value judgments.

So the activity of evaluating lies at the center of human affairs. Even if we do not think of the physical universe as something containing ends or purposes (a teleological conception of the world held by Plato and most classical Greek philosophers), human activities can only be understood in terms of purposes. Such activities include science. The scientific study of the universe and the life it contains is undertaken only because it is valued—whether merely to increase understanding or, as in modern times (for better or worse), to let us harness the world's resources to human needs. We can, in short, neither live as rational beings nor fully understand our personal and social lives apart from the idea of value.

1.4 GUIDING AND DIRECTING CONDUCT

There emerged in human development another important activity—that of guiding and directing conduct. Again, we do not know precisely when or how, but this activity most likely came about in the following way:

Humans have probably always clustered into groups of some sort. No doubt families came first; then tribes, clans, and eventually whole societies. This clustering facilitated our survival, the satisfaction of our needs, and the development of communication. But a part of such communication, almost certainly from the start, was the direction and guidance of conduct—from a mother's warning to her child not to play too close to the fire to a father's instructions to his sons on the hunt. As social relations evolved, the kinds of direction that existed, as well as the circumstances of its use, undoubtedly multiplied, forming the concepts of power, dominance, leadership, and eventually government.

More complex forms of cooperation made increasingly possible the satisfaction of wants and the attainment of broader ends such as education, artistic achievement, and social and political organization. For this reason, the community became increasingly important. Its preservation became essential for the attainment of other values; settled ways of doing things took hold, some rooted in superstition, others in generalizations from experience about what is useful. Although not all were consciously adopted at first, those ways that endured served *overall* (they need not all have done so *individually*) to further the ends or purposes valued by the community and its members.

Accordingly, conduct contrary to established and approved ways of doing things came to be discouraged and often punished. Prohibitions emerged, and certain kinds of conduct were considered *wrong*. Other kinds were permitted or even expressly required and were deemed *right* or *obligatory*. Directives for regulating conduct coalesced over time into rules and principles as settled habits became transformed into customs and practices. Our words "ethics" and "morals," in fact, derive from the Greek and Roman words *ethos* and *mores* respectively, signifying the customs, conventions, rules, standards, and distinctive characteristics of communal groups.

1.5 VALUE JUDGMENTS AND PRESCRIPTIVE JUDGMENTS

Directives expressing requirements and prohibitions in the social sphere at first largely signified what was approved or disapproved by the collectivity. Yet the notions of right and wrong (and associated concepts such as "should" and "should not," "must" and "must not," "just" and "unjust," "duty" and "obligation") provided individuals with the conceptual tools with which to criticize even the customs and conventions of the community itself. The very notions to which the practices of groups gave rise made possible the critical assessment of those practices themselves.

We will never know how it came about, but the recognition (or perhaps invention) of the distinction between what is and what ought to be was an epochal development in human affairs. It created a vastly expanded capacity for reasoning and opened possibilities for the guidance of both personal and social life. Without it, civilization and the institutions of law and government could not have arisen. And morality surely could not have come into being.

Thus it is conceptually possible to question whether infanticide in ancient Sparta, or the burning of widows in India, or the enslavement of Africans by Europeans and Americans was right. Today we can question whether discrimination against women and nonwhites is right, even though these were or still are established practices. Moral thinking became possible with the emergence of the concepts of good and bad, right and wrong.

Here, however, we cross over into controversial ground. Some people deny that one can effectively criticize the customs and practices of other cultures, or perhaps even those of one's own. Morality, they say, is in some important sense relative to the specific social and cultural circumstances in which it arises; right and wrong can only be understood in that context. Still others insist that, although morality is not relative, it derives its meaning only from religion; that omitting the religious dimension in any account of morality's genesis distorts its nature.

Both objections raise serious issues. The first objection raises the issue of moral relativism; the second suggests the possible dependence of morality on religion. But each merits a detailed treatment of its own, and will therefore be discussed separately later (relativism in Chapter 11 and the divine command theory—one version of the religious view—in Chapter 6).

For the present, let me say that in addition to the activity of evaluating we must recognize (1) the importance to human affairs of guiding and directing conduct, a concept which grows out of socialization processes, and (2), in more complex forms, the importance of the perceived need to regulate the conduct of group members. This guiding, directing, and regulating can take the form either of commands and orders or of **prescriptive judgments** about what is right or wrong/what ought or ought not to be done. Both value judgments and prescriptive judgments originate in the practical activities of evaluating and directing.

This importance can be granted, whatever one's views on relativism and the relationship of morality to religion. Therefore, this importance to society of guidance provides a good point of departure for detailing some of the implications of these distinctions. Let us begin by making the distinctions a little clearer.

1.6 NORMATIVE JUDGMENTS AND DESCRIPTIVE STATEMENTS

Value judgments and prescriptive judgments may both be called **normative judgments** to distinguish them from purely descriptive, factual statements about the world. They typically express or presuppose norms or standards rather than simply reporting scientifically verifiable facts. For example, I might say,

1. This is a red car.

I am making a descriptive statement here. I am reporting a fact about the car without any implied evaluation. But if I say,

2. This is a good car.

then now I am making a value judgment, one that presupposes some standard of quality or goodness that I believe the car meets. Now, perhaps I say,

3. You haven't returned the ten dollars I lent you.

Here I am making a descriptive statement. But if I say,

4. You ought to have returned the ten dollars I lent you.

then now I am making a prescriptive judgment.

Although all moral judgments are normative, not all normative judgments are moral. Whether or not they are moral depends on the criteria presupposed in making them. This means that although we associate terms such as "right" and "wrong" with morality, they are often used for purposes other than to make moral judgments.

1.7 MORAL AND NONMORAL JUDGMENTS

To call something "right" in the abstract tells us little. To know what criteria were used for making that assessment, we need a context. Otherwise we simply don't know what "right" means.

There are, for example, right and wrong ways to hold a violin, bake a cake, or throw a football. But they have nothing to do with morality; they have to do, rather, with mastering the violin, making good desserts, or passing a football well. Even more broadly, they have to do with the aims and purposes of music, cooking, and athletics. These activities in turn, of course, are always susceptible to moral assessment, as are any activities we engage in. But our use of normative language in teaching those activities does not normally constitute the making of *moral* judgments.

Thus if I say, "You ought to hold the violin this way," my judgment is prescriptive; I am trying to guide your conduct. But it is not a moral judgment. The criteria presupposed by the judgment are those intended to enable you to produce good music. Or if a parent says to a child, "You shouldn't eat with your fingers," that too is a normative judgment. But it is not a moral judgment. It is a judgment of etiquette, intended to instruct the child in good table manners. Of the four sentences listed in the last section, only the fourth is a plausible candidate for a moral judgment, even though both the second and the fourth are normative.

So value judgments and prescriptive judgments, although both normative, may be either moral or nonmoral. This statement does not tell us what makes judgments moral (other than the fact, of course, that they are made on moral grounds); that is a difficult and controversial issue. But it is enough to indicate the importance of recognizing these distinctions, which are interrelated as shown in the following diagram.

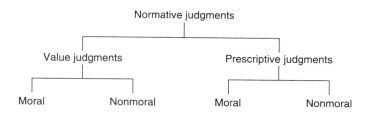

The point is, from the practical activities of evaluating and directing conduct, different frames of reference (or points of view) have emerged that contain criteria for appraising conduct as right or wrong in different areas. These frames of reference include (but are not limited to) etiquette, the law, economics, religion, self-interest, fascism, Marxism, sexism, and racism. The actions they prescribe can and often do conflict, just as anything considered to be valuable can vary radically. White supremacy, for example, is a form of racism that attaches the highest value to the flourishing of the so-called white race, typically prescribing actions prejudicial to nonwhites. Such prescriptions can and do conflict with laws that prohibit discrimination.

Whatever its exact nature, morality has also emerged in human affairs and represents a frame of reference along with the other criteria for appraising conduct listed above. And whatever the most plausible account of how one judges right and wrong from a moral point of view, what is believed to be morally right and wrong often conflicts with what is right and wrong from other perspectives.

1.8 THREE KINDS OF MORAL PROBLEMS

I will use three examples drawn from the experiences of people from different parts of the world to show how conflicts arise.

In the first example, a Chinese woman (from the People's Republic of China) recounts this story about her young nephew:

> I have a 5-year-old nephew. He has never been given any war toys and has been taught not to fight. Last year, he had a hard time in kindergarten. He exhibited behavior at home that we had never seen in him before. He started hitting us and shouting at us, although he had never been struck by us. And he cried more than before. We had the feeling that he was not happy in the kindergarten. When my sister called one of the teachers she said: "We were just about to call you about your son. You should have taught him how to fight; all the other boys want to fight with him. And then he cries and they call him a sissy and fight him even more. You should teach him how to fight or the situation will get worse when he starts school."

My sister replied that it was not her responsibility to teach her son to fight. On the contrary, it was the teacher's responsibility to teach the other children not to fight. It was her responsibility to intervene in fights, stop them and help children to solve their conflicts through nonviolent means. My sister told me it was difficult to teach the teacher from her position as a mother. My sister asked her if she would have given the same advice for a girl student. She admitted that when she wanted to change my nephew's behavior it was precisely because he was a boy and not a girl.[2]

The child is perhaps too young to understand this as a moral problem, but the conflict it creates within him is evident from his behavior.

The moral problem, however, is fully felt by the mother. She finds herself caught between her own convictions about what to teach children about violence and the attitudes of the school (and perhaps of the rest of society). Her child, of course, is himself caught between what she has taught him and what is expected at school. Intertwined with and contributing to this dilemma, are the different expectations for boys and girls with regard to the use of violence, differences that are institutionalized in most societies.

Perhaps the Chinese child was too young to experience his problem fully as a moral problem, but young men from the U.S. during the Vietnam War were not. Many of them found their moral convictions in conflict not only with society's expectations for young men, but also with the legal obligations giving force to those expectations. Many of them thought the war was wrong and refused in conscience to participate. It was clear, however, that they were legally obligated to do so (if, of course, they were drafted and so ordered and if they did not apply for and receive conscientious objector, or CO status). What they judged to be right from a moral viewpoint conflicted with what they were obligated to do from a legal viewpoint.[3]

Not only does morality sometimes conflict with other viewpoints, but some moral considerations seem to conflict with other moral considerations. When they do, morality itself does not speak with one voice. Some of the most wrenching moral problems are of this sort, as shown in the following story of a French youth during World War II, told by the existentialist Jean-Paul Sartre:

I shall cite the case of one of my students who came to see me under the following circumstances: his father was on bad terms with his mother, and, moreover, was inclined to be a collaborationist [with the Nazis]; his older brother had been killed in the German offensive of 1940, and the young man, with somewhat immature but generous feelings, wanted to avenge him. His mother lived alone with him, very much upset by the half-treason of her husband and the death of her older son; the boy was her only consolation.

The boy was faced with the choice of leaving for England and joining the Free French Forces—that is, leaving his mother behind—or remaining with his mother and helping her to carry on. He was fully aware that the woman lived only for him and that his going-off—and perhaps his death—would plunge her into despair. He was also aware that every act that he did for his mother's sake was a sure thing, in the sense that it was helping her to carry on, whereas every effort he made toward going off and fighting was an uncertain move which might run aground and prove completely useless. . . . As a result, he was faced with two very different kinds of action: one, concrete, immediate, but concerning only one individual; the other concerned an incomparably vaster group, a national collectivity, but for that very reason was dubious, and might be interrupted en route. And, at the same time, he was wavering between two kinds of ethics. On the one hand, an ethics of sympathy, of personal devotion; on the other, a broader ethics, but one whose efficacy was more dubious. He had to choose between the two.[4]

Although Sartre speaks as though there were two different ethics here, I would prefer to say that the youth finds himself pulled in two different directions by considerations within morality itself and that the problem is that there *is* no apparent way to settle the question of which considerations should take precedence.

These examples illustrate three different kinds of moral problems: (1) a conflict between morality and conventional beliefs, including societal expectations; (2) a conflict between morality and the law; and (3) a conflict between apparently conflicting obligations within morality itself.

Thus morality represents a point of view that contains criteria for determining right and wrong. And these criteria may conflict with criteria contained in other viewpoints as well as generate apparent conflicts within morality itself. (I say "apparent" conflicts, because it is a disputed issue in ethics as to whether obligations within morality *can* genuinely conflict.)

Historically, the main objective of philosophical ethics has been to explain what the *correct* criteria are for determining moral right and wrong, or what things, including qualities of character, are truly good.

We ordinarily know how to tell whether someone is holding a violin correctly or throwing a football the right way; if we do not, we can ask a violin teacher or a football coach. The criteria of "correctness" are bound up in the activities of studying violin or playing football. Likewise farming, fence mending, cooking, house building, knitting, sailing, housecleaning, lecturing, lawyering, and laundering all have criteria for the right and wrong ways of carrying out these activities. Crops will fail, fences collapse, dinners burn, and so on if we do not conform to the criteria of "correctness." Similarly, we know how to tell what is right or wrong in etiquette or the law (by reading a book on etiquette or consulting an attorney).

But what are the criteria for judging moral *rightness* and *wrongness*? Here there is little agreement. True, there is considerable agreement about what is morally right or wrong, at least within a given society. Few in our society, for example, seriously question whether truth telling, honesty, and promise-keeping are at least generally right, whereas lying, stealing, murder, and rape are wrong. This agreement is probably true even across cultures. But there is much disagreement over *why* they are right and wrong.

For answers to *why* such acts are right or wrong, some people appeal to religion; others, to what society approves or disapproves; and still others to what is beneficial or harmful. Many people, if pressed—including some who lead exemplary lives themselves—could give no coherent, in-depth account of why they are right or wrong. And if they could, they might not agree in their answers, as Plato realized when he pointed out that virtuous conduct in ordinary people is not rooted in knowledge but in right opinion—a second best that serves for practical purposes.

This situation should not be surprising because practical affairs often leave little time for sustained reflection on such questions, even among people who might otherwise be so inclined. What may be more surprising is that there is little agreement on these matters even among philosophers, the very people who make it their business to try to understand morality. Indeed, the history of philosophy presents a succession of competing theories about right and wrong.

Where morality has been thought to consist of rules and principles, philosophy has sought to identify one basic principle in terms of which particular moral judgments can be justified. Where morality has been thought to be primarily a matter of developing character, philosophy has sought to identify those traits that represent true excellence. In either case, this has often meant trying to give an accurate account of what in itself is good and bad. (Many things are good as a means to an end, the way a hammer is good for driving nails; but philosophers have tended to think that only a few things—or even just one—such as pleasure, for example—are good in themselves.)

This approach to ethics is called **normative ethics,** because its aim, in effect, is to identify and explain the most basic moral judgments about right and wrong/good and bad. It does not presume to tell us what people *think* is right or wrong. It aims to tell us what *is* right or wrong.

When philosophers seek to characterize, not what is right or wrong in the most general terms, but what is right or wrong in specific kinds of cases—for example, with regard to abortion, euthanasia, animal rights, racism, sexism, violence, and war—they are engaged in applied ethics, which may be considered a branch of normative ethics. Thus with regard to our three examples, if you took and defended a position on whether young boys should be encouraged to defend themselves by fighting; or whether young men should be required to serve in the military; or whether one should put obligations to one's mother above those to one's country, you would be practicing applied ethics.

The various theories examined in Parts Two and Three are of this normative sort. Taken together, they represent the primary systematic efforts in Western thought to elucidate the content of morality.

Notes

1. *The Works of George Santayana,* vol. 5: *The Life of Reason: Reason in Science* (New York: Scribner's, 1906), p. 156.

2. From Zhuoyun Yan, "Non-violence Education," a term paper written for a course on the theory and practice of nonviolence at the Joan B. Kroc Institute for International Peace Studies, University of Notre Dame, Fall 1991.

3. Whether morality was in fact in conflict with the law would, of course, require determining whether what they *thought* was morally right was actually so. Furthermore, if some of them sought to avoid the draft solely because they did not want to risk their lives, the conflict was not so much between morality and the law (although concern for one's own life can certainly be a moral consideration) as between self-interest (or prudence) and the law.

4. Jean-Paul Sartre, *Existentialism and Human Emotions,* trans. Bernard Frechtman and Hazel Barnes (New York: Philosophical Library, 1957), pp. 24–25.

Discussion Questions

1. Do you agree that morality evolved throughout human history as people gathered together in groups: families, tribes, communities, societies, nations? If you believe that this view is an incorrect one, how would you explain the origin of morality? If you believe it is correct, does it diminish the importance of morality?

2. Do you agree or disagree that the idea of value (goodness) is central to understanding human affairs? Can you think of any area of human endeavor that doesn't presuppose some judgment of value? Would you say that the idea of value is as important to understanding human affairs as the ideas of cause and effect are to understanding the natural order? Why or why not?

3. Think of some examples of normative judgments and descriptive statements from your own experience. What differences do there seem to be between your examples and those cited in section 1.8 and section 1.6?

4. Can you think of a moral problem (either from your own experience or from literature, film, or TV) in which a person is confronted with a conflict between what is morally right and what is legally right? How did the person or persons in question resolve the conflict? Do you believe they made the correct decision? Why?

5. Some people believe that our obligations to family come first. Others think that obligations to our society or country come first. What do you think? Review the Sartre example (section 1.8) and describe what you think the youth should have done and why. What would you do if, out of patriotism, you wanted to join the military—but your parents, out of love for you, wanted you not to?

. . . What is called moral theory is but a more conscious and systematic raising of the question which occupies the mind of anyone who in the face of moral conflict and doubt seeks a way out through reflection.[1]
John Dewey

2 CHAPTER | **Theories of Moral Right and Wrong**

2.1 MORAL LEGALISM AND MORAL PARTICULARISM

Moral rightness may be thought to be based either on rules (and/or principles and commandments) or on particular circumstances, or both. The first of these approaches is legalistic, in that the law is a paradigm of the attempt to regulate conduct by rules, whether they take the form of commandments from God, decrees by a dictator, or statutes enacted by a democratic legislature.

When we judge legal rightness and wrongness, we do indeed appeal to rules because laws can only be formulated in terms of them. Laws permit, prohibit, or require the performance of *acts;* they do not tell anyone what sort of person to be, or what motivation to have.[2] The law does not care whether the person who steals, murders, or rapes is an otherwise good person (although this may be taken into account in sentencing); it is what the person *does* that is important. And acts can be regulated.

Likewise, many philosophers have thought that the key to elucidating morality is to clearly understand the appropriate rules or principles. They believe it is conduct, not character, that morality must regulate, and rules and principles are appropriate for that role. As John Stuart Mill observes, "a right action does not necessarily indicate a virtuous character, and . . . actions which are blamable often proceed from qualities entitled to praise."[3]

This approach may be defined as follows:

Moral Legalism: The moral rightness of acts is determined solely by rules, principles, or commandments.

In this view, an act is right if—and only if—it accords with a correct moral rule (or principle, which may be taken to be simply a very general rule).[4] To know what is right, we must know which rules are correct. Our knowledge of them comes first. Then we must correctly apply those rules to particular situations. (To do so, of course, requires some knowledge about the situation, but it is still the act's accordance with the rule or principle that makes it right.)

Most standard Western ethical theories have been legalistic in this sense, appealing to principles such as the following:[5]

1. **Ethical Egoism:** One ought always to maximize one's own personal good.
2. **Divine Command Theory:** Whatever God commands is right.
3. **Natural Law Ethics:** One ought always to act in accordance with nature.
4. **Kantianism:** One ought always to act on maxims that can be universalized.
5. **Utilitarianism:** One ought always to maximize the general good.
6. **Principle of Justice:** One ought always to act justly.

This list does not exhaust the candidates for principles one might take to be central to morality. There are also, for example, such principles as:

7. **Ethics of Love:** One ought always to act lovingly.
8. **Ethics of Nonviolence:** One ought always to act nonviolently.

These principles have figured prominently in some religious and social movements. But principles 1 through 6 represent what have (arguably) been the main ones, and I discuss each in detail in Part Three.

The quest for a single principle in morality is understandable. As in science, there is a strong impulse in moral philosophy to seek a single, unifying theory—in this case, one that explains morality as a coherent whole. To be able to identify a single principle at the heart of morality would be a major step in achieving that objective. But if a single core principle cannot be identified, then two or more principles—such as 5 and 6 in the preceding list—might have to be acknowledged to be equally basic and not derivable from one another. That is, moral legalism might be *monistic* in recognizing one fundamental principle, or *pluralistic* in recognizing two or more equally basic rules or principles. Either way, these approaches share the assumption that rules or principles are indispensable to morality.

But are rules adequate for guiding conduct? Here are some reasons for skepticism: It is sometimes said that every rule has exceptions. If so, then no rule adequately covers all cases. But if a particular case is an exception, there must be some ground other than the rule for identifying it as an exception. Therefore there must, in that case, be *some* consideration besides what is contained in the rule that is relevant for determining rightness.

Suppose, for example, someone gives you a gun for safekeeping, which you promise to return when he asks for it. One day following an argument with someone else, he comes to you in a rage and demands the gun—obviously bent on doing harm with it. You have promised to return it, and one ought to keep promises (as a rule). But isn't this case, surely, an exception? Something besides the rule is relevant here; namely, the probable harm to someone if you return the gun.[6]

So if rules have exceptions, then simply applying rules to particular situations isn't always enough to determine right and wrong. If, similarly, there should be exceptions to any principle alleged to be the sole, fundamental principle of morality, then that principle (such as the principle of utilitarianism, for example) cannot by itself be adequate either.

It is also clear that rules by their nature are general, whereas practical decisions must be made in particular situations. For this reason, rules can never take into account all the details of actual contexts.

One would need stronger reasons than these to reject rules and principles, of course. But carried to its conclusion, this way of thinking suggests an outlook on moral rightness that is diametrically opposed to legalism. We may call it moral particularism, or "particularism," for short. It can be defined as follows:

> **Moral Particularism:** The rightness of acts depends solely on the situations in which they are performed and is not derived from rules, principles, or commandments.[7]

Aristotle at times sounds like a particularist in this sense, as we shall see in the next chapter (section 3.8). In the twentieth century H. A. Prichard and W. D. Ross were particularists; so may have been the existentialists and the pragmatist John Dewey.[8]

In this view, what makes acts right is not the fact that they fall under some rule or principle, but rather certain features of the acts themselves or of the situation in which they are performed. To determine what is right, therefore, we must judge particular cases on their own merits rather than by appealing to rules and principles. It isn't easy to say, however, what is going on when we do so.

According to one account, we intuit rightness or wrongness (or goodness and badness) in particular situations—the implication being that right and wrong stand for objective properties of acts or situations we are capable of apprehending if we pay attention. In another account, rightness and wrongness consist of emotions of approval or disapproval generated by specific features of particular situations. Either way, insofar as rules have any role at all to play in particularist accounts, they consist simply of generalizations from particular instances of right and wrong, identified independently of the rules (so that if I find promise keeping to be right in this situation, and in the next, and in the one after that, and so on, I could generalize that promise keeping is always right).

You could, of course, take a middle ground that combines features of legalism and particularism. You could say that there are some valid rules or principles but that they do not cover all the kinds of cases in which moral decisions must be made. In that event, it might be said that we should appeal to rules where they are applicable but decide cases on their own merits where they are not.

Legalism and particularism, finally, do not purport to provide us with the content of morality. That is, legalism does not *per se* tell us *what* the correct rules or principles of morality are, and particularism does not presume to tell us what is right in particular cases or even kinds of cases. For that, we need normative ethical theory.

Because the theories considered in Part Three are normative, it is important to understand the nature of normative ethics and how it grows out of the practical activities of evaluating and guiding conduct that (see Chapter 1) lies at the heart of morality. Recall that those activities are expressed in value judgments and prescriptive judgments. The notions of "good" and "bad" are central to the former; those of "right" and "wrong," to the latter.

2.2 RIGHTS-BASED THEORIES

Some philosophers, however, believe morality is primarily a matter of rights; much of the discussion of social issues is therefore conducted in these terms. The Declaration of Independence, of course, states that all people are endowed with unalienable rights by their Creator, which seems to place rights at the heart of morality. Although some contemporary writers contrast so-called rights-based theories with utilitarianism,[9] much of the discussion of justice, even by a utilitarian such as Mill, is framed in terms of rights. And one can speak of a "utilitarianism" of rights (see section 9.2).

Few deny that there are rights or that the language we use to discuss rights is meaningful. But people seriously disagree as to whether or not rights are basic to morality—that is, as to whether right and wrong and duty and obligation are to be understood ultimately in terms of rights. Maybe rights are to be understood in terms of these other notions, or perhaps both rights and these other notions are equally essential to morality.

This raises a complex problem of metaethics. It has to do with the relationship between the concepts of right and wrong, on the one hand, and the notion of rights, on the other hand. It is a problem to which we shall return in Chapter 13. For the present, let us simply note that contemporary moral issues are increasingly framed in terms of the language of rights, and that there is at present no consensus on precisely how rights are to be understood in relation to other moral concepts.

2.3 THE RELATIONSHIP BETWEEN GOODNESS AND RIGHTNESS

A central issue in normative ethics concerns how value and deontic concepts relate to one another (or more simply, how "good" and "right" relate to one another).[10]

Notice the issue's importance. To judge that something is good does not *in and of itself* tell you what you ought to do. It merely assigns value to the thing. You might be convinced that a week in Florida during spring break would be great, but you might not go because you cannot afford it or because you have an honors paper to complete. In other words, without further assumptions you cannot explain how evaluation guides conduct.

To explain how value judgments guide moral conduct, you must be able to show some kind of connection between evaluating and prescribing. That connection could be one of three things:

1. There may be a *causal* connection between evaluating and prescribing. People may just naturally desire what they believe to be good and have an

aversion to what they believe to be bad. In that case, believing something is good might lead you to conclude that it should be pursued. If, further, Plato is right that we desire the good above all else, then to establish that something is good would suffice to lead people to pursue it (or do it, if it is an action). It would also mean that people fail to do what is good only out of ignorance of what the good is or of what will bring it about. It doesn't follow, of course, that people *should* pursue what they find good; but if this account were correct it would leave little ground for plausibly arguing that they should do anything else.

2. There may be a plausible rule or principle saying we ought to do what is good or that we should maximize value. Thus even if not everyone wants what is good, this principle would direct us to promote good. In this view, the connection between evaluating and prescribing is *normative* (it is expressed by a moral principle), although it might also be causal if it led people to guide their conduct by what promotes the good. For example, if either principle 1 or principle 5 in section 2.1 is valid, it provides a normative connection. It does so by prescribing that we promote the good (either our own or that of people generally).

3. There may be a *conceptual* connection, as there is if "right" is definable by reference to "good." This would make all cases of prescribing also cases of evaluating. To make a prescriptive judgment would be to make a value judgment plus perhaps an implied prediction about what would bring about what is good. This would be the case, for example, if it could be shown that "right" actually *means* or can properly be *defined* as "what promotes the greatest good." Then it would be impossible that what is right not promote the good, just as, given the definition of a triangle as (among other things) a three-sided figure, it would be impossible for something to be a triangle and not have three sides.

But another possibility must be taken seriously: that there is no significant connection between goodness and moral rightness at all. In that case, moral judgments of rightness have no connection with evaluations.

If we are correct that evaluating plays a central role in human affairs, it cannot plausibly be said that the idea of goodness does not in general have a bearing on our practical decisions. Nonetheless, while we quite properly let value judgments guide our conduct much of the time, maybe we shouldn't do so when we make moral judgments. If moral rightness does not in fact depend on goodness, then moral judgments must be grounded on something other than the value actualized in conduct.

Another way to put this is to say that while our prescriptive judgments may in general presuppose value judgments, our prescriptive judgments that are moral may not. Let us consider a theory that would say this (examined in detail in Chapter 6).

Suppose there is a God and that God tells us to do some things and not to do others. Suppose further that God's directives determine right and wrong.

In that case, once you knew a certain act had been commanded by God, you wouldn't need to know its consequences or the value of those consequences or anything else in order to know that it is right. (Conversely, if you knew that God had prohibited something, you would know you shouldn't do it.)

You might think that God knows best and that if you do as God says it will bring about the greatest good overall for yourself and others. And, of course, you might want that. But the belief that it would bring about good would not be the reason why any particular act commanded by God was right; that reason would be solely that the act conforms to God's command. The fact that God commanded the act would make it right.

Here, then, is an outlook according to which right and wrong are determined without any consideration of what is good. This outlook makes sound moral prescriptions thus independent of evaluations.

This view still leaves open the possibility that in most of our practical conduct we still have to make value judgments in order to live well. We still have to judge what is good or bad in the way of food to eat, clothing to wear, careers to pursue, and so on. So Plato could still be correct in his claim about how central the process of evaluating is to most of our practical affairs. But in this view, he would be incorrect in extending the claim to our moral decisions.

2.4 AXIOLOGICAL AND DEONTOLOGICAL MORAL THEORIES

This discussion points the way to a central distinction in theories of moral rightness. Some such theories hold that evaluating is primary and that moral judgments depend on value judgments; others hold that prescribing is primary and that moral judgments are partially or wholly independent of evaluations. The first category encompasses **axiological theories**; the second, **deontological theories.**

For example, a metaethical theory that "right" means "approved by my society" is deontological because it makes no reference at all to value or goodness. A theory maintaining that "right" means "promotes the greatest good for my society" is axiological because it defines right in terms of good. Virtually all normative ethical theories are also of one or the other of these types.

There is considerable complexity to these theories. One must grasp it to understand them fully and to understand the more specific issues that divide them. So in the next three sections I detail the interrelationships among these theories. Don't try to memorize all this material now. Just read it through and then refer back to it as you read the following chapters.

2.5 STRONG AND WEAK DEONTOLOGISM

Deontological theories may take either a strong or a weak form. The strong form holds that what is right, wrong, obligatory, or prohibited is independent of what is good or bad. This is true of the view about morality depending on God's commands (even if God commands us to do good, it is God's *commanding* us to do good that makes that act obligatory, not the fact that obeying the command would bring about good).

The weaker form holds that goodness is *relevant* to determining rightness but not decisive. Other things must be considered as well, such as whether you would be acting fairly, honoring a commitment, telling the truth, keeping a promise, or discharging a debt of gratitude. It may be thought that sometimes these other things are of greater moral importance than promoting good. When they are, and when you cannot both honor them and promote the good at the same time, you should, in this view, forgo promoting the good.

Most deontologists hold theories of this weaker sort, but Kant, the most noted deontologist in modern Western philosophy, held the stronger form.

2.6 CONSEQUENTIALIST AND NONCONSEQUENTIALIST AXIOLOGICAL THEORIES

Axiological theories vary according to how they answer three questions: (1) Where is the locus of the good that determines rightness? (2) What is the relevance of any bad that may be actualized along with the good? (3) If consequences are relevant to determining rightness, which consequences for which people or groups are relevant?[11]

Answers to question (1) emphasize the goodness of the act itself, or of its consequences, or of a combination of the two. They thus presuppose a distinction between acts and consequences. Although it is not easy to draw this distinction precisely, everyone agrees there is one, and ethical theories differ according to the importance they attach to it.

Consequentialist theories say rightness is determined exclusively by the consequences of acts; **nonconsequentialist theories** deny this. Like deontologism, nonconsequentialism has stronger and weaker forms according to whether it says that consequences are irrelevant to determining rightness or relevant but not by themselves decisive.

Theories holding that rightness is determined always by the good of the consequences of actions are both axiological and consequentialist or what we may call **teleological.** (They are also sometimes called **utilitarian,** but I'll speak of utilitarianism mainly in connection with theories that stress consequences for people and perhaps for other sentient beings. Teleological theories are also, somewhat misleadingly, sometimes simply called "consequentialist.")

There are other forms of axiological theory. For example, one might believe that right conduct consists at least in part in the performance of good acts. Here the assumption is that acts can be judged good apart from their consequences. Plato and Aristotle seem at times to have thought this, as does the twentieth-century philosopher G. E. Moore. Another possibility is that right conduct is simply the conduct of good people. In this view, character is most important, even if the goodness of acts and consequences is relevant. To speak of someone's goodness or excellence is to speak of virtue, and, as shown later (section 3.11), an ethics that takes virtue to be of central importance is an **ethics of virtue.**

2.7 THE BALANCE OF GOOD AND BAD IN CONSEQUENCES

Question (2) in section 2.6 is important because most acts produce both good and bad consequences. Going to the movies provides you with enjoyment, and that is good. But it also separates you from some of your money, which is bad. Dental work preserves your teeth, and that is good. But it is expensive and unpleasant, and that is bad.

In cases of greater moral significance, welfare provides needy people with money for food, clothing, and shelter (basic needs, as said earlier). And that is good. But other people are taxed to fund the payments, whether they like it or not. And that is bad. Abortion gives women the choice of whether to bear unwanted children, which is good. But it also offends some people's religious and moral convictions, and that is bad. The same is true of most controversial social, political, and moral policies.

Because most acts have both good and bad consequences, teleologists typically say that rightness is determined by there being a predominance of good over bad in an act's consequences. It would matter little that an act brought about more good than another if, in other respects, the act also brought about vastly greater harm. (If working for an hour would earn you ten dollars, but mugging someone would net you twenty dollars, the good of the second act, taken by itself, would be greater than that of the first; but the bad involved would be vastly greater than the exertion of working for an hour.)

To illustrate this point another way, suppose we could quantify good and bad in terms of units (as in fact we cannot do). Let us suppose that each of three acts—X, Y, and Z—brings about a certain quantity of both good and bad:

		Good	Bad
	X	12	10
Acts	Y	5	9
	Z	6	1

Act Y is clearly wrong because it brings about less good than either of the others and is outweighed by the bad it produces. But Z, according to most teleologists, is preferable to X because even though it brings about a smaller quantity of good than X, it also brings about less bad. The balance of good over bad for act Z is $+5$, whereas for X it is only $+2$.

Specifically, teleologists say that an act is right if and only if it brings about as great a balance of good over bad as any other alternative available to the agent, and it is obligatory if and only if it brings about a greater balance of good over bad than any other available alternative.

2.8 THE GOOD OF SELF, OTHERS, AND COLLECTIVITIES

But here we must ask, "Good for whom?" (This brings us to question [3] of section 2.6.) Insofar as we are talking about consequences for people, the possible answers to this question range all the way from the person contemplating performing the act to everyone affected by it.

The position that people should be concerned only with their own personal good—that is, only with the balance of good over bad in the consequences for them personally—is **ethical egoism.** To say we should promote the greatest balance of good over bad for all people affected by our actions (which may include ourselves) is to subscribe to **utilitarianism.** Between these two lie an indefinite number of possibilities.

As noted (section 1.4), people have historically coalesced into collectivities of various sorts: families, tribes, clans, communities, societies, nation-states.[12] In addition to these more or less voluntary associations, people can also be grouped according to genetic or biological traits, such as those defining sex or ethnicity. Moral concerns can be confined to (or considered to give priority to) people comprising any of these groupings. Then the balance of good over bad for those people—and those people only—determines moral rightness.

But need one be concerned only with people? Not necessarily. Sometimes collectivities themselves are considered to be important. Their good, either instead of or in addition to, the good of the individuals who make up the collectivities is an object of concern—and in some cases, of primary concern.

Socrates took such a view as he awaited execution. His friend, Crito, had arranged for him to escape. But he refused, reasoning that to do so would be to flout his death sentence, which, though unjust, had been arrived at in accordance with the state laws. The state (here the city-state of Athens), he contended, is like a parent; people who voluntarily choose to live within its borders and enjoy its protection and benefits have an obligation not to injure it. He would be injuring the state, Socrates thought, by escaping. The state itself, as an entity, was thus an object of moral concern. Plato's representation in the *Republic* of the ideal state likewise assigns it an importance transcending that of the individuals making it up.

In twentieth-century systems, Nazism in Germany and fascism in Italy embodied such an outlook. The fascists under Mussolini exalted the state above the individual. Hitler did the same with the nation (which he took to stand for a *people,* their culture, traditions, and values, whether or not they were part of a state—that is, under a particular government). It was to further the perceived interests of the Aryan race in particular that Nazi policy was framed.

Any collectivity, such as a race, a people, or even humankind as a whole might come to be thus highly regarded. The highest good is then understood by reference to its well-being rather than to that of the individual members (although there must, of course, be *some* connection between the good of the collectivity and that of the members, or else it would be difficult to make sense of the idea of the good of the collectivity).

The collectivity need not even consist exclusively of humans. It might include all beings capable of experiencing pleasure and pain, which would include many animals. Some ecologists even speak of the wider "biotic community" of all living things, including plant and animal life. If this wider community is taken to be of value, moral consideration may extend to it as well.

Many Eastern philosophies have long held such a wider perspective in their emphasis on the essential oneness of all things.[13] The earth or the world as a whole may be assigned such value. Some people even think the earth may have enough characteristics of an organism to be considered a living thing.[14] If so, any concern for all living things requires a concern for the well-being of the earth itself and for its environment; not simply insofar as its condition affects the survival and well-being of ourselves and other species, but for its own sake as well.

2.9 MICRO ETHICS AND MACRO ETHICS

Two types of teleological theory emerge here. **Micro ethics** takes the survival and well-being of individual beings to be the highest good and considers to be right whatever maximizes that good. The beings may be humans—or they may include plants and animals. Micro ethics can have a concern with the good of groups or collectivities, but it does so only insofar as that good is understood to consist of nothing more than the good of the individuals that make up the collectivity. Thus utilitarianism, when understood to be saying that we should maximize value for as many individuals as possible, is a form of micro ethics.

Macro ethics, in contrast, assigns highest value to the survival and well-being of collectivities and entities such as states, nations, races, religions, peoples, nature, and the world. Such entities are considered to be a good in themselves. Macro ethics defines moral conduct (either primarily or exclusively) in terms of what maximizes that good.

Each individual who is part of such an entity (in the case of collectivities) or whose well-being is tied up with that of the entity (in the case of superentities such as the state, the earth, or the universe) may have his or her own good. But the entity *itself* is thought to have a good over and above that of any particular individual and over and above that of the sum of the goods of any group of such individuals. So, national interest, for example, might be taken to represent a good that is more than the sum of the goods of the individuals that make it up. Individuals, in this view, may sometimes have to be sacrificed for the sake of that interest.

Macro ethics, in this sense, presupposes the principle that the good of a whole may bear no regular proportion to the sum of the goods of its parts. Any whole (including nations, states, races, religions, and so on) for which this is true constitutes an **organic unity.**

The concerns of macro ethics and micro ethics need not be exclusive, of course. Ethical egoism is a form of micro ethics. But ethical egoists such as the Epicureans stress the importance of friends and community—not because they attach value to these in themselves, but because they believe they are necessary to one's own good. At his trial Socrates defended himself against the accusation that he had corrupted the young by arguing that no one would do so voluntarily because no one would want to live with corrupt people.

By the same token, a macro ethics that takes the well-being of the biotic community to be the highest good would almost certainly have a concern for the good of individual human beings because they would be a significant part of that community. That community's value, even if not in direct proportion to the good of its individual members, could not plausibly be thought to be determinable apart from the good of individual people.

2.10 OUTLINE

A summary of what we have covered thus far may be found in the appendix. The following schematizes the theories discussed in a way that represents their relationships visually.[15]

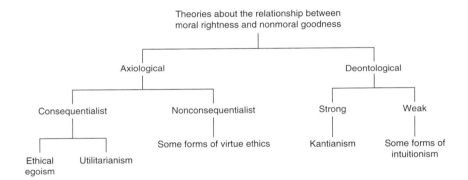

2.11 CHARACTER AND CONDUCT

I have been talking primarily about actions, and the preceding theories all belong to what we may call the **ethics of conduct.** But some of the most important evaluations we make are of *persons,* not conduct. We judge people to be good or bad, admirable or unadmirable, praiseworthy or blameworthy, responsible or irresponsible, honorable or dishonorable, and so on. These all represent ways of assigning value to people as evidenced by their character—their attitudes, habits, motives, dispositions, and traits.

Rather than focusing primarily on conduct, this approach looks for moral guidance to models of good people or to the traits that make up excellence of character. These traits are called **virtues,** and this orientation represents the **ethics of virtue.**

Ancient ethics tended to take the form of virtue ethics in this sense; not that it did not have much to say about conduct, but the emphasis was on understanding what constitutes the excellence of the human person. This emphasis was superseded by much of modern moral philosophy, which increasingly stressed conduct and did so from a heavily legalistic orientation. Thus rules and principles took center stage, a position they occupy to this day. Among contemporary philosophers, however, interest has flared anew in the ethics of virtue, and many believe that the ancients were essentially on the right track in emphasizing virtue. As a result, the ethics of conduct and the ethics of virtue have, in many ways, become competing outlooks. The ethics of conduct remains the dominant orientation, but the ethics of virtue is receiving increasing attention.

We want to look closely at both approaches. The next chapter begins with the classical statement of the ethics of virtue in ancient thought.

Notes

1. *John Dewey: The Later Works: 1925–1953*, vol. 7: 1932, ed. Jo Ann Boydston (Carbondale: Southern Illinois University Press, 1985), p. 164.

2. I am speaking here of human law as it exists in contemporary U.S. society. This does not apply to some conceptions of divine law that seek to regulate one's inner life (thoughts and motivation) as well.

3. John Stuart Mill, *Utilitarianism* (New York: Liberal Arts Press, 1948), p. 21. Originally published in 1863.

4. Rules are often taken to cover only certain types of acts, such as promising or truth telling, and to admit of exceptions. They are also frequently regarded as subordinate to principles, in the sense of requiring an appeal to a principle in order to justify a rule.

5. What follows are only rough approximations of the relevant principles, most of which are elaborated later.

6. As Plato concludes in the example from which this is adapted, in the *Republic* (Stephanus 331).

7. If there is a God, and a command from God makes something right, then whenever God issues a specific command to someone in a specific situation, the rightness of that act depends solely on that situation. This might make it seem that theories based on divine commandment are particularistic rather than legalistic. However, because most theories that appeal to God's commands (see in Chapter 6) deal with commandments to perform certain types of acts (and hence lay down certain rules or principles), I regard such theories as forms of moral legalism. If God's commands make acts right, and God issued *only* specific commands for specific situations, then arguably the divine command theory would be a form of moral particularism.

8. Ross could allow that rules of *prima facie* obligation sometimes determine rightness if it were ever the case that only one rule applied to a particular act. But in fact he believes that every act tends to be *prima facie* right in some respects, and *prima facie* wrong in others, which suggests that more than one rule always applies. W. D. Ross, *The Right and the Good* (Oxford, England: Clarendon Press, 1930), p. 33.

   For good discussions of particularism, see J. Dancy, "Ethical Particularism and Morally Relevant Properties," *Mind* 92, no. 368 (1983): 530–547; and also his *Moral Reasons* (Oxford, UK; Cambridge, USA: Blackwell, 1993). See also David McNaughton, *Moral Vision: An Introduction to Ethics* (Oxford, England: Blackwell, 1988), Ch. 13. Both give somewhat different characterizations from mine; Dancy's argument in particular is too complex to detail here.

9. See, for example, H. L. A. Hart, "Between Utility and Rights," in *The Idea of Freedom: Essays in Honour of Isaiah Berlin*, ed. Alan Ryan (Oxford, England: Oxford University Press, 1979), pp. 77–99; and *Utility and Rights*, ed. R. G. Frey (Minneapolis: University of Minnesota Press, 1984).

10. Following W. D. Ross, in *The Right and the Good*. The issue might, with appropriate modifications, be put as the question of the relationship between value judgments and prescriptive judgments, or even more fundamentally, between the activities of evaluating and guiding conduct.

11. Weak versions of deontologism, recognizing as they do the relevance of goodness, need to answer these questions as well.

12. Not that humans are known ever to have existed in complete separation from one another; but historical evidence shows that they have formed increasingly larger social units over time.

13. Although some Western philosophy from Parmenides through Hegel and Bradley has shown a strong metaphysical bent in this direction (and in Schopenhauer something of an ethical bent as well), it has rarely shown reverence for all life.

14. This is the so-called Gaia hypothesis, after Gaia, the Greek goddess of the earth. See, for example, *The Ages of Gaia: A Biography of Our Living Earth*, by James Lovelock (New York: Norton, 1988).

15. I am indebted to Richard Werner for the essentials of this diagram.

Discussion Questions

1. Section 2.3 examines possible relationships between goodness and rightness. Which of those possibilities seems to you most plausible, and why? Do you ever make judgments of what is right or wrong apart from the consideration of whether they would be promoting something that is good or bad? If so, in what sorts of circumstances?

2. What is the distinction between axiological and deontological theories? What is the distinction between the strong and the weak versions of each?

3. Why is it important to distinguish between the amount of good an act may produce and the balance of *good over bad* that it may produce?

4. Do you think Socrates did the right thing (as represented in section 2.8) by refusing to escape a death sentence on the grounds that by escaping he would be injuring the state? Are collectivities like nations or states capable of suffering injury in a literal sense? If so, how should their well-being be weighed against that of the individuals who make up the collectivity?

5. What is an organic unity? Do you think there are any organic unities? What would be examples of candidates for organic unities?

6. What is the distinction between an ethics of conduct and an ethics of virtue?

Virtues are dispositions not only to act in particular ways, but also to feel in particular ways.[1]
Alasdair MacIntyre

Virtue in Ancient Philosophy

3.1 KINDS OF VIRTUE

Think of someone you particularly admire—a living person or someone from history, fiction, or film. Then ask yourself what you admire about him or her.

The answer will almost certainly be that the person has certain qualities you value, such as trustworthiness, reliability, truthfulness, courage, friendliness, leadership ability, musical, artistic, or athletic accomplishment, and the like; in short, some excellence of character, intellect, or achievement.

Qualities that make for excellence we call *virtues*. These may include **natural qualities** such as strength, speed, or intelligence; **acquired qualities** such as expertise at chess or accomplishment at playing the trombone; **qualities of temperament** such as a good disposition or a sense of humor; **religious qualities** such as faith or piety; and **qualities of character** such as benevolence, kindness, perseverance, courage, or wisdom.

We judge persons as well as actions. And it is with persons that the ethics of virtue is primarily concerned. But the concern is not merely to judge persons; it is to provide guidance for conduct as well. Where the governing imperative in the ethics of conduct is "*Do* what is right," the imperative in the ethics of virtue is "*Be* a good person."

How does one do this? How does one become a good person (or continue to be one if one already is)? This requires asking first what constitutes a good (or virtuous) person.

We may mean merely someone who possesses qualities we admire, like intelligence, a good sense of humor, a quick wit. Or we may mean someone who is *morally* good, who has moral integrity. People can be intelligent, talented, strong, courageous, learned, and many other things we admire, without having moral integrity. Many Nazis had these attributes, but that did not prevent them from doing horrendous moral wrongs. People can possess good qualities and still be unadmirable people.

By a "good person," we usually mean someone who is *morally* good, whether or not he or she exhibits to any significant degree other qualities we admire. Franz Jägerstätter, to take another case from Nazi Germany, was a simple man. Born a peasant, he lacked the education and brilliance of many of the Nazis. But he showed great moral courage in refusing to serve in the German military (for which refusal he was eventually beheaded).[2] In short, he was very ordinary from the standpoint of the usual qualities that make for human excellence; but he was extraordinary in having qualities that make for moral integrity.

So we must distinguish moral virtues or excellences from nonmoral ones. We admire some people for their nonmoral virtues, people whom we might not admire if they did not also have at least some moral virtues.

It is important also to distinguish between natural and acquired virtues. We cannot, for example, just *become* intelligent. We are born with certain intellectual capacities (we can develop them and improve our scores on IQ tests, but it is not otherwise within our power to determine how intelligent we shall be any more than it is within our power to determine how artistically creative we shall be). Many other excellences we can acquire. Given some native ability, we can develop skills at math, music, or basketball. Hard work and dedication are within our control. Through them we can realize our natural potential. Similarly, it is within our power to act morally. We can develop moral character through our own efforts. And although, as we shall see, Plato and Aristotle do not altogether agree, developing moral character requires little in the way of qualities of natural excellence.

Because an *ethics* of virtue, as opposed to a general theory of virtue, aims at providing moral guidance, it is concerned with virtues that can be acquired and that have some warrant to be called *moral*. It might seem that to become morally virtuous requires only that you do what is right. This would make the ethics of virtue depend on the ethics of conduct. But the matter is more complicated than this. We can get some sense of these complexities by considering some important classical theories in the ethics of virtue.

3.2 PLATO AND THE VIRTUOUS PERSON

Chapter 1 noted that evaluating is a central activity in human affairs. For Plato (429–347 B.C.), the idea of goodness is at the heart of this activity. This is important to understanding Plato's account of virtue, which emerges as part of his attempt to counteract the relativistic teachings of the Sophists (professional teachers, some of whom claimed to be able to teach virtue). To do so, he sought to establish an absolutistic foundation for morality.

Some things, Plato says, have a specific function. This is true, for example, not only of the eyes and ears whose functions are to see and hear, but also of artifacts such as tools, whose functions are to cut, chisel, hammer, and so on. Moreover, some living things have functions, and different things of the same kind sometimes have different functions. The function of a thoroughbred horse, Plato might have said, is to race; that of a plow horse, to do heavy labor. All this is part of his teleological conception of the world (see section 1.3).

But the human soul itself, Plato thought, has a *function*. It is to live: to deliberate, make choices, and direct the whole person (which for Plato is a composite of immaterial soul and material body). This living entails the use of reason, which for Plato as well as for Aristotle sets humans apart from animals.

For Plato, a thing's *virtue* or *excellence* is what enables it to perform its specific function well. Any function can be performed well or poorly. If the cornea, lens, and retina of your eye are not in good working order, you have poor vision or none at all. They must work together harmoniously in regulating light to enable you to see. That they are in a state to do that (that they have the power of sight, as Plato puts it) represents their virtue. The same with the ears and hearing. Similarly, speed is what enables the race horse to perform its specific function well, whereas the virtue that does the same for the plow horse is strength. The knife performs well when it is sharp, the hammer when it has a certain heft. To perform well, the ballerina needs poise and grace; the baseball pitcher, speed and control.

3.3 THE SOUL'S FUNCTION

As with other things that have a specific function, the soul has a virtue that enables it to perform its function well. That virtue is justice.

To live well, for Plato, is to live both happily and morally. To do so, we must be just. To see exactly what he means by *justice* requires considering his theory of human nature, which in turn requires saying something about the differences he believes there to be among people.

Some gifted people, Plato believed, have the capacity, given the right circumstances and education, to understand the very essence of goodness, what he called the Idea of the Good. The Idea of the Good is eternal and immutable; it has a reality that transcends the world of sense experience. As such, it provides an absolutistic foundation for morality. No matter what changes take place in human societies, it remains exactly the same. As the idea of goodness is necessary to understanding the world, and specifically to understanding institutions and societies, those who know the good will have a unique grasp of what is best in personal, social, and political affairs.

Just as the grandmaster in chess understands the game, the values and functions of the various pieces, and, to a higher degree than ordinary players, how to play the game well, so a person who understands what Plato calls the Idea of the Good has comparable knowledge about human affairs. Such a person understands what kind of people there are, what their proper function is in a well-ordered society, what the aim of society is, and above all, has good judgment about how to govern the state well in both its domestic and international relations. And just as the grandmaster is the person best suited to play chess well, the person with knowledge of the good is best suited to govern well. That person is a true philosopher; and, ideally, philosophers should be kings.

It is *wisdom*, following on knowledge of the good, that enables such people to perform their specific function of governing well. Others, however, are best suited to serve in the military. They are guardians of the state. The virtue that enables them to perform this function well is *courage*: right opinion (instilled by wise rulers through education) concerning what ought and ought not to be feared. Still others are best suited by nature to be artisans or tradespeople. It is important that their various desires and appetites be controlled, and it is important that there be a shared conviction among them and the rulers and soldiers that the wise should rule. When there is such agreement, Plato held, the state as a whole has the virtue of *temperance*. When, in addition, each of the three classes in society—the rulers, the soldiers, and the workers—performs its proper function well (ruling, providing for the security of the state, and providing for the state's material needs, all in the conviction that the operation of the whole should be superintended by the wise), the state as a whole is characterized by *justice*. Justice is harmony throughout the ideal state.

Much the same is true with regard to individual persons. In the first sustained piece of psychological analysis in Western thought, Plato divides the soul into three parts: reason, a spirited element, and the appetites. Reason is responsible for directing the soul, hence for directing the whole person. The spirited element accounts for anger, indignation, a sense of honor, and ambition in persons who strive for achievements going beyond the mere satisfaction of bodily needs. Finally, each of us has appetites, desires for food, drink, and (beyond a certain age) sex.

Just as in the ideal state, the naturally superior wise persons are best suited to rule, so within the individual person reason is best suited to command the lower parts of the soul. To do this well, reason needs the virtue of wisdom. For the gifted few who have the requisite intellectual capabilities, wisdom issues from knowledge of the good. Others must make do with right opinion. In acquiring right opinion about what ought and ought not to be feared, the spirited element acquires courage. And when the appetites are properly controlled and subordinate to reason (in other words, when they as well as the spirited element "agree" that reason should rule), the whole soul has the virtue of temperance.

What, then, is justice? Justice is that state of the soul in which each of the parts is performing its specific function well and in harmony with each of the other parts. Health is a natural state of the physical body when everything is in order and functioning properly. Justice is the natural order of the soul when each of its parts is in order and functioning properly. When people achieve such inner harmony, they are living well—happily and justly.

3.4 VIRTUE, GOODNESS, AND RIGHT CONDUCT

To achieve this inner harmony is for Plato to actualize goodness within the person. Such a state is good in itself, whatever other consequences this inner harmony might bring. People exemplify goodness and beauty in their character when they are virtuous, and discord and ugliness when they are unjust (just as a fit and well-nourished body radiates health and a neglected, abused one, ill health). And this, Plato thought, suffices for happiness. Virtue, in this sense, is its own reward.

But how does one become virtuous, or maintain virtue once it is achieved? Plato suggests two different answers. He seems not to notice the differences, but they are important to understanding the relationship between virtue and right conduct (or, more generally, an ethics of virtue and an ethics of conduct).

Both answers agree that we become virtuous through *conduct*. We do not just sit down and decide to become virtuous and then somehow, by sheer force of will, bring it about. Some Eastern philosophies advocate meditation as a way to achieve virtue. But even that is usually conceived to be an extended process requiring discipline and commitment. We must *act* in certain ways to bring about and to maintain the desired inner harmony in our souls.

The differences between the two answers suggested by Plato arise when we ask how we are to characterize the acts necessary to produce this inner state. The two answers agree that these acts can be called just or unjust, virtuous or vicious (or, we might say, right or wrong). They differ in that sometimes Plato speaks as though acts were by definition just or unjust according to whether they produce or maintain virtue within the soul; at other times he speaks as though they were just or unjust according to some other criterion, and that character is defined as virtuous according to its relation to such conduct.

Let us explain this, starting with the first possibility. The just man, Plato says,

> . . . sets in order his own inner life, and is his own master and his own law, and at peace with himself; . . . always thinking and calling that which preserves and cooperates with this harmonious condition just and good action.[3]

In this view, it looks as though what is right and wrong (what he refers to in the passage as just and good) are determined exclusively by what produces virtue within the individual. There is no other standard of moral conduct. The ethics of virtue, then, tells the whole story about morality. If we know in advance what virtue is, we can designate as just or unjust those acts that produce it. Our criteria for judging conduct are derived from our criteria for judging character.

At other times Plato speaks as though some acts are known antecedently to be just or unjust. Although these acts promote justice or injustice within a person's soul, it is not their producing those respective states that makes them just or unjust. There must be independent criteria by which we make those determinations. As Plato (*Republic* 444) has Socrates say in the following exchange with Glaucon,

> **SOCRATES:** Why, I said, they [justice and injustice] are like disease and health; being in the soul just what disease and health are in the body.

GLAUCON: How so? . . .

SOCRATES: Why, I said, that which is healthy causes health, and that which is unhealthy causes disease.

GLAUCON: Yes.

SOCRATES: And just actions cause justice, and unjust actions cause injustice?

GLAUCON: That is certain.

To understand fully what constitutes virtue in this view requires first knowing the criteria of right conduct (just and unjust actions). And these criteria are independent of the criteria for a virtuous character (it would be circular to say that virtue in the person is caused by virtuous conduct and that virtuous conduct is what produces virtue). So in this view the ethics of virtue presupposes an ethics of conduct. The ethics of virtue could still be primary, in the sense that being a virtuous person could still be what is most important in morality. But to know how to achieve this state would require antecedent knowledge of what constitutes just or right or virtuous conduct.

So we can formulate two competing views about the relationship between virtue and right conduct suggested by these passages from Plato:

A. **Right conduct** = def. that which promotes, sustains, or issues from virtuous character.

B. **Virtuous character** = def. that which produces, or is sustained or promoted by, right conduct.

The first thesis gives an account of right conduct but leaves unexplained what virtue is; the second explains virtue but leaves unexplained what right conduct is. (One cannot plausibly hold *both* views, of course, for that would explain right conduct by reference to virtue, and then virtue in turn by reference to right conduct.)

Of these two, I suggest that thesis A most nearly represents Plato's position. His continual emphasis of the analogy between justice and health tends to support this suggestion. We do not say that actions or activities are just healthful in themselves (although the above passage is a little misleading in this regard). We think of them as healthful or not according to whether they contribute to health; it is their effects on us that are important. We jog, lift weights, or do aerobics because such activity is good for us. Plato is saying that acts are similarly right or wrong, just or unjust, according to their effects on us, specifically on our souls and character. He may also be saying, though this is less clear (and the analogy with health probably does not hold here), that the conduct of virtuous people is necessarily right. If you want to understand what right *acts* are, look to see which acts are performed by virtuous people.

In sum, if actions promote or sustain virtue, not only in ourselves but in those affected by what we do and in the state as a whole, or if they result from a virtuous character, they are just or right. If they do not, they are unjust or wrong.

Thesis B, in contrast, conflicts with much of Plato's characterization of virtue. He describes virtue in terms of the integrated, cooperative functioning of the parts of the soul, not in terms of just or right actions. True, you must *do* certain things to acquire virtue (at least this is true of those who through study and discipline come to possess virtue through knowledge of the good; others, ideally, have it instilled in them through good education and in practice seem to acquire it inexplicably, as a kind of "gift of the gods"). But Plato speaks as though it is the consequences of those actions—the fact that they tend to promote virtue in people—that make them right, rather than the other way around.

In the end, his commitment to an ethics of virtue is clear when he says, "But in reality justice . . . is not a matter of external behavior, but of the inward self and of attending to all that is in the fullest sense, a man's proper concern." (*Republic* 442)

Although this position does not expressly define right in terms of good, it is characteristically teleological in that most accounts of virtue represent the virtues as good. In Plato's view, virtue is good in itself; what one creates in promoting virtue is goodness. Actions issuing from a virtuous character are right, not only because of any contribution they may make to the virtue of others, but because they help sustain virtue within the person acting. Once you attain virtue, if it is rooted in knowledge of the good and not merely in right opinion, the whole of conduct will sustain and reinforce that condition of moral health. It is a state no one would voluntarily relinquish. For this reason Plato is confident the rulers in an ideal state would not abuse their power.

3.5 SOME PARALLELS IN HINDU ETHICS

Certain aspects of the outlook we find in Plato received expression in Hindu philosophy at the same time, but in a way adapted to the particular cultural and religious context of India.

Whereas in Plato there is a close parallel between the makeup of the individual and that of the ideal state (each, as we have seen, consisting of three parts, with each part possessing its own function), in much of Hindu thought the parallels are not only between the individual and society, but among the *individual, society,* and the *cosmos* as a whole. All are structured in much the same way. The individual is a microcosm of the cosmos. The individual, society, and the cosmos are manifestations of the same, unseen ultimate reality, a kind of creative energy underlying everything that exists.

This account of the cosmos derives from the Vedic writings that preceded Plato by more than 1,500 years. We need not be concerned with its particulars here, but what is noteworthy is the idea that all people are born with a nature that suits them to a certain life and to the responsibilities and duties that life brings. As expressed in a later Indian classic, the *Bhagavad-Gita,* at about the first century A.D.,

> The actions of priests, warriors, commoners, and servants are apportioned by qualities born of their intrinsic nature.[4]

Each person has, in Plato's terms, a certain function determined by the very nature of the person, including intelligence, qualities of character, and physical and mental abilities. For Plato, the proper performance of these functions is necessary for the realization of an ideal state. Indian philosophy, in contrast, holds that each person in the actual world as we know it is suited to a particular role. To live well is to play that role as perfectly and completely as you are able. To do so is to fulfill your *dharma,* a duty arising from the cosmic moral order aligning your particular nature with the particular situation in which you find yourself in life.

This outlook provides the underlying philosophical basis for the Indian caste system. According to this system, four castes make up the social order.

At the highest level are people in whom spiritual qualities predominate— a priestly caste. At the lowest level are those in whom physical capabilities predominate—workers. In between are those in whom intellect predominates, who are best suited for administration and the military, and those for whom their particular capacities suit the roles of merchants and farmers.

These four castes reflect a fourfold division of the makeup of the individual person, who consists of soul, body, intellect, and mind. As the qualities associated with each of these are manifest in varying degrees in different people, the castes made up of such individuals constitute, as it were, the soul, body, mind, and intellect of the social order (and these qualities are manifest throughout the universe). When each caste performs its own function, the spiritual, material, intellectual, and security needs of the whole are provided for. The social whole then achieves a harmony not altogether unlike that which Plato envisioned. In so doing, it exhibits the creative forces at work throughout the universe.

The upshot is that a stratification of society that for Plato is part of the idealized conception of the state is in this strain of Indian thought an imperative for actual society. Individuals by their very nature are defined in terms of their relationship to a larger social whole. That social whole, in turn, is defined in reference to the larger cosmic whole. For this form of macro ethics, individuals cannot be fully known and understood in isolation from the social and metaphysical contexts in which they function.

This approach heavily emphasizes duties in fulfilling one's allotted role in the world, so it arguably represents an ethics of conduct rather than an ethics of virtue. Nonetheless, it does call on the individual to strive for perfection in fulfilling his or her own dharma. This fulfillment represents a form of self-realization. It liberates one from the individuality of personal temperament and character. In this way one acquires awareness of one's identity with the ultimate reality found in all things. And this striving for perfection requires the cultivation of virtues.

The accounts of the virtues vary with different schools of Indian thought, but a characteristic rendering is found in the *Bhagavad-Gita.*[5]

Fearlessness, purity, determination in the discipline of knowledge, charity, self-control, sacrifice, study of sacred lore, penance, honesty;

Nonviolence, truth, absence of anger, disengagement, peace, loyalty, compassion for creatures, lack of greed, gentleness, modesty, reliability;

Brilliance, patience, resolve, clarity, absence of envy and of pride; these characterize a man born with divine traits.

By cultivating these qualities, one can achieve spiritual perfection in this life.

Despite the similarities, the differences with Plato are great. Plato's four cardinal virtues are those of the preeminently rational person. Many virtues of Indian ethics are those of the person striving to transcend rationality. They represent the necessary discipline to attain an intuitive apprehension of the central reality of all things. And it is impossible to do this simply by using reason.

This way of thinking also contrasts sharply with much of more recent Western thought, which is strongly individualistic and views people as essentially self-contained, self-interested units. They create societies through their interactions but have a nature that is essentially definable apart from those interactions. Their duties to the larger whole arise (literally or metaphorically) from contractual arrangements by which they cede some of their rights to the collectivity. Those duties are not an inherent part of the social and cosmic order as they are in Indian thought. Nor are they exemplifications of an idealized conception of the good, as Plato thought. And neither the Indian nor the Platonic conception of the stratification of society fits well with the political conception of justice typical of most twentieth-century Western thinkers, which tends to be equalitarian.

3.6 ARISTOTLE AND THE HABITS OF VIRTUE

Like Plato, Aristotle views the world in terms of ends, purposes, or functions. In nature, the end of the acorn is to become an oak tree. In human affairs, the end of architecture is to produce buildings; of shipbuilding, to produce ships; of medicine, to promote health.

Humans likewise have a function: to exercise to the best of their ability what is distinctive of them as humans, namely, their reason. Reason distinguishes them from animals.

But whereas Plato thinks of the soul as an immaterial substance within the physical body, Aristotle thinks it is nothing more than the living body with a specific form and principle of organization enabling it to perform certain functions. Analyze a human body and you find nothing but the material of which it is composed: bones, tissues, muscles, and (we would say today), ultimately, molecules and atoms. Nature combines these in such a way that an organism comes into being. That organism can see, hear, feel, think, and reason. It also carries on the processes of nutrition, growth, and reproduction. Although differing from modern science about what the basic elements of matter are, Aristotle believes they combine to perform "vegetative," "appetitive," and "rational" functions (all three in humans, the first two in animals, and the first alone in plants). Matter functioning in this way possesses a soul.

Reason has both theoretical and practical functions. In its theoretical use, it serves to gain knowledge; in its practical use, to direct conduct. When one achieves excellence in these two areas—in learning and in the practical affairs of living—one is said to have the virtues of **theoretical wisdom** and **practical**

wisdom respectively. As they are excellences of reason, Aristotle calls them *intellectual virtues.*

Someone might, of course, have one of these virtues and lack the other; or have one to a certain degree and the other to a more or lesser degree. A certain woman might be a brilliant physicist, for example, but be absent-minded, indecisive, and weak-willed in her practical affairs. Her reason might function superbly in theoretical matters, but badly in practical matters. By the same token, another person might lead a well-ordered and stable moral life, but have a limited knowledge or understanding of the world. Reason is functioning at its best when we exhibit both theoretical and practical wisdom.

The soul also has the nonrational appetitive and vegetative functions. So far as these are within our control (as, for example, digestion is not), they need to be superintended by reason. Because our desires and appetites affect how we act rather than what we know, it is practical reason's job to direct the nonrational part of the soul. When reason does this well, as when the person has practical wisdom, it promotes moral virtue. Moral virtues are excellences of the nonrational part of the soul.

Aristotle recognizes many moral virtues, some of which have little to do with what we would consider moral excellences today. For that reason, his overall account of moral and intellectual virtue represents more of a general theory of virtue than a moral theory in particular.

Whereas intellectual virtues represent capacities of reason, moral virtues represent habits, traits, or dispositions of *character,* and they must be acquired by practice. To become a generous person, you must perform generous *acts.* This requires making a conscious effort to do the generous thing in circumstances in which generosity is appropriate. The same with circumstances calling for courage. If you make this effort, over a period of time acting generously or courageously will become habitual. You will just naturally act in these ways, and your doing so will flow from your very character. Then in addition to performing generous and courageous acts, you will have become a generous and courageous *person.* So also with the rest of the moral virtues, including temperance, truthfulness, friendliness, magnificence, justice, and pride (notice the contrast between these virtues and those of the *Bhagavad-Gita* in section 3.5). Aristotle's main virtues are these:

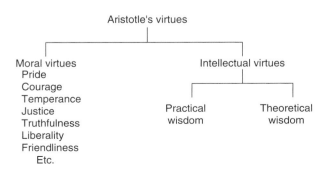

3.7 THE MEAN

How do we know what is right in particular situations? We cannot cultivate the habits of virtue unless we know which acts to "practice." This requires looking at Aristotle's ethics of conduct.

Aristotle's answer to this question is clear, but precisely what the answer *means* is unclear. His answer is that we should act in accordance with what he calls the **mean** (what is often referred to as the **"golden mean"**). In the various situations in which we are called on to make practical decisions, we can distinguish two extremes and a mean between them. We must hit the mean in order to act rightly. Thus, if you eat too much, that is an extreme (an excess), whereas if you eat too little, that is the other extreme (deficiency). If you eat just the right amount, that is the mean. The same with our emotions. If you are always flying off the handle at people, that is an excess, and you are an irascible person. But if you never get angry at all, that is a deficiency, because in some circumstances anger is appropriate. Unlike the ethics of the *Bhagavad-Gita*, Aristotle does not advocate trying to eliminate anger. Getting angry at the right things, at the right time, and in the right place, Aristotle would say, is to hit the mean. When it comes to acknowledging your own accomplishments or merit, to brag shamelessly is obviously an excess, but to be sheepishly diffident is just as bad. You should be confident of your worth, but neither overvalue nor undervalue your merit. That is the virtue of pride.

Notice that the mean is often relative. The right amount to eat will differ for a ballerina and a weightlifter. A generous act may well differ for a millionaire and a beggar on a Kolkata street. The mean is an objective feature of the situations in which we act and not just a matter of subjective feelings or opinion. But because people with their particular needs and temperaments are part of those situations, the mean is often partly relative to them.

3.8 MORAL PERCEPTIONS

But how precisely do we determine *what* the mean is in particular cases? This is the part of Aristotle's answer that is unclear. No one interpretation of what he says coheres with all the rest of what he says.

One answer, I believe, fares better than the others, however; Aristotle says, "such things depend on particular facts, and the decision rests with perception." (*Ethics* 1109b) This suggests that you must consider all the relevant facts of the particular situation in which you find yourself. These include the kind of person you are, what strengths and weaknesses you have, and what your tendencies and predispositions are (the consideration of which characteristics presupposes that you know yourself). You then just "see" what the situation demands.

Aristotle may mean that you must simply decide what is right in such circumstances; there is no criterion beyond that decision by which its correctness can be judged. His position is then a precursor of the sort of view sometimes attributed to existentialism. In that case, it would not be objectivist (though it would still be relativist). But more likely he thinks the decision is based on a perception of a moral quality in the situation. Rather than saying that you perceive the facts and then simply make a decision (where rightness is determined by the decision), he seems to be saying that when you consider all the facts of the situation (including relevant facts about yourself), you simply intuit that for you at this particular time, given your particular character, this is the right thing to do. Your decision to act is based on this perception. What is right is an objective quality of the whole situation (or at least of all those aspects of it that bear on the issue at hand). Aristotle in this view is what Henry Sidgwick called a perceptional intuitionist.

3.9 THE PRACTICAL SYLLOGISM

Sometimes, however, our deliberations require taking account of rules that bear on the proposed action. These rules may themselves become self-evident to us after we perceive the rightness of many instances of the acts they prescribe. Thus, for example, if we see repeatedly that acting courageously represents the mean between cowardice and rashness, we may come to find it self-evident that one ought to act courageously. We would then be in a position to apply that rule to future situations, inferring what is right by reasoning rather than by immediate perception. The twentieth-century intuitionist W. D. Ross gives an account of moral rules tailored very much after Aristotle's in this way.[7]

Thus (though this is not Aristotle's example), we might see the truth of the rule that one ought to act courageously and, finding this is a situation in which our confidence is being tested, conclude that we ought to do the courageous thing. Our reasoning, in that case, might be formalized as follows:

1. One ought to act courageously (major premise).
2. To do X would be to act courageously (minor premise).
3. Therefore: the doing of X.

This represents what Aristotle calls a practical syllogism and illustrates the practical use of reason. Aristotle speaks as though the appropriate conclusion of a practical syllogism is the *performance* of the prescribed action (if one is able, this is the appropriate time, and so forth) and not merely the enunciation of a particular judgment (such as "I ought to do X") prescribing the action.

If you believed that determining what is right always required reasoning from rules, and that correct rules are self-evident, you would be what Sidgwick called a dogmatical intuitionist.[8] But Aristotle probably was not an intuitionist of this sort. He probably did not think that rules always suffice to determine how you should act. When you are aware of a relevant rule, such as that everything sweet ought to be tasted, your reason may apprehend another rule—for example, everything sweet ought *not* to be tasted—that conflicts with it. In that case, some adjudication is necessary to yield a judgment about what this *particular* situation requires.

3.10 ARISTOTLE'S DEONTOLOGISM

Sidgwick observed that "a loose combination or confusion of methods is the most common type of actual moral reasoning." This is probably true. To the extent that Aristotle tries to describe actual moral reasoning, he no doubt thinks it important to reflect the different sorts of appeals that are made in different situations. For this reason he also suggests an altogether different account of how people determine rightness. Sometimes he speaks as though you should look to see what will promote the highest good, either for yourself or the state. But because the good for Aristotle is happiness, and happiness is virtuous activity, you cannot without circularity say that to determine what is right you must see what will promote the highest good. That would be to say that to determine what is right you must look to see what promotes happiness; and to see that requires seeing what promotes virtue; and to see that (at least in the case of moral virtue) requires determining what is right.

Still, there is a case for reading Aristotle as a teleologist (section 2.6). After all, he says in Book I of the *Nichomachean Ethics* that once we know what the highest good is, we will have a target to aim at. This sounds as though he thought we *ought* to aim at the highest good (happiness), and that rightness consists of aiming at it. Furthermore, he sometimes speaks as though practical wisdom's role were to select means to ends that are determined by moral virtue. This suggests that he is using a means-ends model and that right conduct is what promotes the ultimate end of happiness.

Seen in this form, Aristotle appears to be an ethical egoist (ethical egoism is discussed further in Chapter 5). He seems to be saying that each of us desires our own happiness and should strive to achieve that end in all we do. Not that we should not have a regard for the well-being of others; virtues such as justice, liberality, and truthfulness require such regard. But our cultivation of such virtues should be only for the sake of promoting our own happiness.

Some interesting suggestions by contemporary philosopher John Cooper[9] indicate that Aristotle may hold a closely related but less obviously egoistic position. He may believe there is one basic rule, namely,

One ought to pursue the highest good.

and that this rule is known intuitively. But to implement this principle—that is, to determine the means to happiness—requires knowing what is right in particular cases. That in turn requires intuiting the mean.

If this is Aristotle's position, it is a complex one. His basic principle would be teleological, specifying the highest good as the end at which to aim. But his account of how we make our particular moral judgments in specific situations would be deontological. Those judgments would be based on intuition or perception (or intuition of a moral rule from which we infer what is right). Doing what is right would contribute to happiness. It would help you to become morally virtuous, and being morally virtuous would help to create the conditions under which you could fully exercise the rational capacities that must flourish in order for you to be maximally happy. This would still be consistent with your motivation being egoistical, that is, to maximize your own personal happiness. But the criteria of right conduct would not be exclusively egoistic. You could not determine what is right in particular situations by looking at the consequences of acts for your own happiness. You would have to ask what in those situations is right in itself. Having ascertained that, you would *then* know that performing that act would contribute to your happiness.

So this view would, in the last analysis, still be deontological. It would maintain that the goodness of the consequences of actions is not the only thing that determines rightness. What makes your *way of life* right is that it promotes the highest good. But what makes the particular acts that partly constitute that way of life (through the habits their practice creates) right is a matter of perception, not calculation of consequences.

Let me recapitulate the important points of this reasoning. Rather than rightness being determined by what actualizes goodness, the good for Aristotle must ultimately be understood at least in part by reference to right conduct. The good is defined as what we all aim at, and that is happiness. And happiness is an activity of the soul in accordance with virtue (or, as he sometimes says, the most perfect virtue, theoretical wisdom). But to acquire virtue, at least of the moral sort, we must cultivate the appropriate habits. That requires acting in accordance with the mean. The mean is what is right in particular situations and something we determine by perception. (With regard to the intellectual virtues, the story is different; we acquire excellence in our purely theoretical use of reason by learning. Practical wisdom is sometimes represented in purely intellectual terms, as the working out of means to ends, but at other times Aristotle speaks as though it were involved in the selection of ends themselves. So practical wisdom may in part be learned, but in part, like moral virtue, be acquired by practice.)

Although there are different interpretations of him at this point, it appears that, unlike Plato, Aristotle is a deontologist in his theory of rightness. Insofar as taking account of the facts of a situation means considering consequences, as his examples suggest, then he is a deontologist who allows the relevance of consequential considerations in moral deliberation.

If correct, this means that Aristotle is affirming thesis B of the two theses distinguished in section 3.4. Whereas Plato says that what is right must be understood by reference to what produces virtuous character, Aristotle holds that what constitutes virtuous character in the first place must be understood by reference to what is promoted by right conduct (by cultivating the habit of acting rightly).

This leaves us, then, with two competing accounts of the relationship between an ethics of virtue and an ethics of conduct. Both Plato and Aristotle advance an ethics of virtue. But whereas for Aristotle the ethics of virtue presupposes and depends on an ethics of conduct, for Plato the ethics of conduct presupposes and depends on an ethics of virtue.

3.11 MORAL VIRTUE AND RIGHT CONDUCT

Which of these views is correct? If we frame the question from the standpoint of the ethics of virtue, the question is, "Does the ethics of virtue presuppose an ethics of conduct?" (The significance of the question, it should be noted, extends beyond Plato and Aristotle to accounts such as those given by Augustine, Maimonides, Aquinas, Hume, Nietzsche, and various contemporary philosophers who have sought to revive virtue ethics.)

The defender of an ethics of virtue *might* claim that virtue ethics need not even recognize an ethics of conduct. We know from experience what just, courageous, benevolent, temperate, kind, generous, friendly, and honorable people are, and that is all we need know. We need only emulate them. If we become like them, we need not make any judgments about rightness and wrongness. So, this defender might say, we can dispense with an ethics of conduct.

This argument confronts two problems, however. First, it *seems* tacitly to recognize one principle of conduct. It is what tells us to be virtuous. And that looks suspiciously like a judgment to the effect that we ought (morally) to be virtuous. In that case, there would be one principle of conduct, and becoming virtuous would represent compliance with it. If the directive to be virtuous is not a moral directive, then it is hard to see how an ethics of virtue can claim to be a moral position because then we would not meet any moral requirement by becoming virtuous nor fail to meet one by neglecting to do so. Nor would acts performed in the course of becoming virtuous be morally right. So while we could understand such a theory up to a point, it would not add up to a moral theory.

Yet if an ethics of virtue denies even an implied directive to be virtuous (of the sort I attributed to such theories in section 3.1) and claims only to describe virtue without any recommendation as to whether we should try to attain it, then of course the question of whether such a directive is moral cannot arise. But then it is unclear what the point of the theory is and why it purports to be a *moral* (rather than, say, a psychological) theory because it would make no claim to guide conduct, as advocates of virtue ethics have traditionally done.

Apparently, then, however much an ethics of virtue emphasizes character over conduct, it must, if only implicitly, recognize at least one principle of moral conduct. That principle is basic to the theory. It is meant to govern our conduct before we acquire virtue, with a view to getting us to be virtuous. It deals, we might say, with previrtuous conduct. But for that reason it presupposes an understanding of what virtue is. So virtue can still, in an important sense, be the central notion in morality.

3.12 THE PRIORITY OF AN ETHICS OF CONDUCT OVER AN ETHICS OF VIRTUE

But there remains the question of whether acting on that principle presupposes that we understand what right conduct is in particular cases. It will do so if to understand what virtue is requires such understanding. So we must still pursue an answer to the question, "Does an ethics of virtue presuppose an ethics of conduct?"

Notice how the question must now be understood. Let's say we are correct that an ethics of virtue presupposes a directive such as "Be a good (virtuous) person," or as we have most recently put it, a principle such as "One ought to be virtuous."[10] Then, if we ask what virtue consists of, the answer cannot be that it involves following *that* directive, for that would be circular. But it need not be circular to ask if there are independent criteria of right conduct that we must understand in order to become and remain virtuous, hence that we must understand in order to fully comply with the directive. So that is the question before us.

Notice further that a general theory of virtue (as opposed to an *ethics* of virtue in particular) need not answer this question for all virtues. A general theory of virtue (like Aristotle's) may recognize both moral and nonmoral virtues. And it should be possible to explain nonmoral virtues without giving any account of morally right conduct. Being able to kick field goals in football is arguably a form of excellence, but it is good for a reason having nothing to do with morality; namely, helping to win football games. Truthfulness, kindness, and honesty, in contrast, are forms of excellence valued on moral grounds.

Perhaps the clearest case of an excellence valued on moral grounds is what Kant called a *good will*. As Chapter 8 shows, Kant thinks people have a good will to the extent that they act from the motive of duty, that is, respect for the moral law. And this clearly is a moral virtue. The Stoics even identified the whole of virtue with trying to do one's duty; so conceived, virtue was for them the only thing good in itself. But to act from the motive of duty—that is, to try to do what is right because it is right—presupposes some understanding of *what* is right. That understanding must precede acting from the motive. Therefore, some accounting of what is right in the way of conduct is presupposed by the account of this particular moral virtue.

Although we cannot examine the issue at length here, it is hard to see how this conclusion can be avoided for anything that might be considered a moral virtue. Like the ancients, we want to ask not only (1) "What is virtue?" but also (2) "How is virtue acquired?" And as Aristotle realized, it is hard to see how this can be answered satisfactorily without at least tacit appeal to the performance of right acts. Virtue does not just mysteriously spring up in some people. It is not innate. It has to be brought about. This is true even if, as for some Asian philosophies, it is brought about by meditation. Even to meditate is to *do* something. It requires highly developed powers of concentration, and to concentrate is to do something.

If we deny that the actions necessary for promoting virtue are right independently of their promotion of virtue, we are then left without any plausible explanation of why the resultant virtues are moral virtues. Even if we could by sheer act of will produce the internal harmony that Plato identifies with virtue, such virtue would still be the product of some acts. If these acts are not things that it is right to do, or that we ought to do, we are left with no explanation of why that internal state is moral.

It seems, therefore, that an ethics of virtue, understood as an ethics of *moral* virtue, presupposes an ethics of conduct. This does not mean that an ethics of virtue might not still be the most plausible approach to ethics. It may be that morality should focus on the development of character. Maybe our efforts should go primarily into becoming good people, and maybe character is ultimately more important than conduct. Even so, an ethics of virtue still needs an independent account of what constitutes morally right conduct. And that requires attention to an ethics of conduct.

Notes

1. Alasdair MacIntyre, *After Virtue*, 2d ed. (Notre Dame, Ind.: University of Notre Dame Press, 1984), p. 149.

2. See Gordon Zahn, in *Solitary Witness: The Life and Death of Franz Jägerstätter* (Boston: Beacon Press, 1964).

3. Quoted from *The Republic of Plato*, tr. and intro. by B. Jowett (New York: Random House, 1937), 443. Subsequent quotations also from same translation, with Stephanus pagination.

4. *The Bhagavad-Gita*, tr. Barbara Stoler Miller (New York: Columbia University Press, 1986), p. 149.

5. Ibid., p. 133.

6. Henry Sidgwick, in his nineteenth-century classic, *The Methods of Ethics* (Chicago: University of Chicago Press, 1962), Bk. I, Ch. 8.

7. W. D. Ross, *The Right and the Good* (Oxford, England: Clarendon Press, 1930), Ch. 2.

8. *The Methods of Ethics*, Bk. I, Ch. 8.

9. John Cooper, *Reason and Human Good in Aristotle* (Indianapolis: Hackett, 1986).

10. It might be argued that Plato can get by with articulating only a characterization of virtue without needing to presuppose any directive to be virtuous. In his view, virtue is good, and everyone desires the good. If desiring the good means, at least in part, desiring to be good, it may be that all one needs to do is to make clear what virtue is; people will as a matter of course pursue virtue when they understand it. There is no need for a prescriptive judgment directing them to pursue it.

Discussion Questions

1. List some natural and acquired virtues (excellences). Do we admire one kind more than the other? Should we?

2. What, for Plato, are the virtues of wisdom, courage, temperance and justice? Do you agree with Plato that those people with wisdom (derived from knowledge of the Idea of the Good) should rule society? If so, then must we give up democracy? If not, then how can democracy possibly work well?

3. What comparisons are there between Plato's conception of an ideal state and the traditional Hindu conception of a properly functioning actual state?

4. How does Aristotle distinguish between moral and intellectual virtues? What are the two kinds of intellectual virtue? How does the mean play a role in making choices that help in the cultivation of moral virtues?

5. What is Aristotle's practical syllogism? Do you ever make moral decisions in a way that would seem to conform to the practical syllogism? If so, what would be some examples? If not, how do you arrive at moral decisions?

6. Section 3.12 suggests that an ethics of conduct has priority over an ethics of virtue, in the sense that an ethics of virtue needs some independent account of what constitutes right action in order to explain why certain virtues are moral virtues. Would you agree? If so, why? If not, why not?

Happiness, then, is something final and self-sufficient, and is the end of action.[1]
Aristotle

Virtue and Happiness

4.1 PLATO AND ARISTOTLE ON THE NECESSITY OF VIRTUE FOR HAPPINESS

In addition to asking what virtue is and how it is acquired, the ancients asked whether virtue is profitable. They meant, "Does it yield happiness?"

But they not only wanted to know whether virtue leads to happiness. They also wanted to know whether virtue is necessary for happiness. *Must* you be a good person to be happy?

Plato and Aristotle give related but distinguishable answers to this question. Plato sometimes speaks as though it would simply be obvious that virtue is profitable once one understands what virtue is (just as it is obvious that health is good for the well-being of the body once one understands what health is). At other times, he tries to persuade us. For example, he likens a person to a man containing within him a rational person, a lion, and a many-headed beast—these representing respectively reason, the spirited element, and the appetites that make up the soul. (*Republic* 588) He then asks whether it is better that the man rule the beast and the lion, or that one or the other of them rules the man. We are supposed to see that it is clearly better that reason rule than that the spirited element or the appetites rule.

Still again, Plato argues, by comparing the ways of life in which reason, the spirited element, and the appetites predominate, that virtue is more profitable than injustice. He contends that the pleasures of the philosophic life are the only genuine pleasures. The pleasures of lives of ambition and greed (in which respectively the spirit and appetites govern) are spurious. They are like those pleasures we get from quenching thirst or satisfying hunger. We experience discomfort when hungry or thirsty, and eating or drinking relieves that discomfort. The process is pleasurable, but not, Plato would say, because we are experiencing genuine pleasure. It is pleasurable merely because we are alleviating pain. We are all familiar with the bad joke about the person who hits himself on the head with a hammer because it feels good when he stops. Similarly, people who devote their lives to greed and ambition are in this view only more sophisticated versions of such a person (more sophisticated because while they all value relief from pain, the man in the joke self-inflicts it to secure the relief, whereas greedy and ambitious people simply give inappropriate rein to one part of their nature). In contrast, the pleasures of wisdom, which are associated with the philosophic life, are positive in character. They endure and enrich the whole person.

Beyond this, Plato does not tell us much about precisely *what* happiness is. This makes it difficult to assess his claim that virtue is profitable—particularly because he seems to think virtue is sufficient for happiness as well as being necessary for it (although it is possible that this stronger claim was made only by Socrates and not Plato).

It may be true that the thoroughly unjust person, the tyrant, is likely to be insecure, anxiety-ridden, and fearful lest those around him seize his power. And it may be true that the thoroughly virtuous person often glows with happiness. But it is hard to believe that this is always true. The wicked sometimes prosper; the good sometimes suffer misfortune.

In the Old Testament, the Book of Job presses this point. Job is a righteous man who scrupulously obeys God's commandments. Yet he is devastated by misfortune, losing his children, his wealth, and eventually his physical and emotional health. He comes to regret ever having been born.

Although the Book of Job was written in the Near East (by an unknown author) at about the same time Plato wrote in Greece, it emerged against the background of the evolving monotheistic biblical tradition. So there are important differences between Job and the sorts of people Plato describes as virtuous. Job's afflictions are caused by God (though inflicted specifically by Satan). Also, Job's righteousness may have consisted more of proper outward conduct than of the qualities of character of the sort Plato takes to be important.

But despite these differences, the plight of Job challenges Plato's deep-seated optimism about the fruits of virtue. Whether we think a supreme being metes out our fortune or that our fortune is determined by operation of the natural order of things, and whether we think the wicked really often prosper or merely seem to for awhile, the overwhelming weight of evidence—from the genocidal wars of ancient times to the Holocaust and killing fields of the twentieth century—underscores the suffering of the innocent. Whether all these people were virtuous in Plato's sense does not matter. They might have been; and many of them, such as Anne Frank, certainly were virtuous by standards at least as plausible as Plato's. So the case of Job points in the direction of plausible counterexamples to Plato's belief that the virtuous and only the virtuous are happy.[2]

Aristotle, also unaware of the Book of Job, presents an account that makes room for the possibility that virtue does not guarantee happiness. He agrees with Plato that virtue is *necessary* for happiness, but he questions whether it is *sufficient.*

That virtue is necessary for happiness is clear from Aristotle's very definition of happiness. It is, remember, an activity of the soul in accordance with the most perfect virtue (section 3.10). So one must be virtuous to be happy. Also, one must be active to be happy, for happy people are those who function well in the ways distinctive of them as persons, which means they must make full use of their rational capacities. Aristotle believed God's activity to be pure contemplation. The human use of the intellect approximates this divine activity. Thus those with superior intellectual capacities are capable of the greatest happiness.

But for Aristotle, virtue does not quite suffice for happiness. If life is cut short before one has a chance to exercise fully the excellences of which one is capable, one cannot be said to have been happy, nor can those who have been severely deprived of life's material necessities. Although he does not consider such an extreme case, Aristotle would surely have agreed that Job with his afflictions could not be said to be happy (although he might have thought Job achieved a certain nobility in his suffering, of a sort that distinguishes the virtuous from the vicious in such situations).

We need, in other words, a certain length of life and basic material necessities to be happy. And the attainment of these may not be fully within our control. Circumstances play a significant role.

Despite these differences in their conceptions of the relationship of happiness to virtue, Plato and Aristotle agree on three things: (1) that all people desire happiness, (2) that virtue is necessary for happiness, and (3) that happiness comes from perfecting our minds and character, which is largely within our power to do (with the qualification that the highest happiness for Aristotle, and perhaps for Plato, too, is open only to those of superior intelligence).

4.2 PERFECTIONISM AND THE HIGHEST GOOD

Suppose it is true that we all desire happiness. Suppose furthermore that, as Aristotle thought, happiness is final (desired for itself and not as a means to anything else) and self-sufficient (in that once you have it, you lack nothing of importance). Is this really enough, as Aristotle thought, for something to qualify as the highest good?

It is doubtful. Aristotle omits what arguably is a further condition of something's being the highest good: that it be permanent, or at least abiding.[3] Having a certain length of life does not ensure that.

If happiness were fleeting or unstable—if, having achieved it, you might lose it the next day or the next week or the next year—how much better it would be if you could know that once you attained it, it would endure. Job, after all, had been prosperous and happy before misfortune struck. So one might plausibly propose that the highest good should be final, self-sufficient, and permanent.

Insofar as one thinks of happiness as constituting the highest good, it is hard to see how this condition of permanence can be met in this life.[4] Even if the attainment of happiness were largely within our control (which is debatable), whether or not it endures seems not to be. As Job painfully learned, life can suddenly turn sour, happiness turn into misery.

These considerations were recognized by St. Augustine (A.D. 354–430), the first major Christian philosopher. He agreed that everyone desires happiness and agreed further that virtue is necessary for happiness. But he denied that merely perfecting one's character suffices for either virtue or happiness. A good cannot be our chief good, Augustine thought, unless it is one than which no other is better.

Imagine you have achieved some good. If you can imagine some other good that would be even better than it, then the first cannot be the highest good. "If a man feels no confidence regarding the good which he enjoys," says Augustine, "how can he be happy while in such fear of losing it?"[5] But this means that the highest good must be one that cannot be taken away from us against our will, because a good of which that is true will always be better than one that can be taken away. The highest good must be enduring.

Such confidence surely cannot justifiably be achieved in this life. Our lives could end any day; tragedy may strike at any moment. The persons who boarded the flights destined to crash into the Pentagon and the World Trade Center could not have known that their lives were about to end.

4.3 AUGUSTINE AND THE PERMANENCE OF THE HIGHEST GOOD

Consider Augustine's reasoning more closely. Like Plato, he believes we are composed of soul and body, and he believes we must look to the soul to understand virtue. The soul is the body's good; it provides life. And virtue is the perfection of the soul. Virtue is what makes the soul as good as it is capable of being. In this, he is in line with Plato and Aristotle, for whom, as we saw, a thing's virtue is what enables it to perform its specific function well; and that is what represents excellence.

For Augustine, the soul achieves perfection (or in this life approximates it to the highest degree possible) only by following God, and to follow God means to love God. If we do so, then whether or not we are happy in this life we will achieve eternal happiness in the hereafter. We live well (that is, virtuously) if we follow God. We live both well and happily if we reach God—that is, if we achieve salvation. Such blessedness, unlike temporal happiness, cannot be lost against our will. So there cannot be a higher good.

Consider what this implies. We can strive for betterment in various ways, such as by trying to accumulate wealth to secure ourselves against want and need. In contemporary American society, wealth and the possessions it affords are coveted. People often choose careers according to the financial rewards they promise. But we can also strive for betterment (or perfection) in physical development. Aerobics, weight lifting, bicycling, and jogging are ways of doing this. Competitions are ways of honoring excellence in these areas, just as beauty contests are ways of honoring (and sometimes exploiting) physical beauty. Or we can strive to perfect our character. We can try to cultivate the qualities of which Plato and Aristotle spoke or of the sort that are particularly admired today.

But if there is a God—and Augustine assumes there is, in the reasoning under consideration—we can also strive for perfection in loving God. This, according to New Testament teaching, is the First Commandment. It requires loving our neighbor and ourselves as well. So, in addition to the other ideals of perfection (worldly success, physical development, development of character), we can strive to be as perfect as possible in following God's commandment. Although he does not share the Christian view of what it is to know God, or endorse the New Testament conception of what precisely God commands, the Jewish philosopher Maimonides (d. 1204) makes much the same point:

> The prophets have likewise explained unto us these things, and have expressed the same opinion on them as the philosophers. They say distinctly that perfection in property, in health, in character, is not perfection worthy to be sought as a cause of pride and glory for us; that the knowledge of God, i.e., true wisdom, is the only perfection which we should seek, and in which we should glorify ourselves.[6]

For Augustine, to believe in God is to have faith, and with faith comes hope for salvation. Faith and hope, in fact, are presupposed by the perfect love of God. Loving God makes one worthy of knowing what one accepts on faith. To love God is to love one's neighbor and oneself as well. This means trying to enlist others in believing in God. Love in this sense exhibits benevolence, a disposition to do good for others. Their happiness, like one's own—their highest good—can only be achieved through salvation.

The remaining virtues are forms of love. Those who love God, self, and neighbor will have the virtue of fortitude, the willingness to endure whatever one must for the sake of God; they will have prudence as love distinguishes what helps from what hinders it on its path to God; they will have temperance because love will strive to keep itself pure for God, and they will have justice because love will rule all else well in the temporal affairs of this life. Thus where Plato has four cardinal virtues—wisdom, courage, temperance, and justice—Augustine has three: faith, hope, and love, which when fully present will be accompanied by prudence, fortitude, temperance, and justice as manifestations of love.[7]

These virtues are exemplified preeminently in the lives of people such as St. Francis, Martin Luther King, Jr., and Mother Teresa, who represent extraordinary commitments to selflessly follow God's commandments. And it is important to remember that there are commandments here. Even though Augustine believes morality is concerned with the path to happiness, to achieve true happiness requires *being* a certain sort of person, one who is lovingly devoted to God. And that involves complete submission to God's will. The ethics of virtue, as Augustine understands it, is undergirded with an ethics of conduct. We are governed at all times by the commandment to love.

Thus, in this view, both Plato's list of cardinal virtues and Aristotle's larger list of moral and intellectual virtues fail to be genuine virtues. Perfection of mind and character, apart from God, is insufficient. And pride, which Aristotle takes to be the crown of the virtues, representing as it does the trait of those who believe themselves to be justifiably pleased with their own intelligence and character, is the cardinal sin. It is what Milton represents as characterizing Satan's baleful eyes, "mixed with obdurate pride and steadfast hate." It symbolizes the outlook of those who believe they can get along without God and live well and happily by their own resources. What that leads to, in this view, was learned painfully by Adam and Eve.

The view that ordinary virtues are not genuine virtues is moderated, we should note, by St. Thomas Aquinas (1225–1274), the other main figure in classical Christian ethics. He likewise thinks we all desire happiness. And he thinks happiness requires virtue. But, unlike Augustine, he acknowledges human virtues that can be acquired without acceptance of God. Accordingly, there is a kind of "natural" happiness that may be attainable without accepting the Christian outlook on the world.

In a passage that might almost have been written by Plato or Aristotle, Aquinas says,

> Therefore virtue itself is an ordered disposition of the soul, in so far as, namely, the powers of the soul are in some way ordered to one another, and to that which is outside. Hence virtue, inasmuch as it is a suitable disposition of the soul, is like health and beauty, which are suitable dispositions of the body.[8]

For Plato and Aristotle, pre-eminently virtuous people are highly rational. For Augustine and Aquinas, they are devoutly obedient to God. But they are all seen as desiring and striving for happiness. The virtues extolled by both classical Greek philosophy and Christianity are held to be either partly constitutive of happiness or necessary to its attainment.

4.4 DOES EVERYONE DESIRE HAPPINESS? NIETZSCHE ON MASTER MORALITY AND SLAVE MORALITY

But is it really true that everyone desires happiness, or at least desires it above all else? If not, there may be other conceptions of excellence beside those which stress qualities that contribute to happiness.

One finds a good example of such a conception in the world of fiction. In D. H. Lawrence's novel *Sons and Lovers*, a young artist has this exchange with his mother:

> "But damn your happiness! So long as life's full, it doesn't matter whether it's happy or not. I'm afraid your happiness would bore me."

> "You never give it a chance," she said. Then suddenly all her passion of grief over him broke out. "But it does matter," she cried. "And you ought to be happy, you ought to try to be happy, to live to be happy."[9]

What the son's remarks suggest is that some ways of life involve knowingly forsaking happiness or, at any rate, choosing not to pursue it. Perhaps for some people, being creative to their fullest potential requires committing themselves to lonely lives of single-minded devotion to excellence, whether in art, music, literature, science, or philosophy. Such devotion may leave little time or emotional energy for family, friends, or loved ones—the commonly acknowledged ingredients of happy lives.

Much of Friedrich Nietzsche's writings tends in this direction. Nietzsche (1844–1900) writes as though perfection of the self does not come either through being morally good or through religion or loss of individuality by means of asceticism. It comes, rather, through self-mastery and the free exercise of one's creative powers. Plato and Aristotle believed that some people are naturally superior in intelligence; Nietzsche too believed this, and that through such people great achievements have flowered in the course of history. Through them, what is best in humanity will flourish in the future.

But there are obstacles to this occurring, in Nietzsche's view. Those who are superior intellectually, physically, and creatively, he contends, create what is of lasting value among human beings. There are no absolute standards. In their absence, and in the absence of God (whose existence Nietzsche denies), such people are the creators of value (which means morality in its very nature depends on human beings). Although they respect their equals, they despise the weak and do not hesitate to exploit or suppress them—to the point of cruelty and injury if necessary. This is just the way things are; it is the nature of life. Throughout nature, life is the expression of a *will to power:* will to prevail, dominate, suppress. In the superior person, it is not merely the impulse to master others, but also the desire to master oneself as well.

The distinctive qualities of superior people make up the virtues of what Nietzsche calls *master morality:* pride, self-assertion, power, cruelty, honor, rank, nobility. What such people prize is good, and what they despise bad.

The weak have sought over time to overcome the strong. There is a long history of this, in Nietzsche's view. In essence, the weak foster virtues that, when generally accepted, have a leveling effect, holding down the naturally superior and enabling the weak (who are greater in numbers) to gain the advantage. The valuing of equality encourages this, as does the extolling of such virtues as love, compassion, sympathy, obedience, altruism, self-sacrifice, and humility. These are the virtues of slave morality, which are born in resentment of the strong and exemplified in peoples such as the Christians and Jews, who have suffered at the hands of others. The weak elevate qualities that are by nature inferior to the category of the "good," and then label "evil" those qualities that are by nature superior—the virtues of master morality. The standards of good and evil, so defined, reverse the values of good and bad exemplified by the superior, and symbolize the values of slave morality.

In the face of what he sees as the degradation of humanity, Nietzsche urges a "transvaluation of values." What is conventionally "good and evil" is to be transcended in favor of what is by nature good and bad. Only in this way is there hope that the potential of humankind for splendor and achievement will be realized.

Notice that in all this there simply are no standards, religious or ethical, apart from humankind, and that moralities assume different forms depending on the qualities of the persons and circumstances in which they emerge historically. It is important to note that there is also a subordination of the role of happiness. Superior people need not disavow happiness. Unlike the weak, who are guilt-ridden and resentful, they take joy in happiness when they find it, rather than feeling that they do not deserve it. It is just that the pursuit of happiness is not what impels them (particularly if happiness is identified with the pursuit of pleasure). What impels them is the unfettered expression of the will to power—the creative energy surging through them that leads them to accept challenges, overcome hardships, endure suffering, and dominate or ignore others as circumstances dictate. They delight in the spontaneous free play of the forces unleashed by their activity in the world.

The young artist depicted in the D. H. Lawrence quotation does not come anywhere near exemplifying the traits of Nietzsche's superperson. But the issue between him and his mother is one that is at stake in Nietzsche's philosophy. Most people are willing to settle for a comfortable life in the pursuit of happiness. That is what the artist's mother wants for her son—to settle down, get married, and be happy. And that is the life he is certain would bore him. And it is a life that would stifle the energies of Nietzsche's free spirit.

So there emerges here the possibility that not everyone desires happiness above all else. There emerges also the possibility that happiness—contrary to the view of most Western moral philosophers—is not central to a proper understanding of morality. It is not only some individuals who think this. It has been said that whole groups believe this, as anthropologist Ruth Benedict claims when she says, "The Japanese . . . define the supreme task of life as fulfilling one's obligations. . . . The idea that the pursuit of happiness is a serious goal of life is to them an amazing and immoral doctrine."[10] It is possible, too, that virtues that make for happiness (or, at least, that make one deserving of happiness) are not necessarily the central virtues in morality.

But there lurks in all this another possibility. It is that moral virtue—perhaps even morality itself—is not all-important. In the most basic decisions you make in life about the kind of person you are going to be, the choice to become a morally virtuous person is only one option among many, and maybe other options are even more compelling. Nietzsche thought so. He believed that unless humanity is to sink even deeper into the mire of mediocrity, other qualities must flourish in those who have the potential to develop them.

You need not subscribe to Nietzsche's philosophy, however, to take seriously the possibility that morality is not of overriding importance in deciding how to live. Maybe there are qualities of excellence of greater importance than moral virtue.

This view should be distinguished from moral skepticism. It need not question whether there is such a thing as morality or whether we can know what is right and wrong. It concedes all this. It just says that some qualities that make for a worthwhile life are grounded in choices having nothing to do with morality. Just as Lawrence's artist thinks a life of happiness would be boring, so you might think a thoroughly moral life would be boring.

Let us consider, therefore, the possibility that any reflection on what constitutes the ideal sort of person ought to focus more on nonmoral excellences, which, after all, is what Aristotle does. Perhaps that is a more plausible guide to how to live than the pursuit of moral perfection.

4.5 IS MORAL VIRTUE DESIRABLE?

To lead a thoroughly moral life is to achieve a high degree of moral excellence, to approximate moral perfection as nearly as you can. Should you do this? Should you strive for moral perfection rather than for achievement in other areas?

Put this way, the question may evoke skepticism. The idea of someone's trying to be as morally virtuous as possible calls up images of a Goody Two-Shoes setting about to do good throughout the world. No doubt Thoreau had this sort of person in mind when he said, "If I knew for a certainty that a man was coming to my house with the conscious design of doing me good, I should run for my life. . . ."[11]

But need those who strive for moral excellence fit this description? I want to suggest some reasons for thinking they need not.

Morally virtuous people need not to have set about to become virtuous. They need not to have consciously decided to aspire to moral perfection or even to have reflected on their own virtue at all. Rather, they may only have responded to moral considerations when it was appropriate and have *as a result* become moral people. In fact, preoccupation with one's own moral goodness might well stand in the way of leading the kind of life that would result in becoming morally good. Bishop Butler, discussed in the next chapter, argued that a preoccupation with one's personal happiness would likely lead to a *neglect* of the very pursuits that would make one happy. A similar thing may be true with moral virtue. It is possible to become self-absorbed in morality, as well as in anything else. And self-absorption may be incompatible with attaining moral excellence.

Being morally virtuous almost certainly presupposes that one's motives are good, but it does not require that one be motivated to be as morally perfect as possible. Being morally good does not require being self-righteous. When people do self-righteously aspire to moral perfection, the problem is not so much that they become the sort of person many of us would not want to be. It is more likely to be that their self-righteousness becomes self-defeating, and their preoccupation with their own moral perfection prevents them from ever attaining that perfection. This, indeed, may be the deeper meaning of the story of Job.

Does striving for moral excellence require that you must lead a boring life, that you must forgo worthwhile pursuits and must aspire to become a saint? Again, I think not. But let us consider why someone might think otherwise.

If you aspire to a career as a concert pianist, you will have to practice long hours each day. But if you do, you will have little time and energy left over for doing moral good in the world. The same is true with aspiring to become a ballerina, an artist, a tennis star, or a chess champion. Conversely, if you try to be as moral as possible, you must forgo these and other worthwhile pursuits. And this, according to this view, is just the problem. The idea of being a "moral saint" in the manner of Jesus or Gandhi or Mother Teresa is unrealistic, and perhaps even undesirable, for most people. We value the achievements of a Katherine Mansfield, a Mikhail Baryshnikov, or a Michael Jordan, whether or not they are morally good. The world would be poorer without them. And our own lives might be less rich than they could be if we do not cultivate whatever talents and interests we have, whether or not doing so makes us better people morally. As contemporary philosopher Susan Wolf remarks, "a person may be *perfectly wonderful* without being *perfectly moral.*"[12]

There is much truth to this. We don't expect everyone to be a moral saint, and we don't hold it against people if they are not. But it doesn't follow that moral excellence is not an ideal that people should value and, as long as they don't get self-righteous about it, strive to achieve. Nor does it follow that to do so precludes being an interesting and well-rounded person.

Consider the ways in which people might strive for moral excellence. They might live lives devoted to combating injustice, alleviating suffering, promoting social reform—allowing some good "cause" to become dominant in their lives. This represents one kind of moral perfectionism.

In contrast, people might achieve moral excellence by doing what is right as consistently as possible in whatever situations they encounter in their chosen ways of life. This does not require that they pursue any particular type of life (though it certainly rules out certain kinds of lives, such as those of drug dealing or terrorism). Morality does not require of us that we be missionaries, social reformers, or crusaders for justice rather than, say, schoolteachers, plumbers, lawyers, or store clerks. What it does require is that whatever life we choose we conduct ourselves morally in all that we do. We justifiably admire those with the commitment of a Gandhi or a Mother Teresa, but there are many others who live quiet, unheralded lives of extraordinary moral courage and sacrifice. These people are not moral heroes, to be sure, but many of them are moral saints.

The degree of moral excellence you achieve may be measured in part by how much time and energy you devote to expressly moral concerns. But that is not the whole story. It may also be a function of how you live an ordinary life and meet its challenges.

If correct, this means that the moral life, understood as the morally virtuous life, need not be bland and boring. It will, to be sure, be incompatible with the cultivation of some interests (for example, child abuse or racial or sexual harassment). And it *may*, for some, be incompatible with the cultivation of many legitimate talents and interests. Albert Schweitzer almost certainly could have been a better organist had he spent less time ministering unto the sick, and Gandhi might have been a brilliant lawyer had he not devoted himself to liberating India from colonial rule. But morality allows for many different and richly varied ways of life. If it does involve doing good, it surely involves doing good for yourself as well as for others, at least to the point of living a life you find fulfilling.

So, while the overweening self-righteousness sometimes associated with moral virtue is rightly disparaged, it need not characterize moral perfectionism. You can indeed be perfectly wonderful without being perfectly moral. But you *need* not be less than perfectly moral in order to be perfectly wonderful. It is just that, given the shortcomings most of us have, some people can be perfectly wonderful despite not being perfectly moral.

4.6 THE IMPORTANCE OF AN ACCOUNT OF CONDUCT FOR THE ETHICS OF VIRTUE

Even if the preceding argument is a mistaken one and there *are* nonmoral ways of life that are preferable to moral ways of life, and even if it were true that virtue is neither necessary nor sufficient for happiness; still, to make a wise and rational choice about how to live will require an understanding of morality, if only to try to be clear, as Nietzsche does, about what one is rejecting. As the preceding chapter showed, examining the ethics of virtue can only take us so far in this effort. At some point, we need to consider directly what enters into the assessment of *conduct* as right or wrong, moral or immoral. This is necessary for understanding how best to live. Therefore, Part Three focuses on the ethics of conduct.

Notes

1. Aristotle, *Nichomachean Ethics*, Bk. I, Ch. 7, 1097b. *The Basic Works of Aristotle*, ed. Richard McKeon (New York: Random House, 1941), p. 942.

2. In an epilogue of questionable authorship (Job 42:7–17), Job's losses are restored and his fortune doubled after he humbles himself when confronted by God. So it is arguable that the message is, after all, that the righteous eventually prosper. Still, the *fact* of Job's suffering remains, and with it the fact of the suffering of many who seem to deserve it no more than he does.

3. The condition of self-sufficiency needs qualifying, also. If, as Aristotle thinks, there are varying degrees of happiness, one might be happy but nonetheless still desire a higher happiness.

4. Some Asian ethical theories maintain that the highest good consists in perfecting the self through meditation, to the point of a direct awareness of one's unity with the whole of reality. And this achievement is thought to be possible in this life. A Western philosopher such as Kant, in contrast, thinks that happiness is a part, but not the whole, of the highest good, the other part being a good will (or worthiness to be happy). And that is thought to be most likely unattainable in this life.

5. Saint Augustine, "Of the Morals of the Catholic Church," *A Select Library of the Nicene and Post-Nicene Fathers of the Christian Church*, ed. Philip Schaff; *St. Augustine: The Writings Against the Manichaeans and Against the Donatists*, vol. 4 (Grand Rapids, Mich.: Eerdmans, 1956).

6. Moses Maimonides, *The Guide for the Perplexed*, 2d ed., tr. M. Friedlander (New York: Dutton, 1904), p. 396.

7. I am here including faith and hope as virtues, as they clearly represent perfections of the soul and are presupposed by love. But in Augustine's most systematic, early statement of the virtues, he speaks strictly of only four virtues—love, fortitude, prudence, and justice—with the latter three all representing manifestations of love. He also speaks of wisdom, but in a way suggesting that it is all the "rules and light"

that lead to and sustain virtue. See St. Augustine, *On Free Choice of the Will* (Indianapolis: Bobbs-Merrill, 1964), esp. Bk. 2.

8. *Basic Writings of St. Thomas Aquinas,* ed. Anton C. Pegis, vol. 2 (New York: Random House, 1945), p. 415.

9. D. H. Lawrence, *Sons and Lovers* (Avon, Conn.: Limited Editions Club, 1975), p. 272. Originally published 1913.

10. Ruth Benedict, *The Chrysanthamum and the Sword: Patterns of Japanese Culture,* (Boston: Houghton Mifflin Company, 1946), p. 192.

11. Henry David Thoreau, "Walden," in Carl Bode, ed., *The Portable Thoreau* (New York: Viking Press, 1947), p. 329. Originally published 1854.

12. Susan Wolf, "Moral Saints," *Journal of Philosophy* 79 (August 1982): 436.

Discussion Questions

1. Do you agree with Plato and Aristotle that being virtuous (i.e., a moral person) is necessary to being happy? Do you know any immoral people who are happy? Do you agree with Plato (though not Aristotle) that being virtuous is sufficient for happiness? Do you know any moral people who are unhappy?

2. What does Aristotle mean by calling happiness the highest good? Do you agree with him in this? Is there anything you would be lacking if you were happy?

3. Do you agree with Augustine that the highest good must be permanent? If this mortal life cannot guarantee the permanence of happiness, must there be a God and an afterlife, as Augustine thinks, in order for the highest good to be achievable?

4. Is there anything you would rather have than happiness? What about a life of creativity and accomplishment, as discussed in section 4.4?

5. What does Nietzsche mean by master morality and slave morality? Do you think these are accurate characterizations of actual moralities? If so, what should we learn from them? If not, of what interest are they?

6. Section 4.5 raises the question of whether we should strive for moral "perfectionism"—to be as moral as possible. What do you think?

We must therefore study the means of securing
happiness, since if we have it we have everything, but
if we lack it we do everything in order to gain it.[1]
Epicurus

Ethical and Psychological Egoism

CHAPTER 5

5.1 SHOULD WE SEEK ONLY OUR OWN GOOD?

Can it be that morality requires nothing more of us than that we maximize our own good? Ethical egoists believe so. They say that whatever maximizes our own personal good—and only that—is right. To choose always the act that best furthers this end is our sole obligation. Framed as a principle, the view is as follows:

> **Ethical Egoism** (EE): One ought always to maximize one's own personal good as an end.

The egoist is not saying that he or she should simply maximize his or her own good. That would only be to set forth a personal principle and would neither provide guidance for others nor provide a basis for assessing their conduct morally. So it would not be a moral principle, and hence would be an instance of egoism but not of ethical egoism. Nor, of course, are ethical egoists saying that only they and other egoists should maximize their own good. That would be a principle of somewhat broader scope, but of no greater interest to moral philosophy.

The ethical egoist (or "egoist" for short) holds that all of us as individuals should maximize our own good (as an end, and not as a means to anything else) in all we do. This universal claim is supposedly morally binding on everyone.

I should note at the outset some possible misunderstandings of egoism. One is that egoists are egotistical or selfish. Egoists need not be any more conceited than anyone else; they need not brag or flaunt their achievements, nor selfishly disregard the interests, well-being, or happiness of others, nor promote their own good at others' expense. They may do these things, but they need not. Whether or not they do depends on whether they believe that doing so is the best means of maximizing their own good (and whether or not they actually ought to do so will depend on whether they are correct in that belief). If they do not believe that, then they may devote time and energy—even vast amounts of both—to doing things for others and trying to see that the good of others is promoted.

Thus egoists, in other words, may very well be concerned about homelessness, world hunger, or the environment. It is just that if they are, the reason why they are (insofar as they are acting as committed egoists) is once again that they believe that being involved with such issues is the way to maximize their own good. Moreover, if they are correct in that belief, then being involved with such issues will be morally obligatory for them.

This means that you cannot tell whether any given individual is an egoist unless you know something about the person's beliefs. Simply observing someone's behavior is not enough.

Finally, it should not be supposed that the point of egoism is actually to try to bring about the greatest good overall—as, for example, you might be tempted to think if, following Adam Smith, you thought that each person pursuing his or her own good would, as though by the workings of an invisible hand, somehow cause the greatest good to materialize. If you thought this, your fundamental principle would not be ethical egoism at all, but something like the utilitarian principle that one ought to maximize the greatest good. It might or might not be that everyone's acting on EE would bring about the greatest good. But whether it did would be incidental to egoism.

Egoism means what it says: the one, fundamental obligation each of us has is to maximize his or her own good. Nothing else. If doing so brings about a greater good, fine. But if it does not, that is fine also.

It is true, however, that if everyone accepted EE and were successful in doing as it prescribes, then a great deal of good would result. Each person would, in fact, have maximized his or her own good, and that almost certainly would make the world a better place; it might, in fact, be difficult (realistically) to imagine a greater good.

Be that as it may, according to egoism no one has an obligation to bring about such a greater good (other than by making the contribution to it entailed by maximizing his or her own good), and its achievement would simply be a happy by-product of everyone's doing the right thing.

5.2 THREE OBJECTIONS TO ETHICAL EGOISM

But there are serious problems with egoism:

1. First, you may want to ask how likely it is that if people tried to follow a principle such as EE they would be successful in doing what it prescribes. You might argue that a problem with the world is that too many

people already try to act on such a principle, and the result is greed and selfishness.

If this objection assumes that EE entails that people be greedy and selfish, then it is based on one of the misunderstandings just mentioned and can be dismissed on those grounds; EE does not entail that, though it does not rule it out either. However, if the objection assumes only that people would tend to interpret EE as advocating such behavior, and would for that reason proceed to act in the way the objection suggests, then this is a serious practical objection. It raises the question of how people (including those who now act altruistically) would act if they were convinced they should maximize only their own good. It is possible, though by no means certain, that they would act as this objection suggests. But that would have to be shown and could not simply be assumed against the egoist.

In any event, the egoist might reply that the fact that many people might misinterpret, and hence misapply, EE does not invalidate that position. The egoist's aim, after all, is to set forth the correct moral principle (not to guarantee that it will not be misinterpreted, which is not within his or her control). Of course, if it is misinterpreted, that may have bad consequences. The same is true of any moral principle, or of any moral theory for that matter.

2. A related objection carries greater weight. Egoism is a consequentialist position. It prescribes that we maximize value (for ourselves) in the consequences of our actions. This means that to judge correctly what is right in even a single situation requires predicting accurately what the consequences of all the acts open to you in that situation would be. It requires furthermore that you be able to assess accurately how those consequences would affect your own good over the long run. Egoism's concern is not simply with your own good through tomorrow or next week or next year. Rather, it is concerned with your good throughout your life (for which reason the viewpoint of EE is often called prudence). But, (for reasons detailed further in Chapter 9) it is impossible to predict confidently the consequences of even a single act throughout such a long run. There is, in fact, considerable evidence that people make miscalculations all the time about what is to their advantage; at least, many of these people bring ruin on themselves, even when they have been trying to do what is for their own good and have good evidence as to what that is. Thus even if people interpret EE correctly, limitations in our knowledge may make it virtually impossible to apply it correctly.

3. A third objection is more serious still. Even if we assume that people interpret and apply EE correctly, it may be impossible for everyone to do as EE prescribes. Consider why one might think that:

Egoism says that everyone should maximize his or her own good. If I subscribe to EE, I am not only saying I should maximize my good, but I am saying you should maximize yours as well. Sometimes your good may conflict with mine (your pursuit of your good will stand in the way of my pursuit of my good). As Diderot puts it bluntly, "If my happiness demands that I rid myself of all the existences obstructing my desires, then any other individual must be able to rid himself of mine if it obstructs his."[2] If so, then by subscribing to egoism I commit myself to maximizing my own good and, at the same time, to accepting, or acquiescing, to the fact that you sometimes act in ways detrimental to that good.

This has obvious implications for situations in which trust is at stake. You expect the used car salesman to exaggerate the merits of the old car he is trying to persuade you to buy; that is, you expect him to do what he believes to be in *his* interest. If you go to a lawyer (or a physician) for advice, however, you expect to be told what is in *your* interest. If your lawyer subscribes to EE, however, his sole obligation will be to tell you whatever is in *his* interest. That might coincide with what is in *your* interest, but it might not; and if it does not, you will get bad advice. If you confide a secret to a friend and ask that it not be repeated, your friend will quite properly, according to EE, reveal it to others if that would maximize her good.

This basic problem arises even in cases in which you are not soliciting advice or revealing confidences. For example, suppose you are pregnant and do not want the child, but your estranged husband does. Suppose, further, that considering your health, career plans, or just your preferences, your good would not be maximized by your having a child just now, even if your husband takes it at birth and raises it. Applying EE, it seems that you should have the abortion. But if you subscribe to EE, then you are also committed to acknowledging your husband's obligation to maximize his good, which (let us suppose further) would be advanced by your not having the abortion. Your good and his, in other words, conflict. In saying that everyone should maximize his or her own good, you are saying that just as you ought to get an abortion (the means to maximizing your good), your husband ought to prevent you from doing so (the means to maximizing his).[3]

One might deny, of course, that any two people's good can ever conflict in this way, and that apparent conflicts would disappear if we understood better what is genuinely for the good of each party. What is truly for the good of one person, it might be said, cannot be contrary to that of another. So when you judge it would be for your good to have the child, at least one of you must be mistaken; you obviously cannot both have and not have the abortion.

But this assumption of harmony among the goods of all people seems dubious (at least, barring assumptions about an afterlife in which things all work out for the good of everyone). People compete all the time for things they judge to be for their good, whether in love, sports, academics, or business (the "agony of defeat" used to describe failure in sports only slightly over-dramatizes the stakes). In fact, these people may—at least some of the time—be right in their assessment that what would genuinely advance their good conflicts with what would advance the good of another.[4] And if such conflicts are thought to be problematic in the normal course of things, they nevertheless sometimes occur in extraordinary situations—as, for example, if you and another person are stranded on a mountain with only enough food to keep one of you alive during the week it will take the rescue party to reach you.

5.3 THE PARADOXICAL NATURE OF ETHICAL EGOISM

If this assessment is correct, and what is genuinely for the good of some people sometimes conflicts with what is genuinely for the good of others, then we encounter one final problem for egoism. It grows out of egoism's implications for judgments about the conduct of others in situations of such conflict.

Suppose in the abortion case you correctly judge that you ought to have the abortion. How should you judge your husband's conduct? If he is also correct that to have the child (which would require your not having the abortion) would maximize his good, then he, too, is doing what he morally ought. And if you are a consistent egoist, you will have to concede that. This will mean recognizing that incompatible courses of action are both obligatory.

This does not mean, however, that egoism is relativistic, in the sense of entailing that the same act can be both right and wrong at the same time (see Chapter 11). Neither your act nor your husband's is both right and wrong. Rather, both are right. And if either of you judges otherwise, that person is mistaken. The fact that your act is right and your husband is trying to prevent you from performing it does not make his wrong, nor would his acting rightly and your trying to prevent him make yours wrong. (What is odd, though not contradictory, is that each of you would be opposing, and presumably trying to prevent, an action you have to concede is right. And it does seem to follow from this that an egoist cannot consistently promote moral conduct in general.)

But what does this say about one's commitment to egoism? Here is where the paradox arises.

To accept ethical egoism is *to do* something. It is an act along with others one performs in life. As such, it will be either right or wrong. But if egoism is the correct moral principle (and if it applies to all acts, including the act of accepting egoism itself), then you should accept it if and only if doing so would maximize your good. But accepting and trying to follow egoism might not do that if it sets you on a collision course with others equally committed to maximizing their good. If you yield when you come up against such a person—perhaps reasoning (correctly) that each of you is equally in the right—you are not maximizing your good, and hence are acting wrongly (the same, of course, is true of the other person). But if you refuse to yield—perhaps reasoning (incorrectly) that you are in the right and the other person is in the wrong—then there will be no way within morality to resolve your dispute, and the two of you will have to fight it out (literally or figuratively). Either you will prevail (in which case your good will be maximized but the other person's will not) or the other person will prevail (in which case his good will be maximized, but yours will not). Either way, by everyone's accepting and trying to follow EE, some will end up not maximizing their good.[5]

This conflict suggests that even if, by hypothesis, EE were the correct (or true or valid) moral principle, it could not be morally right for everyone to accept it. And it might conceivably even be wrong for anyone to accept and try to follow it, just in case the world is so ordered that virtually everyone encounters conflicts of the sort described—as, arguably, would be true if everyone were an egoist. Whether or not one regards this conflict as a fatal flaw for EE, it renders it deeply paradoxical.

5.4 PSYCHOLOGICAL EGOISM IN HUMAN MOTIVATION

Still, some might argue that EE is the only plausible moral principle because we are so constituted that we cannot act on any other. Our motivation, they say, is thoroughly egoistic.

This view represents **psychological egoism (PE)**, the claim that we are all egoistically motivated in everything we do. Even when we do things for others, the desire to promote our own good is at work. This way of thinking is reflected, for example, in the following passage:

> To observers altruism seems the obvious reason for student participation in community service—but most students won't admit it. The majority mention words like "self-satisfaction" and "self-esteem" when they talk about why they serve, and feel strongly that they gain more than they give. Most would agree with the coed who said recently that the satisfaction she felt in being able to help people was "the most selfish reason of all. . . . Nobody has ever asked me what I'm doing here in the ghetto, but if anyone ever does, I know the answer—I'm here to help myself. Helping people is what makes me happy."[6]

Although the student in this passage stops short of saying that *all* our actions are governed by this motive, such philosophers as Epicurus and Hobbes, and some ordinary people, do say that.

Unlike ethical egoism (expressed in EE), psychological egoism is not itself an ethical position. It concerns what motivates us, not how we ought to act. But like ethical egoism, it need not maintain that people ignore the good of others. Whether they do so will depend, as with ethical egoism, on their beliefs. If you think being considerate and helpful to others is the best way to promote your own good, then (like the preceding student) that is what you will do.

To know whether people are egoistically motivated, we have to know *why* they do what they do. And because psychological egoism is a theory about all human motivation, to know it is true would require knowing why all people behave as they do (at least, when they are acting voluntarily).

So let us take psychological egoism to be the view, not that we are all selfish, but that our conduct is governed always by a single motive, that of self-love, phrased here as a principle:

Psychological Egoism (PE): The sole motive governing all voluntary human conduct is self-love.

Self-love is thus the desire to maximize one's own personal good as the sole ultimate end of all that we do. Egoists often identify this good as happiness, but one might not. One might, like Nietzsche, take one's good to consist of self-realization, which can be understood in terms of creative or intellectual activity that does not entail happiness.

5.5 A CRITIQUE OF PSYCHOLOGICAL EGOISM

Because we cannot tell people's motivation simply from their behavior, this means we cannot tell whether psychological egoism is correct simply from observation. Thus one could not refute psychological egoism simply by establishing the truth of the following:

1. We sometimes act contrary to our own good.

This proposition is indisputably true, but the psychological egoist will correctly point out that there are ready explanations of its truth that do not require assuming that people are motivated by anything other than self-love.

People often, for example, hold mistaken beliefs about what is for their good. First-time drug users no doubt think they can take drugs, enjoy the high, and avoid becoming addicted. They are often mistaken. But that, and the fact that thousands suffer from drug addiction, does not show that their motivation in turning to drugs was not to add to their own good.

If, however, we could establish the truth of the following proposition,

2. We sometimes knowingly act contrary to our own good.

we would perhaps have come closer to falsifying PE. But even this would not be enough. People might knowingly choose actions contrary to their own good, but do so in the belief that doing so is for their good *on balance* or *in the long run*. It makes perfectly good sense to choose actions that diminish our good in the short run (say, by causing us pain or discomfort as when we go to the dentist) in order to maximize our good in the long run (by helping ensure good health). So, to falsify PE along these lines would require establishing a proposition like this:

3. We sometimes knowingly act contrary to our own good, on balance.

Assuming we cannot both act from self-love and at the same time know that our action will be contrary to our good (and so on), establishing proposition 3 would be sufficient for falsifying PE. It would then refute psychological egoism.

But is it necessary to establish proposition 3 in order to show that PE is false? Not at all. It is tempting to assume that if we never act from benevolence—that is, from the desire to do good for others for their own sake—we must therefore always be acting from self-love. But this is not so. Even if we never act from benevolence, we might sometimes act from malevolence (the desire to harm others for the sake of harming them). People who seek revenge against others for real or imagined wrongs are trying to inflict harm on those others. They are not acting benevolently, but malevolently. And they may even be knowingly acting against their own interest if, for example, they have good reason to believe they will be caught and punished. Aiming to harm others—or even aiming to promote their good—is to pursue a different end from your own good.

So even if you are pessimistic about human nature and think that people sometimes harm others out of malevolence (and all that is required is that they *sometimes* do so), that would be enough to refute psychological egoism. And it would do so as effectively as showing that people are sometimes altruistically motivated.

So while to establish proposition 3 would suffice to refute PE, it is not necessary. All that is necessary is to establish the weaker claim:

4. We sometimes knowingly act in a way other than to promote our own good on balance.

Do we ever do this? On the face of it, we do. We certainly speak of such motives as greed, envy, jealousy, revenge, love, kindness, compassion, caring, and the like in characterizing conduct. And great care is taken in criminal trials to try to establish motives for crimes, care which would be pointless if there were just one motive always operating in human affairs.

5.6 BUTLER'S ARGUMENT

An Anglican bishop, Joseph Butler (1692–1752), explored these issues in the eighteenth century. Although he rejected psychological egoism, he nonetheless acknowledged self-love as one of several principles in human nature and gave it its due in determining our conduct. He says at one point,

> Let it be allowed, though virtue or moral rectitude does indeed consist in affection to and pursuit of what is right and good, as such: yet that, when we sit down in a cool hour, we can neither justify to ourselves this or any other pursuit, till we are convinced that it will be for our happiness, or at least not contrary to it.[7]

At first glance, this might seem to concede the truth of PE. But in fact, Butler is conceding that proposition 3 (section 5.5) is false, but he is still adhering to the truth of proposition 4. He is conceding that we never knowingly act contrary to our own good. But he does not think that therefore we are always motivated by the desire to promote our own good. Once we are satisfied an action is not contrary to our good, he is saying, other motives can come into play. And this presupposes that there *are* other motives besides self-love, hence that PE is false.

Perhaps the most compelling consideration inclining people toward psychological egoism is the one cited by the student in the earlier quotation: that we personally derive pleasure or satisfaction from doing things for others. If we assume that pleasure contributes to our own good, it might seem, then, that we are actually seeking our own good when we appear to be acting altruistically.

This, however, does not follow. As Butler argues, the fact that we experience pleasure or satisfaction from actions shows only that we have succeeded in achieving the object of some desire.

If, for example, we are thirsty, the object of our desire is water. The pleasure we get from drinking derives from the fact that we desired *it*, the water; had we not, it would give us no pleasure. It is not that we desired the pleasure and drank the water to get the pleasure. And it is not from the fact that we desired our own good (or happiness, in this case) that we derive the pleasure (even though that pleasure contributes to our good). We derive pleasure because the object (water) is the appropriate one to satisfy that particular desire (thirst). If you are hungry but not thirsty, drinking water will give you no pleasure.

Extending this to the case of altruistic behavior, we can say that, when we are benevolently motivated, promoting the good of others as an end is the "object" of our desire. Hence if we are successful in achieving that end, it is only natural that we should experience pleasure or satisfaction from having done so. But that does not mean the pleasure was the object of our desire. To say so would leave us with no explanation of why we got pleasure. Nor does it mean that self-love was our motive, even though the pleasure we derive may contribute to our own happiness, which is the object of self-love. As Aquinas says: "For pleasure results from the fact that an appetite is satisfied in the good that it has attained. And so there cannot be happiness without attendant pleasure."[8]

So when we find ourselves taking pleasure in doing for others, we should not take that to mean we are selfishly or even egoistically motivated. And if, regrettably, we should find ourselves taking pleasure in harming others, we should not take that to mean we are egoistically motivated either.

This leaves unexplained, however, precisely what the relationship is between happiness and pleasure. Here Butler follows one of the main traditions in the history of ethics by identifying happiness with pleasure or satisfaction. He says, "Happiness or satisfaction consists only in the enjoyment of those objects which are by nature suited to our several particular appetites, passions, and affections."[9]

The picture of happiness that emerges can be represented in the following diagram. Our various desires are shown on one side, their appropriate objects on the other. The resultant pleasure or satisfaction from attaining those objects is in the middle. Happiness, then, is made up of those pleasures or satisfactions. This diagram makes clear what is wrong with psychological egoism. PE contends there is only *one* object of all our desires (taking desires now to signify motivation), namely, our own good. This one motive governs all voluntary human conduct.

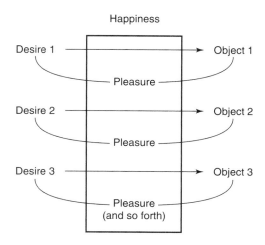

But in fact there are many motives. Conduct involves many desires, each with its own distinguishable object. If happiness consists of pleasure or satisfaction, such a plurality of desires is presupposed to make sense of how we can achieve happiness. Without success in achieving the objects of a substantial number of desires over a period of time, we could not be happy.

This plurality explains how we can derive pleasure from doing good for others without being selfishly or even egoistically motivated. The good of others is one object of our desire. We are simply so constituted as to have a concern for the happiness of others for their sake. That is what Butler calls *benevolence*. If, then, we succeed in achieving the object of benevolence—that is, in promoting the good of others—it's only natural that we experience pleasure or satisfaction from that accomplishment. But that does not mean it was the pleasure or satisfaction or our own happiness that was the object of our desire. We experienced the pleasure or satisfaction *because* we achieved the object of our desire.

This definition, of course, makes happiness a different kind of "object" from others, an internal object. And its peculiar relationship to the rest of our desires and motives has an interesting consequence: if we become preoccupied with seeking our own happiness (that is, if we let self-love crowd out other pursuits), we are likely to neglect the very pursuits that might bring us happiness. There is no way to satisfy the desire for our own happiness other than by satisfying desires for *other* things.

The previous chapter suggested that perhaps being virtuous requires not being preoccupied with being moral. Likewise, it seems that being happy requires *not* being preoccupied with our own happiness. If psychological egoism were correct, and we could not help but be preoccupied exclusively with our own happiness, we would arguably expect to find that no one is happy, which is not the case.

We have been assuming that if psychological egoism were true, it would support ethical egoism. But in fact it would not. If psychological egoism were true, that would mean that we *could not* act from any other motive than self-love, which would mean in turn that we *could not* knowingly pursue any other end than our own good. But if we can't knowingly pursue any other end than our own good, then it's pointless to say (as egoism does) that we *ought* to pursue this end. Only if there is some possibility of our knowingly doing *otherwise* does it make sense to say we ought to do something. And if PE were correct, in the case of seeking our own good there would be no such possibility. Hence, far from supporting EE, PE would render EE useless.

PE would rule out any other ethical principle, as well. It says, in effect, that we have no choice but to always seek our own good. If that were so, any principle prescribing that we do anything else would prescribe that we do something we cannot knowingly do. In that case, it would for all practical purposes deprive morality itself of any significance. Morality would then either (1) prescribe that we maximize our own good, as EE maintains, in which case it would merely tell us to do what we cannot help but try to do anyway; or (2) it would not, in which case (whatever else it prescribes) it would tell us to do something we cannot do.

Notes

1. Epicurus, *Letter to Menoeceus*, in *Epicurus: Letters, Principal Doctrines and Vatican Sayings*, ed. and tr. by Russel M. Geer (Indianapolis, Ind.: Bobbs-Merrill, 1964), p. 53.

2. Denis Diderot, "Natural Right" in *Nature and Culture* (in Liester Crocker, ed., *Diderot's Selected Writings*), p. 42.

3. Strictly speaking, these acts would be only part of the means to the attainment of the end in each case, because many other acts would presumably have to be performed before their respective goods were maximized.

4. I am assuming throughout this discussion that not only would their good be furthered by the acts in question, but also that by these acts their good would be furthered to a greater extent than by any other act, so that the act in question is obligatory.

5. Not only that, but if you are each doing what you are obligated to do, then it would be wrong of either of you to do otherwise; compromise is therefore ruled out.

    The egoist might object that all this presupposes that one or the other of the parties to such a conflict has miscalculated the means to the end of maximizing his or her own good, and that this miscalculation makes the contrivance of such an outcome possible. This is correct, of course, but it is the egoist's own theory that virtually guarantees that someone will miscalculate in situations of this sort.

6. "Activists Who Don't Make Headlines," *Rochester Review*, Spring 1969.

7. Sermon XI, "Upon the Love of Our Neighbour," in A. I. Melden, ed., *Ethical Theories* (Englewood Cliffs, N.J.: Prentice-Hall, 1967), p. 266.

8. *Summa Theologica*, I–II, Q4, a. 3.

9. Butler, Sermon XI, p. 260.

Discussion Questions

1. It's sometimes thought that ethical egoists are selfish, inconsiderate people. Why is this not necessarily true? Can you tell whether someone is an ethical egoist just by observing his or her behavior? Why?

2. Grant that people often come into conflict with one another in the pursuit of what they mistakenly believe is their happiness. Do you think people would come into conflict if they all pursued what was in fact their happiness? If not, why not? If so, are some people destined by circumstances to be unhappy?

3. Do you agree with the argument of section 5.3 that ethical egoism is paradoxical?

4. How is psychological egoism different from ethical egoism? Can we tell from a person's behavior whether he is a psychological egoist?

5. It's often thought that psychological egoism is true unless it can be shown that people sometimes act altruistically, that is, from the motive of benevolence toward others. Section 5.5 argues that this claim is false. Do you agree? Why?

6. Section 5.6, following Butler's analysis, argues that happiness is an elusive thing to achieve, and that preoccupation with achieving it may actually obstruct its attainment. Does this argument seem to you to be correct? Why or why not?

Nor is it only in human things that what ever is commanded by God is right; but also in natural things.[1]
St. Thomas Aquinas

6 CHAPTER | The Divine Command Theory

6.1 THE CASE OF ABRAHAM AND ISAAC

Suppose there is a God who is perfectly good, all-knowing (omniscient), and all-powerful (omnipotent). And suppose God loves us, wants what is best for us, and has made known what that is.[2] But suppose that rather than just conveying the wish that we would do certain things and refrain from doing others, he reveals his will through commands and prohibitions.

If you want to obey God and also do what is right, you will have no problem, at least not as long as what God commands seems to you to be right. But suppose you have a child, and one day God commands you to kill your child. What would you do?

This happened to Abraham in the story of Genesis when he was told to sacrifice his son, Isaac. Although restrained at the last minute by an angel of God, Abraham was prepared to slit Isaac's throat. Although in ancient times child sacrifice was sometimes practiced, today people who harm or kill children (or others), saying God told them to do so, are imprisoned or confined to mental institutions. Even people who simply claim God talks to them are viewed with suspicion. So if there is a God, there is always the question of how you know that what you *think* is God's will, is in fact so.

In addition to the problem of knowing whether you have correctly identified God's commands, there is a more fundamental difficulty. It may exist even if you correctly understand what God commands.

6.2 GREEK AND CHRISTIAN VIEWS OF HUMAN NATURE

Let us first put the problem in broader perspective. Plato and Aristotle, as well as most Greek moral philosophers, thought that human beings are basically rational and will do what is right if they understand what that is (although Aristotle allows for weakness of will). They also generally thought that, with qualifications for differences in intelligence and for misfortune caused by chance, people have it within their capacity to lead a good life. There is nothing inherently evil or corrupt about people.[3]

According to traditional Christianity, however, the human soul has been corrupted by original sin, which has been transmitted to all descendants of Adam and Eve. Moreover, we are limited in our capacity to see for ourselves what is best in the way of individual and social conduct, a deficiency that can be offset only by divine revelation. God must let us know what he wants of us, which he does most conspicuously through commandments.[4] We are also deficient in our capacity to do what God requires of us, and for this we need regeneration through divine grace. Grace is required for people limited in both intellectual and moral capacities who cannot live well and achieve supreme happiness on their own.

6.3 GOD'S COMMANDS ACCORDING TO JUDAISM, CHRISTIANITY, AND ISLAM

Many Jews think God's commandments are those of the Old Testament, principally the Ten Commandments. Many Christians think all the commandments reduce to the New Testament commandment to love. Moslems think both Christians and Jews are wrong and that not until God spoke to Mohammed (through the angel Gabriel) did the full story that began with Adam and Eve unfold. For Moslems, God's directives are not exclusively those of either the Old or the New Testament (or a combination of the two), but of the Koran.

God may be thought to issue commands of a general sort, addressed either to everyone or to certain peoples, as in the Ten Commandments, or to specific individuals at specific times, as in the case of Abraham. Or God may be thought to issue basically one commandment only, addressed either to everyone or to specific peoples. The New Testament teaching from the Sermon on the Mount, for example, requires that you love God, your neighbor, and yourself—and is often understood to require this of everyone, not just followers of Jesus.

Now if you believe in God and are prepared to obey God unquestioningly, you will simply do as God directs, no matter what the consequences. Shiite Moslems, for example, who have been persecuted for centuries, have a history of extolling self-sacrifice in the service of God. Many of them believe that select individuals, known as Imams, infallibly represent God's will to others. Thus during the Iran-Iraq war, Iranians, who are mostly Shiites, went to their deaths by the thousands in the conviction that they were carrying out God's will as conveyed by the Ayatollah Khomeni.[5]

Again, leaving aside whether one can know what God commands or even have a warranted belief about what that is, such actions as those of the Shiites show what an unqualified commitment to obey God entails. Some, such as the Danish philosopher Søren Kierkegaard, have thought this conclusion absurd. But they have also thought it inescapable.

When you question whether some things God commands (or might command) are *actually* right, serious philosophical problems arise. Let us see why.

6.4 THE RELATIONSHIP BETWEEN GOD'S WILL AND MORAL RIGHTNESS

If you want both to obey God *and* to do what is right, you have to make some assumptions about the relationship between moral rightness and God's will. You might, for example, think that

  1. Whatever God *approves* is right.

If God is loving, you could be confident that whatever he approves will be best for you; or, if not best, at least good. The problem is that we cannot be sure we know everything that God approves and disapproves; his ways, after all, "pass all understanding," as it says in the Bible. So it might seem that

  2. Whatever God *permits* is right.

is a better approximation. But although this seems plausible in one sense, in another it does not.

If we take "permits" to mean "could prevent but does not," it would seem then that everything that happens, both in nature and in human affairs, is right. God, after all, being omnipotent, could prevent anything whatsoever from happening (if nothing else, he could always cause the universe to stop existing, which would put a stop to everything). But he obviously is not preventing what is taking place right now from happening, and has not prevented anything that has happened from the beginning of the world to the present.

Taking "permits" to mean "could prevent but does not" would thus deprive morality of virtually all significance because there would no longer be a contrast between right and wrong in human experience. So this definition will not do, although it highlights two dimensions of the problem of evil, concerning: (1) why God allows so-called natural evils such as earthquakes, hurricanes, and HIV viruses to exist when he presumably could prevent them; and (2) why he allows people to engage in wrongdoing when he could prevent that as well.

On the other hand, if we take "permits" to mean "expressly allows," proposition 2 becomes more plausible. Then it would cover only those cases in which God says (to an individual, a group, or everyone), "You may do this" or conveys to them in some other way that they have authorization to do it. Thus if you believe with the Old Testament that God made a covenant with Abraham giving to him and his descendants[6] the land of Canaan, you might well—as some Israelis do today—take this to represent God's express permission for those descendants ever after to claim the land as their own. Not only has God not prevented it when he could have (and hence has permitted it in the first sense), he has expressly authorized it (hence permitted it in the second sense as well). But others—like many Palestinians—who claim the same land, while they may have to concede that God has permitted that settlement in the first sense (as they will if they believe that God could have prevented it but did not), do not concede that God permits it in the authorizational sense.

Anyone who holds that proposition 2 should be understood in this authorizational way may be said to hold a **divine permission theory (DPT)**, which is one way of understanding the relationship between God and morality.

Sometimes, however, this relationship is specified even more narrowly. Sometimes it is said that

3. Whatever God *commands* is right.

The emphasis here is not on what God permits you to do but on what God *requires* you to do. If God merely *permits* you to do something, you may do it or not as you choose; there is nothing wrong with not doing it. But if God commands you to do something, it is wrong not to do it. For this reason, "right" in proposition 3 has the force of "mandatory" or "obligatory," and although we sometimes use "right" in this way, it will help avoid confusion if we substitute the word "obligatory" instead. This gives

3′. Whatever God commands is obligatory.

If something is obligatory, then, it is morally required in the sense that you are not only permitted to do it, but you would be wrong *not* to do it. It is something you *must* do.

Proposition 3′ represents what is called the **divine command theory (DCT)**. Now, if God permits some things that are not commanded, then DCT isn't enough to spell out fully the relationship between God's will and moral conduct. Some actions will be left over, so to speak, whose moral status is unaccounted for. So for the sake of convenience, let's take DCT to be expressed by the following principle:

> **Divine Command Theory (DCT):** Whatever God permits, prohibits, or commands is right, wrong, or obligatory respectively.[7]

This principle considerably extends the range of human conduct covered by the theory. Depending on how broadly you understand God's expression of divine will, this principle may cover all conduct.

Finally, note that although God's commandments are usually discussed in the context of Judeo-Christian religious traditions, the DCT could be used equally to legitimize any form of moral legalism. If God commands obedience to any of the legalistic principles considered earlier (section 2.1),[8] compliance with those principles then becomes obligatory. Thus ethical egoism, utilitarianism, the categorical imperative, and so on, could become the required principle for everyone to follow if God so commanded.

We have, then, a complex set of possibilities (see diagram), depending on how many commands God is believed to issue and to whom.[9]

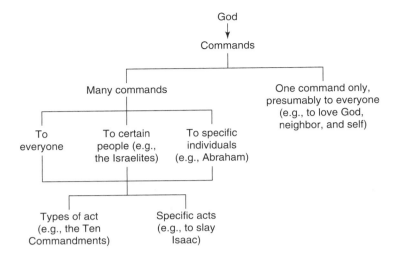

6.5 A PROBLEM FOR THE DIVINE COMMAND THEORY

The problem for such a theory is connected with one that emerges in a discussion between Socrates and Euthyphro in Plato's dialogue, the *Euthyphro*. Euthyphro proposes to define "piety" as "what is loved by all the gods." Socrates then asks him, "Do the gods love piety because it is pious, or is it pious because it is loved by the gods?" Euthyphro doesn't get the point, which Socrates proceeds to explain at length. We need not concern ourselves with the details of that explanation, but we can adapt the underlying concern in Socrates' query to the case at hand. We can do this by asking, "Does God command what is right *because* it is right, or is it (what is right) right because God commands it?"

Assuming that these exhaust the plausible alternatives, one or the other of the following must be true:

1. God commands what is right because it is right.

or

2. What is right is right because God commands it.

That is, either there is something about right acts (or types of acts) that leads God to command them, or there is something about God's commanding acts (or types of acts) that *makes* them right. To say both alternative 1 and alternative 2 are true would be circular.

It is alternative 2 that creates a problem for cases such as that of Abraham and Isaac. In the biblical account, we are clearly meant to believe that God's commanding Abraham to slay Isaac makes it obligatory for Abraham to do so. Yet many people believe it would be wrong to kill one's own child in cold blood, even if told to do so by God. As contemporary ethicist Nel Noddings writes,

> For us, then, Abraham's decision is not only ethically unjustified but it is in basest violation of the supraethical—of caring. . . . Abraham's obedience fled for protection

under the skirts of an unseeable God. Under the gaze of an abstract and untouchable God, he would destroy *this* touchable child whose real eyes were turned upon him in trust, and love, and fear.[10]

So we might ask, why not then opt for alternative 1 right at the outset, and say that God commands what he does *because* it is right?

The reason is that alternative 1 has its own problems. To say that God commands acts because they are right implies that rightness somehow exists independently of God. It is as though in the moral scheme of things there were three things: God, the moral law, and human beings; and God, understanding the moral law better than we do, tells us to do those things that are right and forbids us to do those things that are wrong.

In one sense this is unproblematic. If God knows what is right and wrong (as we would expect, if he is omniscient), and if he only issues commandments that accord with this knowledge (as we would expect, if he is good), we could hardly do better than to obey him. He would be like Plato's philosopher king elevated to the status of divine perfection, and the whole of humanity would be like citizens of Plato's ideal state. So long as people followed God, they would act with right opinion in accordance with the perfect wisdom of the supreme being.

But this alternative has a troubling consequence. It would mean that something exists independently of God, namely the moral law. And if morality governs the conduct of all rational beings, then even God would be constrained by that law; moral considerations would be binding on him as well as on anyone else. And that would seem to limit God's power and, thereby, his perfection. (Of course, if God is perfectly good, he has no inclination to do wrong and no reticence about doing what he ought, and hence moral constraints would be no burden on him; but he would still be bound by them.)

So we need to take alternative 2 seriously. The problematic cases it raises are of two sorts: The first are those in which God clearly commands certain acts that seem not to be right. The second are those in which, although God has not commanded certain acts, they would seem wrong even if God *were* to command them.

6.6 COMMANDS TO DO WHAT SEEMS IMPOSSIBLY IDEALISTIC

Cases of the first type actually break down into two sorts. First, there are cases, such as that of Abraham's, in which what God commands seems wrong because it is so terrible. We need to discuss cases of this sort in greater detail and will return to them later. Second, there are cases in which what God commands seems wrong, not because it is terrible, but precisely because it seems so good as to represent an ideal of conduct that is out of the reach of ordinary mortals. The very commandment to love, set forth by Jesus in the Sermon on the Mount, in fact, has seemed to some theologians to represent an impossible ideal. If so, and if "ought" implies "can" (if, that is, we can be obligated to do something only if it is something we *can* do), then it doesn't seem right that

God should command us to do it (though strictly speaking in this case it's not the act but God's commanding it that doesn't seem right).

Christians faced this second problem early on. In saying that you should love God and yourself and your neighbor, Jesus made clear that this obligation extends to enemies as well; you should love your enemies and turn the other cheek. This seemed to most early Christians to mean that they should refrain from violence and war.

St. Augustine, however, sought to explain Christ's sayings in such a way as to render them compatible with war and killing (as well as with the citizen's duties to the state). He thought that such conduct was permissible for Christians under some circumstances and that the conflict with the teachings of Christ is only apparent.

6.7 AN ATTEMPTED RECONCILIATION OF THE COMMANDMENT TO LOVE WITH HUMAN JUDGMENTS OF WHAT IS POSSIBLE

We can focus on the problem in the following way. Starting with the principle of DCT and adding to it the command to love our enemies, we get the following argument to the conclusion that loving our enemies is obligatory:

1. Whatever God permits, prohibits, or commands is right, wrong, or obligatory respectively (DCT).
2. God commands us to love our enemies.
3. Therefore, loving our enemies is obligatory.

If you accept premise 1, as Augustine does, and premise 2, as any Christian must who takes the New Testament at face value, you must accept the conclusion (3). It is impossible for premises 1 and 2 to be true and the conclusion (3) to be false. How, then, can Augustine reconcile the conclusion with Christians who resort to violence?

Augustine's answer—one that many Christians have used ever since—is to argue that we must properly interpret the commandment to love. When we do, he thinks, we find it leads to an understanding of the conclusion that makes it compatible with Christian participation in war.

What God requires of us in the commandment to love, according to Augustine, is that we adopt the correct inner attitude. This means we must have a loving spirit. This is what Christ had in mind in the Sermon on the Mount, not the performance of outward acts.

Let us explain this. We can view acts in terms of their external, physical components, or in terms of their internal and mental components. The physical components consist of bodily movements that can be seen and verified (we can see someone pull a rabbit out of a hat, but we may not know why he—or she—did it). The interior components will include the motives explaining why he did what he did and what his intention was in doing it.

From an external standpoint, giving alms to a beggar may involve little more than placing coins in his or her hand. But the intention may be of various sorts: to ease the plight of this particular person, to discharge an obligation imposed by the Koran (if you are a Moslem), or to impress your friends with how compassionate you are. Similarly, the motives might be compassion, duty, or self-interest.

The point is that, however we draw it, there is a distinction between the interior and the exterior aspects of actions. Western law recognizes this in connection with illegal acts when it distinguishes between the *actus reus*, the external, material components of the act (the woman picked up the blouse and walked out of the store without paying), and the *mens reus*, the conditions defining a culpable state of mind (she did not forget to pay for it, but rather intended to steal it). To be guilty of a crime, it is not enough simply to have done what the law prohibits; you must also have done it in a certain frame of mind.

In Augustine's view, God is most concerned with our frame of mind, or more specifically, with the state of our soul, which is where evil arises. Evil is the will's turning away from God; it is being motivated by a desire for pleasure and possessions—or by an aversion to pain—rather than by love of God. No matter how proper an external action may be, if it is done from an evil motive, it violates the commandment to love God. This is why Aquinas emphasizes that divine law is required for human guidance. It is needed to regulate the inner life that human laws cannot govern (human law can make you pay taxes, but it cannot make you do so cheerfully).

By the same token, no matter how apparently contrary to customary standards your outward actions may be, if they spring from loving devotion and obedience to God they are permissible. Augustine says, "When God commands anything contrary to the customs or compacts of any nation to be done, though it were never done by them before, it is to be done; and if intermitted it is to be restored, and, if never established, to be established."[11] The appeal to custom counts for nothing when custom conflicts with God's commands.

Pushing this reasoning to its limits, Augustine contends that what God's command requires is that we adopt a loving attitude toward our enemies, which he takes to be compatible with killing them in wartime (if God commands it or if other conditions defining a just war are met). Whether you can in fact do this, and love your enemies at the same time you kill them, is of course problematic. But whether or not this can be made plausible, if we understand premise 2 in this way, we see how Augustine thinks he can accept the conclusion (3) and, at the same time, accept Christian participation in war. As noted earlier (section 4.3), what is important is the perfection of your soul. Simply doing certain external acts is not enough, and sometimes it is not even necessary. What is necessary at all times is that you do *whatever* you do in the spirit of loving devotion to God.

6.8 DOES GOD EVER COMMAND US TO DO WHAT IS WRONG?

We have considered a case in which a divine commandment seems to require us to be too good, to do what is humanly impossible by refraining from violence when violence seems necessary. Now let us look at the other side of the problem, which concerns cases (such as Abraham's with which we began) in which God commands acts that seem to us *too* violent, or too contrary to standards of human decency. These, moreover, concern commands to perform specific acts rather than, as with loving our enemies, certain types of acts.

There is evidence in the Old Testament not only that God commanded the slaying of an innocent child, but also that he commanded theft and adultery in particular cases.[12] So we can formulate an argument paralleling the previous one, framed in terms of particular acts rather than types of acts.

1'. Whatever God permits, prohibits, or commands is right, wrong, or obligatory respectively (DCT).
2'. God has commanded particular acts of slaying the innocent, theft, and adultery.
3'. Therefore in these particular instances the slaying of the innocent, theft, and adultery are obligatory.

6.9 AN ATTEMPTED RECONCILIATION OF GOD'S COMMANDS WITH HUMAN JUDGMENTS

The Argument of Aquinas

Let's look at the way in which Aquinas handles these problems.

In the case of the slaying of an innocent, Aquinas seems to accept the entirety of the argument. That is, he accepts that God so commanded Abraham, accepts that God's commanding it made the act obligatory (at least up to the point at which God rescinded the command), and accepts the conclusion that such slaying was indeed obligatory (and, presumably, would have been right had God not intervened to prevent it).[13] Aquinas says,

> All men alike, both guilty and innocent, die the death of nature; which death of nature is inflicted by the power of God because of original sin, according to *I Kings* ii.6: *The Lord killeth and maketh alive*. Consequently, by the command of God, death can be inflicted on any man, guilty or innocent, without any injustice whatever.[14]

Insofar as the problem is that DCT seems to render permissible an act that is in fact wrong, Aquinas here takes the bull by the horns and simply denies that the act in question *is* wrong.

His handling of the cases of apparent theft and adultery is different, however. Here he says,

> In like manner, adultery is intercourse with another's wife; who is allotted to him by the law emanating from God. Consequently intercourse with any woman, by the command of God, is neither adultery nor fornication.—The same applies to theft, which is the taking of another's property. For whatever is taken by the command of God, to Whom all things belong, is not taken against the will of its owner, whereas it is in this that theft consists.[15]

Whereas he is prepared to say that slaying an innocent person is obligatory if commanded by God, he does not say that particular acts of adultery or theft are obligatory if commanded by God. Instead, he says (in effect) that acts that *would* constitute adultery or theft under normal circumstances do not do so when commanded by God (had he characterized the slaying of Isaac as an apparent instance of murder, which it is, he could have used the same argument in that case). The reason in the case of apparent adultery is that since marriage is consecrated by God's law so that a woman is allotted to a man by this means, no command by God pertaining to this relationship can violate that bond. Therefore, intercourse with another man's wife, if commanded by God, is not adultery.

The case of apparent theft is even simpler. You do not steal something unless you take it from its rightful owner. Since everything belongs to God, taking what God tells you to take cannot constitute theft—even if by human laws what you take belongs to someone else.

Given this, Aquinas would deny premise 2′ in section 6.8. In his interpretation, God has neither commanded theft nor adultery in these cases. If premise 2′ is false, one can consistently accept premise 1′, but deny the conclusion 3′.

So there are three possible lines of reply to the objection that DCT renders right certain actions that are in fact wrong. The first involves reinterpreting God's commandments in such a way that you can comply with them even while performing outwardly the acts (like killing your enemies) they seem to prohibit. The second involves conceding that something God has commanded *seems* wrong to us (as with the slaying of Isaac), but denying that it *is* in fact wrong. The third involves arguing that when certain acts are properly described (as with the cases of alleged theft and adultery), the appearance of wrongness disappears.

6.10 WOULD GOD'S COMMANDING THE TORTURE OF A CHILD MAKE IT RIGHT?

The second major sort of case to consider concerns not actual commands of God that are contrary to what we think right, but commands that, were God to issue them, *would* violate our most deeply held convictions about morality. Here the relevant premise is

1″. If God were to permit X, then X would be right.

Why put 1″ in the subjunctive in this way? Because if we take alternative 2 (section 6.5) as entailing only premise 1 (section 6.7) and premise 1′ (section 6.8), we could reasonably conclude that we need worry only about what God has commanded or might plausibly be expected to command in the future; and we would not have to concern ourselves about what he *could* command (such as that we listen to Muzak the rest of our lives), but that if he is merciful we can be pretty sure he will not. And it is precisely things that God could command that generate the problem.

The problem, to be sure, is not a practical one. Without reason to believe that God ever will command outrageous things, we almost certainly will never have to contend with such problems in our actual conduct. So why worry about them?

They are worth worrying about philosophically because unless we know what to say about them—or can satisfy ourselves that such speculation is pointless—we fail to understand fully the relationship between morality and God's will.

The problem is not basically that God might tell us to do things whose point we do not understand or that seem wrong to us. After all, once again, God's ways are believed to "pass all understanding." The problem centers about what to say of the possibility that God might tell us to do something that *is* wrong. If that is even a possibility, then both DCT and DPT are inadequate (since they claim that God's commanding or permitting something *makes* it right; these expressions of God's will are the sole right-making characteristic in morality).

To be sure, you might wonder why it is necessary to speculate about far-fetched cases. The Bible is replete with examples of genocide, murder, undeserved suffering, adultery, and theft—either commanded or authorized by God. If those acts (or, as we saw in the case of adultery and theft, acts that would normally be examples of these kinds) are right when commanded by God, what would *not* be?

In any event, philosophers and theologians have considered even more horrific acts, such as the torture of a child. If God were to command the prolonged and unremitting torture of a child, would it then be right? Would it be morally incumbent on us to put aside all our feelings of sympathy and compassion, grit our teeth, and set ourselves to the gruesome task?

Notice that for this to provide us with any sort of test of DCT, we have to assume that the prolonged and unremitting torture of a child *would* be wrong; if we just say that it *seems* wrong; there is no problem.

So let us assume that it *would* be wrong. If that is the case, and DCT could conceivably authorize it, then DCT is inadequate as a moral theory.

The assessment of this problem involves complexities we cannot do justice to here, but I want to consider one possible response to it. It consists of denying, not only that God would ever command the gratuitous torture of a child, but also that God *could* ever command such a thing. If God could never command such an act, then no such act could ever be made right by God's commanding it, hence there could never be a case—even in principle—in which the DCT conflicts with what we know to be wrong. So DCT could never be refuted by such a consideration.

The reason why it is supposedly impossible that God could ever command child torture is that God, by his nature, is supremely good. His commanding such an act would be at such variance with his nature as to make it impossible that he should ever do it.

6.11 WHAT DOES IT MEAN TO CALL GOD GOOD?

What might it mean to say that God is good in this sense? It might mean that God is intrinsically good, which would entail that his goodness depends solely on the properties that make up his nature (for the distinction between intrinsic and extrinsic value, see section 9.4). But this seems unhelpful. In addition to the properties of being omnipotent and omniscient, God also has the property of being perfectly good. To say that he is intrinsically good—meaning that his goodness depends solely on the properties that make up his nature—would be to say that his goodness depends (at least in part) on his goodness, which is circular.

Suppose instead we say God is intrinsically good in the sense that his goodness is independent of his relation to anything else. This leaves it open whether his goodness depends on anything at all. His goodness, in this view (as well as in the first), would remain just as it is even if the whole of creation ceased to exist.

But if we say this, it is hard to see how God's goodness can be incompatible with anything he tells us to do. When we imagine him commanding us to do something, we are considering him in his *relationship* to something else, namely, to us and to possible acts we might perform. And by hypothesis his goodness is independent of such relations. If God is immutably good in his nature, it should not matter whether or not he tells us to torture children. His goodness would remain unaffected because it is in no way conditional on what we do or what effects we have in the world.

It would seem, therefore, that God's commanding child torture could conflict with his goodness only if by his goodness we mean *extrinsic* goodness. A thing has extrinsic goodness only by virtue of its relations to other things. So if God is extrinsically good, there must be some relationships in which he stands to other things that account for that goodness. What might such relationships be?

It is tempting to say that the moral law is a candidate. If a person conscientiously abides by the moral law (assuming there is such a law), we might call the person good.[16] But his or her goodness would be extrinsic because it could only be understood by reference to something else—namely, the moral law. We cannot say this in alternative 2 (section 6.5) (the view that what is right is right because God commands it). In that view, remember, there is no moral law apart from God. It is what God commands that determines what is right, hence determines what the moral law is. So we must have some other conception of what it means to say that God is extrinsically good.

There are two main possibilities here. The first is that it means that God is morally good. The second is that it means that God is a loving God. Let us begin with the first possibility.

If God is morally good, then he is supremely good and represents the ideal of moral perfection. This means we have to say more than that he merely tries always to do what is right and never knowingly does what is wrong. Since he is omniscient, he cannot fail to know whether what he is doing is right, and since he is omnipotent, he cannot fail to do what is right if he sets himself to it. In this he differs from us. Even exceptionally moral people sometimes fail in their efforts to do what is right, as when they are prevented by circumstances beyond their control. And even the most virtuous people probably *sometimes* knowingly do something wrong (even thinking sinful thoughts will do; remember the Bible speaks of adultery in the heart). God, however, if he is morally good, invariably does what is right.

Can we make sense of this using the version of DCT we have been considering? I don't think so.

If it is God's permissions, prohibitions, and commands that make acts right, wrong, and obligatory respectively, then God is, in effect, the creator of morality. Nothing is right or wrong unless God issues some directive regarding it. So unless he issues directives to himself with which he can then either comply or not, God stands outside of morality, and his own actions are neither right nor wrong. But if God's actions are neither right nor wrong, then it cannot be the case that God always does what is right.[17] Since always doing what is right is a necessary condition of God's being morally perfectly good, it follows that we cannot say God is morally good.

It is still true, however, that God never does what is wrong. But the reason is not one that confers any moral credit on God—it is not that he *could* do wrong but chooses not to. The reason is that he *cannot* do wrong. The notion of wrongness, like that of rightness, simply has no meaningful application to God's conduct (a stone never does what is wrong either, and it likewise derives no moral credit for that because a stone, too—though for other reasons than God—can do no wrong).

If God is not morally good, then his being morally good cannot explain why he cannot command child torture. And if we can't explain why God cannot command child torture, we have not shown why, according to DCT, child torture would not be right if God commanded it.[18]

Note that this does not mean we can't make sense of the possibility that God might tell us to do something wrong but not mean it—that is, not intend that we actually do it. After all, God was apparently just testing Abraham to see how obedient he was; God did not actually want to see Isaac killed (considering that he intervened to save Isaac). But even if God could direct us to do what is wrong (not intending that we do it), *that in itself* would not be wrong. In fact, it would fully accord with God's will.

6.12 IS GOD EXTRINSICALLY GOOD BECAUSE HE IS A LOVING GOD?

So God's commanding child torture could conflict with his goodness only if by this we mean extrinsic goodness. And we have considered the possibility that God is extrinsically good by virtue of his relationship to the moral law. Let's now consider a second possibility; that God would not tell us to do horrific things because he is a loving God. If God is good because he is loving, his goodness is extrinsic because being loving can be understood only by reference to something else—the object of one's love (unless one loves only oneself).

The problem with this is that it is difficult to reach agreement as to what constitutes loving behavior. We all have a pretty good understanding of what constitutes loving, caring, compassionate behavior among individual persons—as in a mother or father's love for a child, love between a wife and husband, or love between a committed couple. If this is what love means, then indeed it is incredible to suppose God could be loving and at the same time tell us to torture a child. But *is* this what love means, at least for Christians?

Remember Augustine's problem. He argued that you can love your enemies and still kill them. If killing on such a scale as warfare is compatible with loving those on whom you inflict such suffering and death, why should it be thought that God's infliction of pain, suffering, and death (or his ordering such infliction by others) on one individual is incompatible with God's love? If *we* can perform horrific acts against our fellow humans as long as we maintain the proper inner spirit of love, why can't God do the same? And does not this deprive the idea of love of any real meaning?

We can't have it both ways. If we exonerate ourselves for the performance of indescribably cruel acts, we cannot then turn around and say of similar acts that God could not command them because he loves us.

But suppose we stick consistently to what seem to be the implications of loving behavior as experienced in personal relations. Suppose we acknowledge that it requires at least our rethinking our conduct toward enemies and foreigners and people we do not like. If we ask whether God would ever command someone to torture a child, it is hard to make a case for saying he would (excluding cases in which he tells someone to do it without intending that the person actually carry out the act).

But this, of course, is not what is at issue. Those who ask whether God's commanding child torture would make it right need not have the slightest inclination to believe God ever would command such a thing. Their disagreement is only with a moral theory that would have as a consequence that if he did, such an act would be right. Moreover, to show that God would never do something does not show that it is impossible for him to do it. For all we know, God may (for aesthetic reasons) never create a pink and orange universe. But he could do so if he wanted.

Apparently, therefore, *if* (as we have been assuming but have not argued) it is a shortcoming of DCT that torturing a child would be right if God were to command that act, then none of the replies we have considered succeeds in meeting that objection.

6.13 CAN "RIGHT" BE DEFINED BY REFERENCE TO GOD'S COMMANDS?

Notice that nothing in all this explains why it should be thought in the first place that God's commanding something makes it right. We do not have time to explore that issue in detail, but I want to consider briefly one proposed explanation.

It consists of saying that right simply means "commanded by God." But as others have pointed out this only pushes the problem back. Anyone who questions why God's commanding something makes it right is going to want to know why anyone should accept this definition, in which case the definition itself will need justifying. And the problems involved in trying to justify it will likely turn out to be as formidable as those in answering the original question directly.

Certainly not everyone means this by "right." Atheists pretty clearly do not (unless as a grounds for saying that because there is no God there is no right and wrong). The very fact that the issues we have been discussing need to be taken seriously suggests that merely establishing that something is (or might be) commanded by God does not suffice to establish its rightness conclusively. But it should do so if "right" means nothing more than "commanded by God." Then, to say of an act (such as Abraham's projected slaying of Isaac) that it is commanded by God would *ipso facto* be to answer the question of whether or not it is right. And to say,

1. God commanded Abraham to slay Isaac.

and then to ask,

2. But is it right?

would be a pointless question. It would simply be to ask,

2'. But is it commanded by God?

which is already affirmed in the first statement (1). As G. E. Moore would have put it, the question is not an open question.

Moreover, if we accept the definition then,

3. Whatever God commands is right.

becomes true by definition. Statements of which this is true are often called *analytic,* and there is serious question as to whether an analytic statement of this sort can function as a prescriptive principle. And, after all, we are looking at DCT insofar as it purports to set forth the basic principle of morality, sufficient (given enough facts and subsidiary rules, if they are necessary) to enable us to make all our determinations of moral rightness and wrongness.

Put in its baldest form (and a little uncharitably), the problem is that if the definition is correct, then judgment 3 in effect says nothing more than

3'. Whatever is commanded by God is commanded by God.

and 3' not only does not tell us anything we did not already know, but is also useless for guiding conduct. Hence it can hardly qualify as a moral principle. What we are looking for in the ethics of conduct is some directive or set of directives to enable us to distinguish right from wrong; or if not directives, then some account of how we should go about making determinations of rightness and wrongness.

So, to be plausible, the connection between rightness and being commanded by God must be something other than the definitional one. And unless or until such an account is forthcoming, the DCT is inadequate.

6.14 CONCLUSION

I noted earlier (section 1.5) that one approach to morality would maintain that it cannot adequately be understood apart from religion. The DCT represents one version of that approach. It is one that maintains that morality in a very direct way is dependent on religion in that we cannot make sense of moral judgments of right and wrong—and perhaps even of the meanings of "right" and "wrong"—apart from God's commands. If what I said is correct, this view is mistaken; at the very least, it faces formidable obstacles in being made plausible. This does not mean that religion may not yet have an important bearing on morality. But it does mean that the bearing cannot consist of the strong connection maintained by DCT.

Another major attempt to base ethics upon a religious foundation maintains that while God may not guide our conduct through commandments—or, at any rate, may not do so all of the time—he nonetheless has ordered the natural world and our own nature so that, through reason, we may ascertain for ourselves what is right and wrong. This approach represents a long and influential tradition from which have evolved secular as well as religious ethics. It is called *natural law ethics*. We shall turn to it in the next chapter.

Notes

1. St. Thomas Aquinas, *The Summa Theologica*, I–II, Q. 94, Art 4. *Basic Writings of St. Thomas Aquinas*, vol. 2, ed. Anton C. Pegis (New York: Random House, 1945), p. 780.

2. For convenience I occasionally refer to God as "he." This should not, however, be taken to mean that God is a male, since God—if there is such a being—is neither male nor female. You should be mindful that such a use is considered by some to represent a gender bias in favor of males, which is not intended here.

3. Plato thought that most people would do best to follow the guidance of the wisest people and that, at least ideally, the wisest people should have leadership roles in the broader social scheme of things.

4. God also, in some views, imprints on our natures an intuitive understanding of certain precepts the following of which will enable us to live well, at least in our relations to others. Relatedly, it is sometimes thought that God has given us certain natural inclinations that serve the same purpose. As we shall see in the next chapter, these views represent conceptions of natural law, a manifestation of God's eternal law for the governance of the whole of creation as it pertains to the guidance of human beings. Such natural law is essentially immutable and provides the backdrop against which to understand and measure human laws. It is known to us by looking within, to our understanding and our natural inclinations, whereas God's commandments come to us, as it were, from outside.

5. Although the Ayatollah Khomeni was called an Imam, most Shiites did not regard him as on an equal footing with the twelve historical Imams. Nonetheless, Shiites who went willingly to their deaths in human waves on the battlefield apparently believed they were carrying out God's will.

6. The covenant is only with his descendants through his son Isaac, who biblically constitute the Jewish people, and not his descendants through his son Ishmael, who biblically constitute the Arab peoples.

7. If one understands the notion of permission in still a further sense (beyond what God expressly or tacitly allows), meaning that God allows the performance of any actions that are not prohibited and the nonperformance of any that are not required, one could formulate the DCT thus: Any act is permissible if and only if it does not violate any of God's commandments.

8. Excluding the principle of the DCT itself.

9. The possibilities are considerably more complex than I am representing here. God might, for example, give one command only, and that to certain peoples or groups; or he might command everyone to perform specific acts, either collectively or individually, and so on.

10. Nel Noddings, *Caring: A Feminine Approach to Ethics and Moral Education* (Berkeley: University of California Press, 1984), p. 43.

11. St. Augustine, *The Confessions*, Bk. III, Ch.8, in Philip Schaff, ed., *A Select Library of the Nicene and Post-Nicene Fathers of the Christian Church*, vol. 1 (Grand Rapids, Mich.: Eerdmans, 1956).

12. On this topic, see *Basic Writings of Saint Thomas Aquinas*, vol. 2, ed. Anton C. Pegis (New York: Random House, 1945), pp. 779–780.

13. This, incidentally, may distinguish the case of Isaac from that of Job. Whereas Job's friends implied that he *must* have sinned in order to deserve such punishment, and hence must not have been innocent in God's eyes (despite appearances to the contrary), there is no hint that Isaac is anything but truly innocent.

14. *Basic Writings of Saint Thomas Aquinas,* vol. 2, ed. Anton C. Pegis (New York: Random House, 1945), p. 780.

15. Ibid.

16. Allowing for the qualification that a person's simply consistently *doing* what is right, without doing it for the right reason, might make us hesitant about calling the person good. This is Kant's view, as we shall see in Chapter 8. And it is the view of many who emphasize the ethics of virtue rather than exclusively the ethics of conduct.

17. It would also follow, paradoxically, that God cannot ever do what is right either.

18. You might argue that it is actually God's willing things that makes them right, rather than his commanding them, and that in this view—which might be called a **divine will theory (DWT)**—you can make sense of saying that he always acts rightly. This, however, encounters other difficulties. Arguably, another condition of God's being morally good is that he never chooses to do wrong. This presupposes that he *could* do wrong. But, in DWT, for God to do what is wrong would require that he act contrary to his own will. And it is not clear that we can make sense of that. It would require that we be able to distinguish between God's willing and his acting, and it's doubtful we can do that. To will is *to do* something. And to do something is to act. In the case of people, we can speak of their willing (in the sense of intending) to do something and then failing to do it (they can be impeded or change their minds). But unlike us, God does not have to set about to do what he wills. His will is directly efficacious (at least if he wants it to be; he might choose to work through others, or through historical processes, as some have thought; but then his willing *that* is directly efficacious). For God to *will* what is wrong would be for him to *do* what is wrong. And if God, being good, cannot will what is wrong, then it makes no sense to say that God could do what is wrong.

Discussion Questions

1. Would you kill your own child, as Abraham was prepared to do, if you believed in God and were convinced that God had commanded you to do so? Would love of God require such obedience? Should love of God supercede love for your child?

2. What problem for the Divine Command Theory arises from the attempt to answer the question of whether God commands what is right because it is right, or whether what is right is right because God commands it? How would you answer this question? Why?

3. How does Augustine (section 6.7) attempt to reconcile Christian love of one's enemies with willingness to kill one's enemies in war? Do you find his reasoning plausible?

4. Aquinas (section 6.9) uses different arguments to try to either justify or explain away God's biblical commands to kill, commit adultery, and steal. What are his arguments? Do you find them convincing?

5. If we don't have any reason to believe that God would command such things as the torture of a child, what point is there, philosophically, in worrying about what to say if he did?

6. What might it mean to say that God is good? Do you think any of the answers considered in sections 6.11 and 6.12 convincingly resolve the problems facing the Divine Command Theory? Why or why not?

The root of evil is this: not being in accord with nature.[1]
Augustine

7 CHAPTER | **Natural Law Ethics**

7.1 MORALITY AND NATURE

Common sense readily distinguishes between things found in nature and things that are not. Trees, rocks, rabbits, and squirrels are found in nature. Computers, stereos, and cars are not. Nor are socks, cities, sororities, or shopping malls. They're all products of human activities. Sometimes they come into existence through express design, sometimes through activities directed to other ends.

But what about right and wrong? Are they found in nature or are they human creations as well? They obviously aren't found under rocks or growing on trees. You can't see them, feel them, or hear them the way you can the sunset, the wind, or the thunder. So they can't be "found" in any usual sense. The only sensible question can be whether they are *grounded* in nature—whether morality is in some sense part of the natural order of things as opposed to being a "social construct." Taking the question in this way, we can ask: Can we determine what is right and wrong by understanding nature properly?

The natural law tradition answers that we can. It holds that morality is part of the natural order of things.[2] Some things—the most important things for individual and social conduct—are right or just by nature, apart from the opinions or practices of humans. Other things, like dress and manners, are right merely by custom or convention. One of the early characterizations of natural law is by the Roman statesman Cicero:

> This, then, . . . has been the decision of the wisest philosophers, that law was neither a thing contrived by the genius of man, nor established by any decree of the people, but a certain eternal principle, which governs the entire universe.[3]

An eternal "law" of this sort—a form of Moral Legalism—governs all persons everywhere, always, and without exception. For this reason eternal law is universal, absolute, and opposed to ethical relativism (notions we shall explain further in Chapter 11).

Two questions spring quickly to mind. First, what does natural law ethics mean by "nature?" Second, how does natural law tell us to act? We shall take up the first question now and deal with the second in section 7.8.

7.2 WHAT DOES NATURAL LAW ETHICS MEAN BY "NATURE"?

Sometimes the natural law tradition understands nature to refer to the natural order as a whole—"cosmic nature," as we might call it.[4] And sometimes this tradition understands nature to refer to human nature in particular. Often, the source of natural law is thought to be God. This is true of much ancient and medieval thought, as well as contemporary Catholicism. Sometimes God is thought to be immanent in, or even identical with, nature (as in Stoicism). At other times he is thought to be independent—a being who is the creator of the universe (as in Christianity). But in some recent and modern versions of natural law ethics the assumption of a divinity is thought unnecessary to natural law. So there are religious and secular versions of natural law ethics depending on whether God or nature alone is thought to be the ultimate source of natural law.

With the development of the nation state in the sixteenth and seventeenth centuries, interest grew in the nature of international law and in the justification of political and legal obligation. Accordingly, the natural law tradition spawned theories that belonged more nearly to social and political or legal philosophy than to ethics. And even as an ethical theory it became complex. It recognized the need to account for duties to oneself as well as to others; and, in the case of duties to others, it recognized the need to account for obligations binding absolutely on all people everywhere, as well as conditional obligations that presuppose certain human institutions (for example, particular forms of government). It was largely out of the exploration of these conditional obligations that natural law thinking gave rise to social and political philosophies. Thus we can outline in the following way the various forms natural law thinking has taken:[5]

Outline of Natural Law Theory

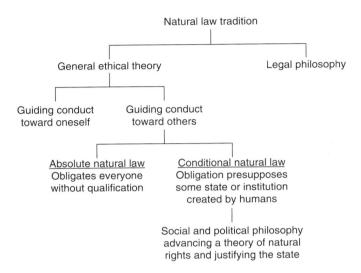

In what follows, we shall consider natural law thinking as an ethical theory, focusing primarily on the forms it takes in ancient Stoicism and in Christianity.

7.3 STOIC NATURAL LAW ETHICS

In its simplest form, natural law ethics sets forth a directive for conduct: *Live in accordance with nature.* But this has meant different things at different times, depending on how nature has been understood and whether its source was thought to be divine.

For the Stoics, God is diffused throughout the world. Indeed, God is identical with nature (the view we call **pantheism**). Nature's laws and processes are accordingly thought to be rational. Thus to live in accordance with nature doesn't mean to "get close to nature," say, by going out and living in the woods, as Thoreau did; it means to conform to the principles of a rational order. It means to live rationally. This idea that moral conduct is basically rational conduct (and, conversely, that immoral conduct is irrational conduct) is one of the main contributions of Stoic thought (and ancient Greek thought, in general) to the history of ethics.

But what does living in accordance with nature mean in concrete terms? How do we know what accords with nature? In the hundreds of years in which Stoicism flourished, the answers to these questions varied. We shall put together a composite of what was most central to them.

Knowledge of what accords with nature requires philosophical (including what we would call scientific) understanding of the world as a whole, including the behavior of animals. Thus it also requires understanding human nature. In the quest for such understanding the Stoics are **empiricists**. They believe that our knowledge of the world is derived from and tested by sense experience. We can't, for example, reliably judge what accords with nature simply by sitting and thinking about it. We need understanding of our own nature. This requires exploration of three topics:

1. Desires and aversions
2. Beliefs
3. Pursuits and avoidances

We all desire some things and have aversions to others. Pleasure, money, success, friends, and the like are among the things most people desire. Pain, poverty, ill health, and death are among the things to which most have an aversion. But it's one thing to desire or be repulsed by something; it's another to actually pursue or avoid that thing (you might desire sweets, for example, but pass up that extra dessert to avoid unneeded calories; and you might have an aversion to pain but willingly have dental work to preserve your teeth). Obviously our proper pursuits and avoidances must be of concern to ethics, since they make up our conduct. Pursuits and avoidances might even be said to make up all our voluntary conduct.

But whether we should *pursue* any particular object of desire or *avoid* any particular object of aversion depends on the correctness of our beliefs about them—particularly about whether they are good or bad. So three things are essential to living rightly: (1) understanding human desires and aversions; (2) having correct beliefs about which of them (or, strictly speaking, which of their objects) are good or bad; and, on that basis, (3) making wise decisions about how to act—that is, about which desires we should seek to satisfy and which aversions we should respect by avoiding their objects.

Here the Stoics believe that proper understanding of desires and aversions requires asking the questions: which things are good, which are bad, and which are indifferent in themselves? To this, they give an astonishingly simple answer.

Virtue, they hold, is the only thing good in itself. Vice is the only thing bad in itself. *Everything* else is indifferent. Everything. This means that every single item cited above as among the things most people desire (pleasure, money, good health, and so on) is indifferent, of absolutely no value in itself. And every single thing cited as among the things to which most of us have an aversion (pain, poverty, ill health, death) is not in itself bad. *Accordingly, the only proper object of desire is virtue, and the only proper object of aversion is vice. We live in accordance with nature insofar as we desire only virtue and sustain an aversion only to vice.*

The implications of this are far-reaching. Many people would say that pleasure is the only thing good in itself (for the distinction between intrinsic and extrinsic value, see section 9.4). This view was held by the Epicureans, who were influential at the time of the Stoics. And many people who don't believe that pleasure is the only thing good in itself at least believe that it is one of the things that is good in itself. But consider what another Roman Stoic, Seneca (4 B.C.E.–65 C.E.) says, contrasting pleasure with virtue:

> Virtue is free and indefatigable, and accompanied with concord and gracefulness; whereas pleasure is mean, servile, transitory, tiresome, and sickly and scarce outlives the tasting of it: it is the good of the belly, and not of the man; and only the felicity of brutes.[6]

But right away questions arise. We're trying to understand what it is to act in accordance with nature. At least part of the answer is that it is to act in accordance with *human* nature, but, as we've seen, virtually everyone desires money, good health, friends, pleasure, and the like. The Stoics certainly knew this. If we restrict our desires to virtue, aren't we neglecting desires that, whether or not they're a part of our nature, are nonetheless universal? And is it wrong to have an aversion to pain, disease, loneliness, and death—which virtually everyone does?

So we must ask not only (1) What is it to pursue virtue? but also (2) What do we do about the fact that most of us desire all sorts of things besides virtue and have an aversion to all sorts of things besides vice? Are we wrong to do so?

Let us take question (2) first, because this kind of concern leads the Stoics to draw further distinctions *within* the category of the indifferent, between things to be preferred and things to be rejected—despite the fact that both things are neither good nor bad. And here, in the category of things to be preferred, the Stoics include the very things most of us desire: pleasure, good health, money, and so forth. In the category of things to be rejected, they include those things most of us have an aversion to: pain, ill health, poverty, and the like. (They also recognized, within this category of the indifferent, things that are absolutely indifferent, such as whether you have an odd or an even number of hairs on your head.)

So the Stoics make provision for selecting and avoiding many of the things conventionally pursued and avoided. But they do so with this stipulation: that one's selections are to be made with the understanding that none of the things preferred is good in itself, and none of the things avoided is bad in itself. Why, then, we may ask, should we prefer any of them or reject others?

Here the Stoic answer isn't altogether clear. Perhaps it's because Stoics believed that certain things (for instance, good health, pleasure) would contribute to happiness, and others (ill health, pain) would detract from it. But happiness for the Stoics is thought to be *peace of mind*, consequent upon living virtuously. And peace of mind isn't conveyed so much by good health, money, pleasure, and so on. It's conveyed by understanding that virtually nothing that can befall you in life (other than slipping into vice)—whether it be poverty, illness, or misfortune—is really bad; that most of these things are out of our control,[7] and, if experienced, are borne with calmness and understanding. When we call people "stoical" today, we mean precisely that they can endure suffering, hardship, and misfortune without complaining or losing their bearings in life. So it's unlikely the Stoics locate the justification for our preferences in a belief that satisfying those preferences promotes happiness.

More likely, the Stoics think that we should prefer certain things because it is natural to do so; that if we understand human nature, we find we're so constituted as to (generally) prefer pleasure to pain, good health to ill health, and so on. All these things relate to self-preservation. The Stoics emphasize that animals have an instinct for self-preservation. So, presumably, do we. This reflects part of how we both are constituted by nature. So in preferring good health to ill health, pleasure to pain, and so on, we are acting in accordance with nature—now understood as the natural, biological constitution of humans as well as animals.

If this is correct, the Stoics are saying that to live well we must desire virtue and only virtue for itself. Other things may be sought but only insofar as they accord with our nature—and then only with the understanding that they aren't good in themselves. By the same token, the sole proper object of aversion is vice, along with other things like poverty, ill health, and death, which should be avoided, not because they are bad in themselves, but only because it accords with our nature to do so. If we do this and become virtuous, the Stoics believe, we'll achieve the peace of mind that constitutes happiness.

7.4 THE STOIC CONCEPTION OF DUTY

So far, Stoic ethics clearly emphasize virtue. In what sense is it an ethics of conduct? Here we first have to ask what it is to pursue virtue (question 1 posed in section 7.3). To answer this question requires elaborating on the Stoic conception of the natural order of things.

We have said that the Stoics conceived of God as a rational principle immanent in the world. For this reason, they think of cosmic nature as an interconnected whole that doesn't do harm to itself. We share in this principle by virtue of the fact that, unlike plants and other animals, we have intelligence. The implications of this are spelled out by one of the later Stoics, the Roman Emperor Marcus Aurelius:

> If our intellectual part is common [to all persons], the reason also, in respect of which we are rational beings, is common: if this is so, common also is the reason which commands us what to do, and what not to do; if this is so, there is a common law also; if this is so, we are fellow-citizens; if this is so, we are members of some political community; if this is so, the world is in a manner a state.[8]

Marcus Aurelius is saying that by virtue of our possessing reason, whose function is to tell us what to do and to refrain from doing and that is essentially the same in all human beings, there is a "common law" governing all human beings everywhere, whatever state or region they may live in. As human reason is part of the divine reason of the universe as a whole (and because reason is orderly and consistent), what it dictates is essentially the same for all. Thus there is a "natural" law to be apprehended, if only we attend carefully to what reason prescribes.

Therefore, it is reason that informs us what is good and bad in itself (virtue and vice, respectively, as we have seen) and what is indifferent and that directs us to pursue essentially only the good and avoid essentially only the bad (allowing, as we have also seen, for preferences within the category of the indifferent). More than that, this common rationality and the common natural law governing all persons means there is a common brotherhood of all persons—that all human beings, wherever they are from and whatever government they live under, are brothers and sisters. Morally, they are equals. (The Stoics stand out from much of ancient philosophy by proclaiming the equality of women and men.) This means that they constitute a kind of community beyond the particular political communities of human creation, and the world as a whole is a kind of state. Built into the very order of cosmic nature is the fact that humans are social and political beings and belong, in a sense, to one and the same universal community.

How does this relate to the question of how we are to live virtuously? The Stoic answer is that to live virtuously, we must do our **duty.** What does it mean to do our duty? The Stoics cannot say, as many ancients said, that to do our duty we must promote the good. The good, remember, is virtue, and we're asking what it is to pursue virtue. So we can't say that to pursue virtue is to do one's duty and then, when asked what it is to do one's duty, turn around and say that it's to promote the good. That would be circular. So the Stoics are deontologists in their account of duty. And so their ethics—though it gives an important place to virtue—isn't primarily an ethics of virtue (see section 3.11).

Instead the Stoics understand duty in terms of what is required by our relations with other people. Thus, parents have duties to their children, simply by virtue of the fact that they stand in the relation of parent to those particular human beings; and children have duties to their parents simply by virtue of the fact that they stand in the relation of being children of those particular adults. Similarly, husbands and wives have duties to one another established by the relations in which they stand, as do citizens of the same state—and as do all humans by virtue of sharing a common rationality with all people and being members of a universal brotherhood of all human beings.

This is the natural order of things. By acting in accordance with those duties, we act, in a sense, in accordance with the rational nature of the universe. Like most Greek ethicists, the Stoics believe that human beings basically desire what is good and right and depart from it (and do wrong) only involuntarily because of ignorance of what is truly good and right. So if we understand properly what is natural—not only with regard to how we as humans are constituted but also with regard to how the whole universe is constituted—we will do what is right, and thereby achieve virtue and the peace of mind that constitutes happiness.[9]

7.5 CHRISTIAN NATURAL LAW ETHICS

With the rise of Christianity, natural law ethics was adapted to the Christian world view. Part of that world view holds that there is a God who is not identical with the universe, as with the Stoics, but the **creator** of all things. Moreover, God, in this view (as we have seen in section 6.1), is perfect: all powerful (omnipotent), all-knowing (omniscient), and perfectly good. If God, being perfectly good, wants what is best for us—as Christians have traditionally thought—how does he convey what that is?

There are two main possibilities here. The first is that God reveals his will by commanding us to do what he wants and forbidding us to do what he doesn't want. This is the Divine Command Theory of ethics considered in the previous chapter. The second is that God provides us with the capacity to determine on our own what is best for us (that is, what is morally right and wrong), at least in certain areas.

Christian natural law ethics combines these answers. It says that God makes his will known to us through revelation and also through natural law. Through revelation God conveys to us certain things directly and explicitly, which, with our limited powers of understanding, we couldn't otherwise know on our own. According to this view, the Bible represents the revealed word of God, and we are explicitly guided regarding what to do or not to do in certain areas by divine commands or prohibitions contained in the Bible. But this is not the only way God discloses his will. God has so ordered things that by proper use of our reason ("right reason," as it is called), we can determine what is right or wrong—at least in our relations with one another—on our own. And in so doing, we are doing God's will, because God wants what is best for us. In this view, certain things are intrinsically right or wrong—that is, right or wrong *in themselves*. They aren't right or wrong because God (or anyone else) commands or prohibits them.[10]

7.6 SAINT THOMAS AQUINAS

Natural law ethicists differ among themselves in the particulars of their accounts. We shall consider the account of St. Thomas Aquinas (1225–1274). Although we considered some important arguments of his relating to the divine command theory (see section 6.9), he is usually placed in the Natural Law tradition.

Contrary to the Stoics, who were deontologists, Aquinas is a teleologist in his ethical theory (see section 3.10). In his view there is one, transcendent, highest good, which is God. And it is ultimately by reference to God that all else is to be understood. But while God is the highest objective good, there is a subjective good for humans. And Aquinas understands this good to be **happiness.** Following Aristotle, he understands happiness to be something at which we all aim. But there are two kinds of happiness: natural happiness, which we are able to achieve on our own, and supernatural happiness—contemplation of God—which we can achieve only with divine grace. How do we achieve these ends—either that of natural happiness or the transcendent end of supernatural happiness? Here is where virtue enters.

7.7 HUMAN AND THEOLOGICAL VIRTUES

Virtue enters here because it involves habits that perfect us to perform good acts and achieve happiness. Aquinas again follows Aristotle in appealing to the idea of habit when characterizing the virtues. But Aquinas distinguishes, as Aristotle does not, **theological virtues** from **human virtues.** The theological virtues of faith, hope, and charity (love) are habits (or dispositions) perfecting the intellect or the will. Faith perfects the intellect so that it can accept divine principles; hope perfects the will so that it can yearn for salvation; and love perfects the will for devotion to God and one's neighbors.

Human virtues, Aquinas says (following Aristotle, again), are either intellectual or moral. The intellect is concerned with truth and falsity. **Intellectual virtue** consists of habits that perfect the intellect in the consideration of truth (that is, that dispose the intellect to apprehend truth correctly). Some things, such as the principle that a whole is greater than its parts, we know intuitively; others we know by deduction from such principles. Understanding is the virtue associated with our knowledge of self-evident principles; science is the virtue associated with deductive knowledge. Wisdom oversees both ways of knowing truth and judges the various sciences as well as their basic principles. But, in addition to working well in theoretical areas, our intellect must also work well in practical matters. Art is right reason about things to be *made*. Prudence, in contrast, is right reason regarding things to be *done*. It concerns the whole of one's life and involves the right choices of means to ends.

Now, one can be disposed to use the intellect well (have an "aptness" to do so, as Aquinas would say), without in fact doing so or doing so consistently. One can know a lot, in other words, without using that knowledge or using it to good ends. We must choose to use our intellect well. This requires **moral virtue,** which is habit that perfects the appetitive part of the soul (which governs choice) to do well and attain happiness. Temperance is keeping our passions from leading us to act contrary to reason (say, through lust); fortitude is keeping our passions from preventing us from doing what reason says (say, through fear). Justice, less directly connected with the passions, is giving each person his or her due with regard to the various transactions in which we engage. One can have moral virtue without the intellectual virtues of wisdom, science, and art; but it requires understanding and prudence (which is akin to moral virtue).

The four cardinal human virtues are prudence, temperance, fortitude, and justice. In outline form, Aquinas's conception looks like this:

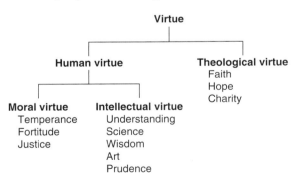

We need virtue for well-being and happiness—human virtue to achieve natural happiness, theological virtue (and divine grace) to achieve supernatural happiness. To achieve the theological virtues we need Divine Law, which consists of "precepts about all those matters whereby men are well-ordered in their relations to God."[11] (Human law can't effectively govern all aspects of our lives because [as we saw in Section 6.7] it can't govern our thoughts and intentions; for this we need Divine Law.) So how do we achieve human virtue?

Here is where natural law enters; natural law is the participation of the eternal law (God's plan for all of creation) in rational beings. It is by virtue of natural law that we discern the difference between good and evil. By acting in accordance with natural law we act rightly in our relations to other persons and things. (However, this doesn't suffice to make us well-ordered in our relations to God.) Indeed, Aquinas says that "[e]very act of reasoning is based on principles that are known naturally."

Reason operates in one or the other of two ways, depending on whether natural law is thought to be expressed in natural inclinations that are a part of human nature—or in propositions whose truth is apprehended by reason, either intuitively or by inference.

For example, we might say, as Aquinas does, that we have a natural inclination to good in accordance with the nature we have in common with all substances—that is, we have a natural inclination to preserve ourselves. Hence what pertains to self-preservation is a part of natural law. Or we might say we have a natural inclination to good in accordance with the nature we share with animals (nonhuman animals, if you like). Thus whatever pertains to the natural aspects of animals (for example, to reproduction and the education of offspring) is part of natural law. As rational beings, we're capable of understanding our own nature and distinguishing between inclinations that are natural and inclinations that are not (for example, a desire for drugs).

At the same time, reason also is capable of seeing the truth of a self-evident precept like *good is to be done and evil avoided*. Indeed, all the other precepts of natural law flow from this, Aquinas believes. And reason is capable of proceeding from this precept to conclusions about what it implies in particular cases—such as that we should seek to know the truth about God, should live in society with one another, should honor our father and mother. To follow our natural inclinations to good, and to implement principles we find to be self-evidently true, is to act in accordance with our nature. And that, in this interpretation, is to live in accordance with nature.

Yet, even though we are using our rational human capacities to determine what is intrinsically right or wrong, we are, all the while, conforming to God's will as represented in his ordering of things. God's plan for the governance of creation is his eternal law. The participation of that law in human beings, as we have said, constitutes natural law. So we are not only acting in accordance with human nature when we follow natural law, we're also acting in accordance with the natural order of creation as designed by God. So, as with the Stoics (though with many points of difference), Christian natural law theorists are looking to both human nature and cosmic nature in trying to understand natural law.

7.8 PROBLEMS FOR NATURAL LAW ETHICS: HOMOSEXUALITY AND SEXUAL HARASSMENT

Two main problems exist for natural law ethics. The first is how to specify precisely what is and is not in accordance with nature. The second is how to bridge the apparent gap between Is and Ought (see section 13.12).

Consider the first problem as it relates to a specific moral issue, that of discrimination against gays and lesbians. A common objection to homosexuality is that it isn't "natural." But what precisely does this mean? It might mean (1) that it isn't found in nature among other (nonhuman) animals, or (2) that it varies from the norm with regard to sexual behavior, or (3) that it uses sex organs for purposes that are not part of their proper function.[12] (See section 3.2 for Plato's view that all things have a proper function.)

In sense (1), homosexuality *is* natural because it is found among other animals. (Konrad Lorenz, for example, reports homosexuality among geese, and it's also reportedly rampant among bonobo apes.)[13] But in sense (2), it is *not* natural, because—despite disputed data on the prevalence of homosexuality—heterosexuality is clearly the norm. In sense (3), homosexuality may or may not be natural depending on what the proper function of sex organs is. If it is to procreate and only to procreate (which, of course is false, since sex organs play a role in eliminative functions as well), then clearly gays and lesbians don't use sex organs for this purpose, since they don't procreate. But then neither do most heterosexuals use them for procreation most of the time. (The fact that there are more than a million abortions performed in the United States each year suggests—disregarding changes of mind—that the parties involved did not intend to procreate.) If, however, people properly engage in sex for a variety of reasons—from the expression of love, on the one hand, to simple enjoyment, on the other—then there is nothing unnatural about gays and lesbians doing so as well.

But it might be urged that there's a fourth sense in which homosexuality isn't natural, namely (4) that it uses sex organs exclusively in ways that *couldn't* be part of their proper function. This would differentiate these uses from that of most heterosexuals. This claim, as with (3), would be correct if one took procreation alone to be the proper function of sex (since gay and lesbian lovemaking could not, even in principle, result in pregnancy). But it would not be correct if one supposed sex to have other proper functions.

Finally, it might be urged that homosexuality is unnatural in the sense (5) that it represents a personal preference of a lifestyle that goes against how humans are constituted to live properly. But this claim runs up against the possibility, as many believe, that homosexuality isn't a lifestyle but an *orientation,* genetically determined (or at least set by genetic disposition), over which one has little or no control.

None of this resolves one way or the other the issue of whether or not homosexuality is natural; but it points out the difficulties in making clear what one is saying if one claims that it is unnatural.

But suppose that the difficulty of specifying precisely what is "natural" could be overcome. Suppose we agreed that the sense implied by (1) is the correct one, so that if a practice were found in nature it could properly be designated a natural practice, and if it could not, it would be unnatural. Here natural law ethicists would still have to show that what is found in nature is right and ought to be practiced, and what isn't ought not to be practiced. (In discussing the Is/Ought problem in section 13.12, we shall consider inferences from the fact that something *is* the case to the conclusion that it *ought* to be the case; here we are now including reasoning from the fact that something *is not* the case to the conclusion that it *ought not* to be the case.) But can we go from *is* to *ought* (or from *is not* to *ought not*) in this way?

That we cannot in any obvious way is apparent. Consider another problem that illustrates this situation. Sexual harassment—repeated, unwanted sexual attention—is a common problem in the contemporary world. But there is evidence that it's widely practiced among animals. It has been reportedly found among birds, bees, chimpanzees, sea otters, dung flies, elephant seals, and baboons.[14] But surely the fact that sexual harassment is practiced in nature doesn't imply that it ought to be, much less that it ought to be practiced by humans. Similarly, even if it could be shown that only heterosexual sex was natural, that would not by itself be sufficient for establishing that only heterosexual sex ought to be practiced.

More specifically, with regard to the previously stated approaches in which homosexuality might correctly be said to be unnatural, approach (2) wouldn't seem to warrant any conclusions about its being wrong. Musicians, athletes, and scholars depart radically from the norms with regard to musical performance, athletic achievement, and numbers of books read; but surely that is to their credit, since the norm with regard to these activities provides no plausible standard by which to evaluate rightness and wrongness.

With regard to approaches (3) and (4), suppose one could establish convincingly that the proper function of sex organs is to procreate and that homosexuality is unnatural in the sense that it either doesn't, in fact, use sex organs for that purpose (approach 3) or that it couldn't do so (approach 4). Would it follow that other uses are wrong? Not necessarily. Arguably, the proper function of the mouth is for eating and drinking, the legs for standing and walking. But we do not for that reason say that kissing, chewing gum, waltzing, and high jumping are wrong. Most people use the mouth and legs for functions other than their "proper" ones—some of which *couldn't* be proper functions (for instance, one couldn't get adequate nutrition and hydration by kissing or chewing gum; and while one might conceivably get around by waltzing, one couldn't, even in principle, do so by high jumping).

We shall see (Chapter 11) that a problem for ethical relativism is that the mere fact that certain things are approved (or accepted, or practiced) in any given society is not sufficient for showing that they ought to be. Generalizing this, we may say that the mere fact that something is found throughout nature as a whole isn't sufficient for showing that it ought to be accepted or acquiesced in—much less that it is wrong to fail to accept it or acquiesce in it. If so, then it seems we can always ask why we should act in accordance with nature, as natural law ethics tells us to do, even when we are in agreement about what is natural and what is not. It may be that natural law ethics (in some of its many forms) can provide an answer to this; but to the extent that it supplements the appeal to nature with other considerations, it begins to weaken its warrant for being called a natural law ethics, for then other considerations (besides what accords with nature) begin to be determinative of right and wrong.

7.9 NATURAL LAW AS SOCIAL, POLITICAL, AND LEGAL PHILOSOPHY

It's easy to see now how the natural law tradition could develop into both a legal philosophy and a social and political philosophy. Once one supposes that there is a natural law—in the sense of a moral order grounded either in human nature or in cosmic nature (or both)—then it is a short step to concluding that human laws (often referred to as positive laws) are subject to appraisal by such law. Human laws are created by fallible humans at different times and under varying circumstances. Natural law is unchangeable and has God as its source. So it's reasonable to conclude that, just as the acts of individual persons are justified only insofar as they accord with natural law, so human laws—the enactments usually of groups of persons—are likewise justified only so far as they accord with natural law. This has become a central tenet in natural law (conceived of as a legal theory). (At its minimum, it represents the view that positive law is to be judged ultimately by moral standards.) By the same token, it was easy for natural law to evolve into a social and political philosophy. For it is widely regarded by natural law theorists that we humans are by nature *social* beings, and hence that it accords with nature that we should come together in communities—eventually forming societies and states. This process requires justification, and that justification has to show the process of forming communities, societies, and states as according with nature.

Here one of the main tendencies in Western thought has been to emphasize the uniqueness of the individual and to see the justification of social and political organizations as deriving from individuals' free acts. Given that the individual came to be viewed as possessing by his or her very nature certain rights or claims against others—"natural" rights, or more often, human rights—one can see how free, rational, individuals in possession of rights by their very nature could be seen to be justifiably governed only if they consent to be governed and only if they freely give up some of their rights (or, more properly, freely agree not to exercise some of those rights), in exchange for the benefits of living in society under government. Both of these tendencies—the one to view human law as subject to evaluation by a "higher" natural law, the other to view human beings everywhere as possessing inviolable human rights—were, of course, central elements in the founding of the United States.

7.10 IS GOD NECESSARY FOR ETHICS?

Once natural law ethicists begin to think of some acts as right or wrong in themselves, rather than because they're commanded by God, and begin to think of human nature as being possessed of inalienable rights, the role of God in ethics begins to recede into the background. The way is then open to eliminating God altogether from the picture.

One such way is to hold that rightness and wrongness are in some sense part of the real, objective world but not necessarily the "natural" world of the sort that can be studied by science. This thinking gives rise to a **moral realism** of the sort sometimes found in Ethical Intuitionism (see section 12.2). As W. D. Ross (1877–1971), one of the twentieth century's leading intuitionists, says, "There are not merely so many moral codes which can be described and whose vagaries can be traced to historical causes; there is a system of moral truth, as objective as all truth must be. . . ."[15] If we are able, without divine assistance, to know such truths—and if, knowing them, we are capable of following them without divine grace—then right and wrong are, in some sense, part of the nature of things, but they don't follow from any divinely ordered system.

Another way to try to eliminate God from a central role in ethics is to locate morality, not in the nature of humans *per se,* but in the very nature of rationality (which might include nonhumans, such as God, angels, and extraterrestrials).

This possibility of explaining ethics without appeal to God is hinted at (unintentionally, to be sure, since he was a devout believer) by Francisco Suárez (1548–1617), who writes that:

> the dictates of right reason constitute natural law; and, accordingly, the man who is guided by them is said to be a law unto himself, since he bears law written within himself through the medium of the dictates of natural reason.[16]

Another element is added to this thinking shortly thereafter by the Dutch jurist, Hugo Grotius (1583–1645):

> The law of nature is a dictate of right reason, which points out that an act, according as it is or is not in conformity with rational nature, has in it a quality of moral baseness or moral necessity; and that, in consequence, such an act is either forbidden or enjoined by the author of nature, God.
>
> The acts in regard to which such a dictate exists are, *in themselves* either obligatory or not permissible, and so it is understood that necessarily they are enjoined or forbidden by God.[17]

With Suárez we have the idea that man (humans) is in some sense a "law unto himself," since we have the principles of right and wrong written within us. With Grotius we have the idea that at least certain acts are right or wrong *in themselves,* apart from being commanded by God. (Note that he does say they are commanded by God, but the point is that God commands them *because* they are right; it's not God's commanding them that *makes* them right [a distinction we discussed in section 6.5].)

Consider an extension of this reasoning. If by virtue of our rational nature we can discern what is right and wrong in some cases without looking to the commands of God or trying to interpret cosmic nature, then perhaps we can do so in all cases. And if we can do so in all cases, what need is there in ethics for the idea of God at all? If each person is a law unto himself or herself, then, to understand ethics, isn't it enough to understand human reason—or even just the idea of rationality itself, whether found in humans or not?

This is the core idea explored by Immanuel Kant. While he does think we must postulate the existence of God in order to fully explain morality, he doesn't think we need the idea of God in order to explain the nature of our duties. He would say that interpreting morality as something that depends on the will (commands, prohibitions, or permissions) of anyone, including God, undercuts the autonomy of morality. It reduces morality to something else. Morality tells us what *ought* to be. To describe what someone tells us to do or not to do—even if that someone is extraordinarily wise, like Plato's philosopher king, or even infinitely wise and good, like God—merely tells us what *is* the case. It simply reports some facts, even if they are of a special sort. And no such set of facts *by itself* can tell us what we ought to do. Morality stands on its own. There is something mistaken about trying to reduce it to anything else.

But Kant's conception of the autonomy of morality not only maintains that morality doesn't depend on God's will, it also maintains that morality doesn't depend on any empirical facts about the world, either. So although his theory is in many ways a logical extension of natural law ethics, it goes beyond natural law ethics in stripping ethics of a naturalistic foundation. It is to Kant's theory that we shall turn next.

Notes

1. Saint Augustine, *On Free Choice of the Will* (Indianapolis: The Bobbs-Merrill Company, Inc., 1964), p. 126.

2. I shall speak of the natural law tradition, rather than natural law theory, since the tradition encompasses a variety of loosely related theories that have little in common beyond the shared belief that right and wrong—and sometimes good and bad, justice and injustice—cannot be fully understood without reference to nature or to what is natural.

3. *The Treatises of M. T. Cicero*, trans. C. D. Yonge (London: George Bell and Sons, York Street, Covent Garden, 1876), p. 431.

4. In using "cosmic nature" in this way, I am following Julia Annas in her discussion of Stoicism in *The Morality of Happiness* (Oxford: Oxford University Press, 1993), p. 159.

5. In these distinctions, I am following generally the seventeenth-century writer, Samuel Pufendorf, *De Jure Naturae et Gentium Libri Octo*, Vol. II, trans. C. H. Oldfather and W. A. Oldfather (Oxford: At the Clarendon Press, 1934), Ch. III, Book II, "On the Laws of Nature in General," pp. 229f. In this section I speak of "conditional" obligations where Pufendorf speaks of "hypothetical" obligations.

6. *Seneca's Morals of a Happy Life, Benefits, Anger, and Clemency*, trans. Sir Roger L'Estrange (Chicago: W. B. Conkey Company, no date), pp. 141, 142.

7. The Stoics were fatalists, believing all events were predetermined. This is a fascinating part of their philosophy that we cannot go into here and that they never fully reconciled with their ethics, which seems to presuppose free choice.

8. Marcus Aurelius, *Meditations*, in *Meditations of Marcus Aurelius, Epictetus: The Enchiridion* (Chicago: Henry Regnery Company, 1956), p. 32.

9. Other aspects of the Stoic outlook, such as their fatalism, create problems for their ethics, but we shall not go into them here.

10. According to some natural law ethicists, God does as a matter of fact command or prohibit acts that are right or wrong, but he does so *because* they are right or wrong. It's not his commanding or prohibiting them that makes them right or

wrong. Since God has ordered things so as to make it possible for humans to act rightly by following natural law, he can't—because of his perfect goodness—in consequence will that we not do what is right and refrain from what is wrong; hence he can't fail to command what is right and prohibit what is wrong. See Francisco Suárez, *A Treatise on Laws and God the Lawgiver,* Book II, *On the Eternal Law, the Natural Law, and the Ius Gentium,* Ch. VI, in *Selections from Three Works of Francisco Sußrez,* Vol. II, trans. Gwladys L. Williams, Ammi Brown, and John Waldron (Oxford: At the Clarendon Press, 1944), p. 206.

11. Saint Thomas Aquinas, *On Law, Morality, and Politics,* eds. William P. Baumgarth and Richard J. Regan (Indianapolis/Cambridge: Hackett Publishing Company, 1988), p. 87.

12. I am adapting this discussion from some points made by James P. Sterba in his *Morality in Practice,* 5th ed. (Belmont, CA: Wadsworth Publishing Company, 1997), pp. 388–389.

13. John Schwartz, "Making Love, Not War: If We Had Studied Bonobos Earlier, We Might Have Some Different Ideas About Male Aggressiveness," *The Washington Post National Weekly Edition,* July 28, 1997.

14. Natalie Angier, "Sexual Harassment: Why Even Bees Do It," *New York Times,* October 10, 1995.

15. W. D. Ross, *The Right and the Good* (Oxford: At the Clarendon Press, 1930), pp. 14f.

16. Francisco Suárez, *A Treatise on Laws and God the Lawgiver,* Book II, p. 184.

17. Hugo Grotius, *De Jure Belli Ac Pacis Libri Tres,* Book I, Ch. 1, Sec. X, in James Brown Scott, ed., *The Classics of International Law* (Oxford: At the Clarendon Press, 1925), pp. 38, 39.

Discussion Questions

1. What different meanings does natural law ethics give to the term "nature"?

2. What do the Stoics mean by the rule: Live according to nature? What does this rule imply with regard to the topic of desires and aversions? Do you find plausible the Stoic view that nothing is intrinsically good other than virtue, and that nothing is intrinsically evil other than vice? Does this conflict with our common-sense value judgments?

3. What is the Stoic conception of duty? Is it ultimately an axiological or deontological account (as explained in section 2.4)? Do you agree that there is a common brotherhood of all persons by virtue of their shared rationality?

4. What, for Aquinas, is the distinction between theological and human virtue? What is his distinction between moral and intellectual virtue? How does his distinction between moral and intellectual virtue compare with Aristotle's (section 3.6)?

5. Section 7.8 suggests that two contemporary moral problems, homosexuality and sexual harassment, pose problems for natural law ethics. What are the problems? Do you think natural law ethics can resolve them? How?

6. In the previous chapter we explored the notion that God is essential to ethics. Section 7.10 of the present chapter suggests reasons for thinking that the idea of God may be unnecessary for ethics. What do you think? If there is no God, are "all things permitted?"

*Is it not of the utmost necessity to construct a pure
moral philosophy which is completely freed from
everything empirical?*[1]
Kant

8 CHAPTER | **Kantianism**

8.1 MORALITY IS NOT FOUNDED ON HAPPINESS

Ethical egoism, as described, stresses the consequences of actions for our own personal happiness. Divine command theory stresses the authority of God and obedience to his will. The first theory has problems with consistency, as it would commit us to a principle that, if generally accepted, would lead others into pursuits that can be detrimental to our own good. The second theory, by linking rightness to an external authority, would seem to commit us to allowing that some actions we believe are terribly wrong are (or could be) permissible.

Immanuel Kant (1724–1804) stresses consistency. Indeed, he says that "[c]onsistency is the highest obligation of a philosopher and yet the most rarely found."[2] And he insists that moral judgments cannot be derived from external authority, not even God's. His theory is complex and difficult, however, and there is little agreement about how precisely to interpret it. In what follows, I shall present a way of understanding it that I believe renders it as plausible as possible; an interpretation that is Kantian in spirit rather than in exact detail.

Suppose someone tells you to lift a 200-pound weight or to run a mile in under five minutes. Some people can do one or the other of these things, and a few do both. But even if you can do these things, you might fail on a particular occasion. There might not be a weight handy, or you might strain your back. Whether you succeed, in other words, is partly out of your control. Virtually all of us, however, could *try* to lift 200 pounds or to run a mile under five minutes. That much is within our power.

Now suppose someone tells you to be happy. Is that within your power? It certainly is within your power to try. But it may not be fully within your power to succeed. If you die young, you will not have had much of a chance (and remember, Aristotle said we need a certain length of life to be happy). If you are imprisoned for life under conditions of extreme deprivation, you may fail to be happy. The same possibility exists if you are tormented by anxieties throughout your life.

The point is that happiness arguably depends at least in part on circumstances beyond our control. More importantly for our purposes, we can never know for certain how what we do will affect either our own happiness or that of others in the long run. That is a matter of the consequences of actions, and we can never be certain what those will be.

For this reason, Kant believes we cannot properly base morality on the concept of happiness. And the fundamental principle of morality cannot be one prescribing that we promote happiness, whether of ourselves or others. If we can never know for certain what the consequences of our actions will be, then if promoting happiness were the only right thing to do, we could never know what is right. The same would apply to any theory that understood rightness to consist of the production of certain states of affairs in the external, social world. In any event, happiness, though it is a component of the highest good for Kant, is not good without qualification. The other component of the highest good, and the only thing that is good without qualification, is a good will.

8.2 THE GOOD WILL

What is important for Kant is that we *try* to accomplish certain purposes. Whether we succeed is often beyond our control. We have done our duty if the purposes are morally correct ones and we have tried to achieve them.

But that is not all. As important as it is to try to do what is right, it is equally important to do it for the right reason. For us to deserve any moral credit, so to speak, for doing what is right, we must do it *because* it is right.

Suppose a friend of yours has gotten the answers to a chemistry exam in advance and slips you a copy as you go into the exam. If you refuse it, or throw it away, you have done the right thing. Maybe no one else will know what you did, but it is the right thing nonetheless. Suppose, however, that the only reason you do not cheat is because you are afraid you might get caught. You have still done the right thing, but you have not done it because it is right. You have done it because you think cheating is too risky. In this case, even though your act was right, you as a person deserve no moral credit for having done it. If you would have cheated had you thought you could get away with it, you as a person are no better than if you had cheated.

So Kant insists that to derive any moral worth from our actions we must do them from the right motive. And the only motive that confers any moral worth on us is the motive of what he calls duty: doing what is right because it is right. This does not mean that all other motives are bad. It is just that they have no *moral* worth, of either a positive or negative sort. If you are in love, you may go out of your way to be considerate of the person you love, and this may be the right thing to do. But if you do it from love, not duty, no moral worth attaches to what you do (for Kant all other motives besides that of duty come under the heading of inclination, and reduce ultimately to self-love).[3]

Those who act from the motive of duty are said to have a good will. They try to do what is morally right because it is right. They may not succeed in actually accomplishing what they intend by acting; as we have seen, we can never know with certainty what effects our actions will have. But we do have control over what we *try* to bring about in the world and over whether we are responsive to moral considerations in the process. This is what is important morally.

A good will, furthermore, is for Kant the only thing unconditionally good in itself. Its goodness does not depend on its being successful in achieving its purposes. It is even conceivable, he says, that external circumstances should be such that the good will never achieves its purposes. But even then, he says, the good will would still "sparkle like a jewel with its own light, as something that had full worth in itself."[4] This it would do even if no one knew of its existence.

In fact, Kant believes we can never know for certain what other people's motives are (or even our own, for that matter); hence we can never know whether they have a good will. As we saw in connection with psychological egoism (section 5.5), we cannot tell just from observing people's behavior what motivates them.

This gives Kant's approach to ethics an internal orientation, which sets it apart from ethical egoism and from any theory that bases morality on the production of certain consequences. In this it is similar to Augustine's theory. At the same time, he does not intend the theory to be subjectivistic; it does not base morality on our feelings or emotions. It is not the fact that you *fear* getting caught that makes cheating wrong. And it is not the fact that it makes you feel good that makes caring for your newborn baby right. And it is not because God commands you to do certain things or because society approves of them that they are right, either. Neither feelings nor emotions make acts right—nor are acts made right by their consequences or by the authority of anyone, human or divine.

To understand what makes acts right requires examining Kant's concept of duty, and that requires considering his conception of rationality.

8.3 THE CONCEPT OF DUTY

In our ordinary thinking about morality, Kant thinks, we regard the notion of moral duty as having an absoluteness about it. If I have a genuine moral duty to do something, it is binding on me whether I like it or not. It is not merely a matter of preference or how I feel about things. I cannot justifiably avoid doing my duty simply by deciding it would be inconvenient. Nor can anyone. What is a duty for me must be a moral duty for anyone who is like me in relevant respects and similarly situated; it is not variable from person to person, as the extreme relativist thinks (section 11.2).

If this is how we think of moral duty, then moral principles must have an absoluteness about them as well, and must apply to everyone alike. This does not mean they apply only to human beings. Moral principles are not merely universal. If all people desire happiness, then the ethical egoist's principle would be universal because it would apply to all people. But morality is not limited in principle to human beings. Why not?

Those aspects of our nature that bring us within the scope of morality are the facts that we are capable of following rules, drawing inferences, generalizing, and making free choices. We are capable of altering our conduct because we recognize the truth of some propositions and the importance of certain interconnections among them. These are the capacities that make us rational beings. This way of thinking on Kant's part is in keeping with much of natural law ethics (section 7.10).

Rationality, Kant thinks, is central to the whole idea of morality. But human beings may not be the only rational beings. If there is a God, God is rational, and if there are angels, they are rational too. If, as many astronomers believe today, there is extraterrestrial life, it may be rational. But such life, if it exists, will not be human (the typical science fiction account of aliens from outer space represents them as intelligent but very different from us in nature and appearance).

Now, any being that is capable of deliberating, following rules, and making free choices is subject to the moral law. If you can freely and reflectively choose to do one thing rather than another, then it always makes sense to ask whether what you choose is morally right. It is this, not your physical appearance or your particular desires—much less your background or history—that establishes the relevance of morality to your conduct. Even if you were constituted so as not to desire your own happiness, it would still make sense to assess the rightness or wrongness of what you do.

8.4 OBJECTIVE PRINCIPLES AND HYPOTHETICAL IMPERATIVES

Given that morality applies to all rational beings, we still need to ask what morality requires of us as human beings. Kant answers, in effect, that morality requires that we act as fully rational beings would act. Moral conduct is rational conduct.

We do not know whether there are in fact other rational beings besides ourselves, but if there are, we know that by virtue of being rational they will be capable of making decisions and choices, and they will have ends, purposes, and desires (although these may be for quite different objects from those we desire).

Now, to be rational is perhaps above all to be consistent. For example, if you are rational you will do what is necessary to achieve your aim or desire (other things being equal), since it is consistent to do what is necessary to achieve that aim. It is a principle of rationality that to desire an end is to desire the indispensable means to its attainment. Knowing that, we can formulate various objective principles, which are simply principles expressing how a fully rational being would act given certain aims or desires.

From our own experience, we can readily formulate such principles for rational beings who have the same sorts of desires we do. Some of these concern everyday affairs:

1. A fully rational being who wants a car to run will put gas in it.
2. A fully rational being who wants to get from New York to San Francisco in the fastest way possible will fly.
3. A fully rational being who wants to make an early class on time will set an alarm.

Kant would call these "objective principles of skill." They cover a range of practical situations. Others relate specifically to the desire for happiness:

4. A fully rational being who wants to be happy will not smoke cigarettes or use drugs.
5. A fully rational being who wants to be happy will be considerate of others.
6. A fully rational being who wants to be happy will not drive at excessive speeds.

The assumptions in principles 4 through 6 are, of course, that to risk lung cancer, drug addiction, alienation of others, or auto accidents is likely to be counterproductive to the pursuit of happiness. Principles of this sort Kant would call "objective principles of prudence."

What is the relevance of such principles to our conduct? The answer is that how a fully rational being would act is normative for how we, as imperfectly rational beings, *ought* to act.

If a fully rational being who wanted to get from New York to San Francisco in the fastest way would fly, then if I want to get there in the fastest way, I ought to fly. That judgment—

If I want to get to San Francisco from New York in the fastest way possible, I ought to fly

—is what Kant calls an imperative. It consists of two parts. The antecedent (the "if" clause) refers to the desire in question, the consequent (the "then" clause) refers to what ought to be done to satisfy that desire.

Notice, however, that the "ought" in the consequent is binding on me only if I have the desire mentioned in the antecedent. If I am in no hurry to get to San Francisco, there is no reason why I should fly; it is not incumbent on me as a rational being to do so. I could just as well drive or take a train. And if I want to enjoy the countryside, that is what I should do. For this reason, Kant speaks of such imperatives as *hypothetical*. The validity of the "ought" depends on my having the appropriate desire.

Hypothetical imperatives, we can see, can be derived from the corresponding objective principles; they depend on verifiable truths about means to ends. Where the desire is variable among people and for the same person at different times—as in the preceding case (and in the corresponding hypothetical imperatives derivable from objective principles 1 through 3)—Kant speaks of the imperative as a problematical imperative (or sometimes a technical imperative or imperative of skill).

The various "oughts" derivable from principles 4 through 6 likewise presuppose that one has the appropriate desire. The difference in these cases is that we know all human beings desire happiness, so the antecedent of the resultant hypothetical can always be assumed to be true. This means that in principle 4 we can just as easily say,

> If you want to be happy, you ought not to smoke or take drugs.

or

> Given that you want to be happy, you ought not to smoke or take drugs.

Either way, the validity of the "ought" still presupposes the desire. If there are beings who are indifferent to their happiness, these considerations would give them no reason to do or refrain from doing the acts in question. Because in our case we can always affirm the desire, Kant calls these hypothetical imperatives "assertorical" (or "pragmatic" or "prudential").

Ethical egoism, in his view, reduces morality to hypothetical imperatives of this sort. It tells us what we ought to do only on the assumption that we want to be happy. And it is for this reason that it is inadequate as a moral principle. Recall that Kant takes it to be part of our common-sense understanding of duty that duty be absolute; that is, unconditional. This requires that moral principles be absolute; they must apply alike to all conceivable rational beings. But the assertorical imperative applies only to beings who, like us, desire happiness. And its implementation in particular cases depends always on an estimate of consequences. Because we can never be altogether certain what the consequences of our acts will be, ethical egoism would mean that we could never be certain what is right.

For example, if you live in New York and have a job interview in San Francisco, you might judge that it is in your best interest—that is, most conducive to your happiness—to fly rather than postpone the interview and drive. But if you fly and the plane crashes, you were wrong, and would have done better to postpone the interview. Or if, thinking the plane might crash, you drive instead and the car crashes, then you were wrong about that. For morality to apply to all conceivable rational beings, and for us to know for certain what is right and wrong, morality cannot be grounded in either human nature or estimates of empirical consequences. It must be grounded in reason.

To see how this can be, let us distinguish a third type of objective principle. In addition to the objective principles of skill and prudence, there are also objective principles of morality. But whereas the principles of skill and prudence express how a fully rational being would act who had certain desires, the objective principles of morality formulate how a fully rational being would act *irrespective* of desires or preferences. Thus we can say,

7. A fully rational being would tell the truth.
8. A fully rational being would keep promises.
9. A fully rational being would not cheat.
10. A fully rational being would act benevolently toward others.

No mention need be made here of such a being's having any particular desires, not even the desire for happiness. A fully rational being will do certain things and refrain from others simply by virtue of being rational.

If, now, these are things that a fully rational being would do categorically (that is, unconditionally—irrespective of desires or preferences), then they prescribe what we, as imperfectly rational beings, categorically *ought* to do, irrespective of our desires or preferences. Each of us, in other words, can reason as follows:

1. A fully rational being would keep promises.
2. Therefore, an imperfectly rational being ought to keep promises.
3. I am an imperfectly rational being.
4. Therefore, I ought to keep promises.

Imperative 4 is for Kant a categorical imperative. It does not require the specification of a desire in an antecedent. The validity of the "ought" does not depend on any empirical condition, either subjective (my desires or preferences) or external (the consequences of promise keeping for my or anyone else's happiness).

So moral imperatives (or moral judgments, as we would say) are for Kant categorical imperatives. They cannot be merely hypothetical. We cannot avoid their normative force by disavowing any interest or desire in doing as they prescribe.

But how do we know precisely which judgments are categorical in this sense? To find out, we need to ask how a perfectly rational being would go about making choices among actions and here, therefore, we need to introduce a new concept.

8.5 SUBJECTIVE PRINCIPLES OR MAXIMS

Whenever we choose to perform an action, we are, as it were, choosing a type of action. We are committing ourselves to doing this *type* of act in this *type* of circumstance. We are acting for a reason, and if we encounter another situation that is similar, the same reason applies to it. Otherwise our conduct overall would be fragmented and disconnected; there would be no continuity to what we do and no consistency in our lives. The living out of rational life plans would be impossible.

Another way of putting this is to say that we commit ourselves to a kind of rule whenever we perform a voluntary action, one that might be stated something like this: "In circumstances of this sort, I will perform this sort of act." This does not mean that we invariably adhere to such rules. Sometimes we are inconsistent, and at other times we change our minds and deliberately redirect our lives through new commitments. Nor does it mean we always (or even most of the time) have such a rule expressly in mind when we act. It is rather that, if we reflect on what we are doing, or considering doing, we can in principle always specify some such rule for every act, a rule that states what we propose to do, and perhaps why.

Kant calls rules of this sort "subjective principles," or more often, "maxims." They are subjective in that they claim no validity for others and have no applicability beyond our own conduct. But every voluntary action has one. It is part of the very idea of rationality that actions be constrained by such rules of consistency. This would be true even of perfectly rational beings. They would act on maxims as well.

Therefore, to understand the way in which the notion of rationality grounds judgments about how we should act, we need to recognize

1. Subjective principles (maxims)
2. Objective principles
   a. Skill   } Conditional
   b. Prudence
   c. Morality   } Unconditional

Insofar as they are rational, there is no difference among perfectly rational beings. Rationality is the same in all of them (see the Stoic Marcus Aurelius, section 7.4). This means that, *as* rational beings, they cannot consistently choose to perform actions whose maxims could not be accepted by other rational beings. Otherwise, they would be committing themselves to rules of action that would conflict with the very rationality they themselves embody.

We may put this by saying that a perfectly rational being would act only according to those maxims that could at the same time be universal laws—that could, in other words, be acted on by all conceivable rational beings in relevantly similar circumstances.

8.6 THE CATEGORICAL IMPERATIVE

Now, if that is how a perfectly rational being would act, then it is normative of how we, as imperfectly rational beings, *ought* to act. This yields what for Kant is *the* categorical imperative, the basic principle of morality:

> **Categorical Imperative 1 (CI$_1$):** Act only according to that maxim by which you can at the same time will that it should become a universal law.

I say that this is *the* categorical imperative. Kant sometimes uses the notion of categorical imperative to stand for particular categorical moral judgments, as in, "You ought to tell the truth" or, "You ought to keep promises." But he also uses it to stand for the basic moral principle from which these particular judgments are derived (how, we will consider in a moment). Matters are complicated further by the fact that he gives several different formulations of the categorical imperative, two others of which we shall consider shortly.

Let us pause for a moment to take account of the significance of the CI$_1$. In the CI$_1$, we have arrived at Kant's fundamental principle of morality. It is his holding to such a principle that makes him a moral legalist. Our moral judgments (particular categorical imperatives) must be derivable from the CI$_1$.

Notice furthermore that the CI$_1$ makes no reference to goodness. It does not tell us to promote the good of anyone—not of ourselves, or of people generally, or of the world as a whole. If we are motivated to follow this principle, we will in fact be cultivating the only thing that is good in itself, namely, a good will, because we will be trying to do what is right because it is right.[6] But the CI$_1$ does not tell us to estimate the good that will result in order to decide what our duty is. It is not concerned with consequences or with goodness. So in addition to being legalist, Kant's position is nonconsequentialist and deontological.

8.7 APPLYING THE CATEGORICAL IMPERATIVE

What exactly does the CI$_1$ mean, and how does one apply it to particular situations in order to determine what is morally right? Or, in Kantian terminology, how does one apply *the* categorical imperative to derive *particular* categorical imperatives?

This is the most vexing part of Kant's ethical theory, and to critics and admirers alike the least satisfactory. Let us try to understand the thinking that underlies it.

Remember that all the preceding is by way of trying to explain how moral conduct is essentially rational. If we do what is morally right, we are acting as a fully rational being would act; if we knowingly do wrong, we are acting irrationally.

Now, how can an act be irrational? Although we often speak of acts as irrational, strictly speaking an action cannot be irrational by itself. Considered in one light, an act is just another event along with all the others that take place in the world. As such, it is neither rational nor irrational. Only if we view an act in a broader context does it make sense to speak of it as either rational or irrational. This broader context must include the act's interconnections with other actions, and specifically its connection with the concept of a rational being. In other words, it makes sense to speak of acts as rational only in a sense that presupposes an understanding of what it is for beings to be rational.

Thus (to take an example of a verbal act), if we simply reflect on the words, "I promise to give you your money back next week," we cannot say whether the act of uttering those words is rational or not. We need to know something about the context: who has spoken the words, to whom they were spoken, what was communicated thereby, and so on (it makes a difference, for example, whether they are uttered in a play, or spoken solemnly from one friend to another). That is, we need a context that involves rational beings, purposes, and desires.

Suppose the context is the following: You need money quickly, and the only way you can get it is to borrow it. You know someone who is trusting, so you ask her for a loan. Unknown to her, however, you plan to leave town within the next few days and don't intend to repay it. In this context, your uttering the words in question constitutes the making of a promise—a deceitful one, however—and as such represents a transaction between two rational persons (nonrational creatures do not have a concept of promising). What takes place can fully be understood only in terms of the idea of rationality. In this situation, you are using the rational practice of promising, and the other person's rationality as well, to further your own ends. The very effectiveness of the transaction for your purposes presupposes this rationality.

To show why it is wrong to make such a deceitful promise, we must show it is irrational. But the act of speaking those words just by itself, as I have said, is neither rational nor irrational, so something must link that act with other possible acts and with the relevant features of rationality embodied in those persons involved in the transaction.

Here is where the notion of a maxim comes in. First we must state what the maxim of such an act would be, as in the following example: "If I find myself in need of money, I will borrow it and promise to repay it, knowing that I will never do so." This is a kind of rule to which you would be committing yourself by performing the act in question in the context we have imagined. You would, in other words, be committing yourself to acts of a certain *kind* in situations of a certain *kind*. The maxim shows that beyond the particularity of the act there is a generality provided by the rule. This makes it possible to begin to consider the act rationally.

Because a fully rational being would act only on maxims that could be made universal laws for all rational beings, the CI directs us, as imperfectly rational beings, to do likewise. That is what we ought to do.

What does this mean in this case? We have specified the maxim of the act. We must now consider what it would be like if it were a universal law—that is, if it were adopted by all rational beings so that *everyone* made it a rule that when in need of money they will borrow it and promise to repay it, intending all along not to do so. What would that be like?

Clearly, if everyone acted on that maxim no one would lend money. Everyone would know in advance that it would never be repaid. If we take the notion of "promising" to extend to all kinds of financial transactions that might not involve the actual uttering of just those words, the institutions of banking, finance, and investing would collapse because all such institutions presuppose trust that certain agreements and commitments will be honored.

That might be disastrous or even catastrophic, you might say. But why would it be irrational?

Here we need to specify one additional factor, the purpose for which you made the deceitful promise in the first place. That purpose, obviously, was to get money. But now we can see that there is a kind of contradiction here. It is between your purpose and the universal acceptance of the maxim by which you would be acting in trying to achieve that purpose. If the maxim were universally accepted, you could not achieve your purpose, for no one would lend money. In performing the act, you would be using a means (a deceitful promise) to an end (getting money), which would be undercut by the universal acceptance of the very maxim to which the act would commit you. You would at one and the same time be doing one thing (committing yourself to the universal acceptance of the maxim) that if universally done would conflict with another thing you are also doing (trying to borrow money).

Here is the inconsistency (Kant speaks of it as a "contradiction"). As consistency is a requirement of rationality, you would in this case be acting irrationally. Because the act is irrational, it is contrary to duty, and wrong.[7]

The example of the deceitful promise illustrates what Kant calls a "perfect duty." But he recognizes also what he calls "imperfect duties," such as a duty to develop one's talents. Let us consider briefly how these differ.

Suppose a person decides to quit school at an early age, concluding that it is not worth his while to learn to read and write well, or to do math, or to use a computer. His maxim, if he gives it any thought, might be something like, "I'll neglect developing my abilities, skills, and talents if I feel like it." Could one universalize this maxim? In one sense, yes. One can imagine a world in which everyone acted on that maxim; it would simply be a world in which people were uneducated and lazy. Unlike the case of the maxim involved in the deceitful promise, there is no "contradiction" involved in trying to conceive of such a world. It is relatively easy to do, in fact. But what Kant says we cannot consistently do is will that such a world actually come about. Why not? Because we all have various aims and objectives in life (ultimately we all want to be happy, and our other aims and objectives are connected with this desire), and if we don't develop our abilities and talents the attainment of these other objectives will be impossible. Consider why:

Most of us would like to own a home and a car, have money for vacations and travel, and have enough leisure time to pursue our interests. Some want to practice medicine or law or to pursue careers in music, acting, or business. But if we don't develop certain abilities or talents we won't be able to achieve any of these objectives. We won't be able to compete in the job market, or if we do get a job, we will be unlikely to gain advancement. If our aims require a college degree, we won't even get into college. Moreover, if everyone acted on the same maxim, there wouldn't even be the opportunities for good jobs and education in the first place. Those opportunities exist only because other people have developed their abilities and talents. The company with which you might hope to get a job wouldn't exist if the management and other workers (or others in their place) hadn't made it a going concern; the university where you might hope to get a Ph.D. wouldn't exist if others hadn't studied history, science, philosophy, literature, and so forth, before you. There could be such a world. But given the aims virtually all of us have, it is not one we can consistently will to come about.

The fact that we cannot consistently will the universal acceptance of this maxim would make action in accordance with it wrong. The same with the duty not to disregard the happiness of others. We can conceive of there being a world in which everyone did that. But we cannot consistently will that such a world come about—because we ourselves, at one time or the other, must depend on others for help and sympathetic concern; it would not be forthcoming in a world in which everyone was indifferent to the happiness of others.[8]

Although Kant has considerably more to say about the distinction between perfect and imperfect duties, in each case it is the inconsistency—hence the irrationality—of what one would be committing oneself to in the performance of the act that makes it wrong. But the inconsistency is located in a different place, so to speak, in the two cases.

8.8 TREATING PERSONS AS ENDS

I have said that although Kant believes the categorical imperative is the one basic principle of morality, he believes it admits of different formulations. These are all intended to be equivalent, in the sense of yielding the same moral judgments (particular categorical imperatives) for particular situations. The formulation just considered, which is the one most often discussed in connection with Kant, may be regarded as a principle of consistency.

Another important formulation (CI$_2$) may be considered a **principle of humanity**. It says,

> **Categorical Imperative 2 (CI$_2$):** Act so that you treat humanity, whether in your own person or in that of another, always as an end and never as a means only.

Kant here stresses the rational nature of humans as free, intelligent, self-directing beings. In saying they must never be treated as a means only, he means we must not, as we often put it today, "use" people. We must not manipulate them or turn them to our own purposes. They, like ourselves, are not objects or instruments merely to serve the ends of others, nor are they to be lied to or deceived. To treat them thus is, in effect, to fail to respect their autonomy and to deny the rational nature they have in common with us. A community of rational beings can function harmoniously only if its members respect in one another the conditions under which rationality can flourish. This is to respect one another as ends.

In our previous example, to make a deceitful promise to a friend is to use that person as a means only. By deliberately deceiving her, you deprive her of the chance to evaluate fully in a rational way the issue that is put before her when you ask for money. You maneuver her into unwittingly serving your purposes by getting her to do what she would not do if she understood the situation clearly. That is what makes the act wrong according to this second formulation of the categorical imperative.

You might object that we cannot help but use other people as means. When people deliver our mail, collect our trash, cut our hair, grade our exams, or cook our meals, they function as means to our ends. Does this not violate the categorical imperative?

Not necessarily. CI$_2$ prohibits treating people as *mere* means. It does not prohibit their being treated as means at all. People cannot live in complex social arrangements without many of these people much of the time—and perhaps all of them some of the time—serving as means to the ends of others. But it is possible to respect people as ends at the same time that they serve in these capacities. They can, for example, be paid well, allowed to choose freely which occupations to engage in, and accorded respect in the performance of their duties. That people are often exploited and oppressed does not of itself show that there is anything wrong with treating them as means. It shows only that there is something wrong with treating them as mere means.

8.9 THE WILL AS UNIVERSAL LAWGIVER

The third formulation of the categorical imperative (CI₃) may be called the **principle of autonomy**. It says,

> **Categorical Imperative 3 (CI₃):** Act only so that the will through its maxims could regard itself at the same time as universally lawgiving.

The central thought here is that when we act morally, it is *we* who freely choose, who freely make our own moral decisions. We are autonomous moral agents. In acting on maxims that can be universalized (that could be universally accepted by all rational beings), we are, as it were, legislating for all rational beings. It is as though we were, each of us, individually universal lawgivers. Stripped of the particulars of physical differences and attributes of character, and considered solely as rational beings, we are all essentially the same. The rational nature embodied in all of us—including intelligent life in outer space, if there should be such—is the same throughout. When we choose, it is as though we were choosing for all rational beings, and when we do so we are acting autonomously.

If we allow our choices to be made for us by anyone else, we compromise our autonomy (Kant says we then act "heteronomously"). We cannot look to society, government, religious leaders, a monarch—or even God—to tell us what our moral decisions should be. We must ourselves legislate morality. So ethical relativism is a totally inadequate moral theory, appealing as it does to the practices or customs of a society as the determinants of right and wrong.[9] It means that the divine command theory[10] is also inadequate. Kant allows that we need to postulate the existence of God in order, ultimately, to make complete sense of morality. But that is because we need to assume the existence of God to explain how all things can be ordered in such a way that we can make endless progress toward achieving the highest good (which consists of a good will combined with the happiness one deserves by virtue of having a good will) in the afterlife. It is not that God's commands constitute rightness.

Not only that, but we cannot allow our choices to be determined even by our own inclinations—our desires, preferences, wishes. These all reduce ultimately to self-love and if self-love were our sole motive (as the psychological egoist maintains) we could not achieve a good will. To achieve that, we must act from the motive of duty. Only then do we derive moral worth from what we do. I suggested earlier that if psychological egoism were true we should expect that no one would be happy. We might say, in a Kantian spirit, that if psychological egoism were true we should expect that no one would be moral either.

Schematizing this part of the discussion, we can see the interrelationship among the different kinds of imperatives in the following way:

Imperatives

I. Hypothetical:
   A. Problematical (technical, skill)
   B. Assertorical (pragmatic, prudential)
II. Categorical:
   A. The basic principle of morality, with formulations emphasizing
      1. Consistency
      2. Humanity
      3. Autonomy
   B. Particular moral judgments of duty

8.10 KANT NOT A CONSEQUENTIALIST

We have seen the complex conceptual apparatus Kant thinks lies behind our commonsense notion of duty. His account represents the most formidable attempt in the history of ethics to show how morality is thoroughly rational.

Although Kant's theory is sometimes contrasted with theories of virtue, note that it has no necessary incompatibility with such theories; in fact, although we have not considered it, Kant himself has a theory of virtue, stressing the importance of developing character and virtues such as conscientiousness and beneficence.[11] It is just that overall his theory is best considered an ethics of conduct because of the importance it assigns to conduct as well as to rules and principles.

It has also seemed to some that despite its apparent deontological orientation, Kant's theory is in fact ultimately consequentialist because it requires that we consider the consequences of universalizing our maxims. This, however, is mistaken. Kant does not say that rightness is determined either by the consequences of acts or by the consequences of our universalizing them. What he says is that we must reflect on what the world would be like if our maxims *were* universally accepted; that we must consider whether such a world would be rationally conceivable and one that we could consistently—if it were in our power to do so—will into being. But considering what the consequences would be if our maxims were universally accepted does not itself have consequences in the actual world. This considering is done by reason alone. What *do* have consequences in the actual world, of course, are actions we perform as a result of determining what our duty is. But these are not themselves the consequences of our universalizing our maxims (though they are consequences of our choosing to perform the actions after assessing their rightness by rational means). What the actual consequences would be if we performed certain actions does not enter into the process by which we determine rightness at all. For that reason, Kant is not a consequentialist. And because no consideration of what the value of the consequences of our actions would be enters into the determination of rightness, he is not an axiologist either.

But if it is not a sustainable objection against Kant that despite himself he was a consequentialist, there are other problems for his theory (only two of which we have space to mention here).

The first problem is that his whole theory founders unless we can make sense of the saying that every voluntary action has a maxim. As we have seen, the notion of a maxim is pivotal in the whole rational process by which we determine rightness.

The categorical imperative purports to govern all conduct. And it is presumed not to be difficult to determine what it prescribes. But it requires that we specify correctly the maxim of proposed actions. The problem is that prospective actions do not come with one and only one maxim unmistakably attached to them. Whether I describe the maxim of my action as "moving my arm in situations of this sort" or as "paying a bribe in situations of this sort" may make a difference to whether I can universalize it. Every act seems to admit of having many different maxims associated with it, and which of these we take to be the correct one can make a difference to the ultimate determination of the rightness of the act.

Even before that, whatever we do admits of being characterized as any one of an indefinite number of actions. In some circumstances, the action that a person performs might be characterized as that of either moving his arm, swinging a racket, hitting a tennis ball, or returning a serve. And all these might be correct characterizations. In more serious circumstances, what someone does might be characterized as moving a finger, pushing a button, following orders, or launching a nuclear missile—again, each with equal correctness. So what is the "act" that is our proper concern when it comes to determining rightness—and what is its maxim? Is it, "If I want this system to operate, I will press this button"? Or, "When given orders in situations of this sort, I will comply"? Or, "When ordered to initiate a nuclear attack, I will do so"? Whether you could consistently will that all rational beings act on your maxim might well depend on precisely which of these you take to be the maxim. The first might lead you only to consider an efficient world in which people make things run in the intended way by starting them properly. The third might lead you to consider a world in which everyone is willing to initiate the destruction of civilization if ordered to do so.

But even if this problem were surmounted, there is a another problem that is more fundamental. It lies in Kant's assumption that how fully rational beings would act is normative for how we, as imperfectly rational beings, ought to act. What is presupposed by Kant's reasoning is a principle on the order of "One ought to act as a perfectly rational being would act." This would then enable one to conclude that we ought to act in this way.

In other words, to get from

1. A fully rational being would do X.

to

2. An imperfectly rational being ought to do X.

we need a premise such as

1. One ought to act as a fully rational being would act.

But once we formulate an assumed premise of this sort, we see it has problems. Many people would question whether focusing on fully rational conduct is at all the way to approach morality. Some, like Hume (who wrote before Kant), would say that reason by itself is utterly incapable of guiding conduct, since it can only deal with relations among things. Hume put this rather dramatically when he said that "[r]eason is, and ought only to be the slave of the passions, and can never pretend to any other office than to serve and obey them."[12] Reason can show us the way to selecting correct means to our ends, but it cannot select our ends for us. For that we need our "passional" nature (feelings, emotions, desires). It is how we feel about ends that leads us to adopt or reject them. And some feminists would maintain that this whole Kantian conception of reason, as objective and free of historical and social contexts, is essentially a male conception, one that fails to do justice to women's experience, which is rooted in feeling, connectedness, and caring (see Chapter 14).

These problems are not necessarily fatal to Kant's theory, but they need to be reckoned with. In any event, Kant's is a powerful theory and represents perhaps the paradigm of moral legalism.[13] Its most serious problems, in my judgment, are those afflicting all legalist theories, as we shall see in Chapter 12.

Notes

1. Immanuel Kant, Preface, *Foundations of the Metaphysics of Morals*, ed. and tr. Lewis White Beck, *Immanuel Kant: Critique of Practical Reason and Other Writings in Moral Philosophy* (Chicago: University of Chicago Press, 1949), p. 51.

2. Immanuel Kant, *Critique of Practical Reason and Other Writings in Moral Philosophy*, ed. and tr. Lewis White Beck (Chicago: University of Chicago Press, 1949), p. 135.

3. Ibid., p. 133.

4. Ibid., p. 56.

5. I say "in principle," because although theoretically such prudential imperatives are like imperatives of skill, they differ in an important respect, in that the concept of happiness central to them is indeterminate. Because of the contingent, empirical character of the idea of happiness, we can never be certain what actions will further it in the long run. Kant says, "But it is a misfortune that the concept of happiness is such an indefinite concept that, although each person wishes to attain it, he can never definitely and self-consistently state what it is he really wishes and wills. The reason for this is that all elements which belong to the concept of happiness are empirical, i.e., they must be taken from experience." (Ibid., p. 77).

6. Meaning now by "right" what is mandatory or required, not merely what is permissible.

7. Note that this shows only that it is wrong to act on this particular maxim, which is associated with a false promise. This does not show that breaking a promise for another reason, such as to save someone's life, is necessarily wrong. To determine that you would need to consider the nature of the maxim in that case and whether it could be successfully universalized. Also note that, although Kant thinks that a pure

moral philosophy is free of anything empirical, to derive specific duties from the categorical imperative requires some empirical knowledge—in this case, for example, about what must be the case for human beings to make promises successfully.

8. There is more to Kant's distinction between perfect and imperfect duties. For example, there is leeway with regard to which actions will satisfy an imperfect duty in a way in which there is no leeway in the case of perfect duties.

9. Cultural relativism would be mistaken because it takes the way in which imperfectly rational beings have behaved for centuries (as reflected in their customs and practices) as normative of how they ought to act. And extreme relativism would be mistaken because (in at least some of its forms) it takes the feelings and emotions reflecting the self-love of imperfectly rational beings to be normative. Each makes morality dependent in an essential way on human nature or the human condition. See Chapter 11 for a detailed discussion of these issues.

10. Understanding by the divine command theory here, any theory that asserts thesis 2 from section 6.5.

11. This has tempted some to view his theory as primarily an ethics of virtue. See, for example, Onora O'Neill, *Constructions of Reason: Explorations of Kant's Practical Philosophy* (Cambridge, England: Cambridge University Press, 1989), p. 161.

12. David Hume, *A Treatise of Human Nature*, Pt. III, Sect. III.

13. It is important not to misinterpret this. Kant himself speaks of legality in connection with the outer character of acts, their moral rightness. His emphasis on moral worth requires that actions be done from the motive of duty. Still, Kant's whole theory rests on a conception of a supreme principle of morality in a way that makes it a form of moral legalism as we have defined it.

Discussion Questions

1. Much of ethical theory attempts to ground ethics on the notion of happiness. Kant rejects these attempts. Why?

2. Why does Kant think that a good will is the only thing unconditionally good in itself (though he thinks that a good will combined with happiness is the Highest Good)? Are there similarities between Kant's conception of a good will and the Stoic conception of virtue? Insofar as a good will rests upon motivation, what are the practical problems in knowing whether anyone (including yourself) has a good will?

3. What is Kant's conception of an objective principle? What kinds of objective principles are there?

4. What is Kant's distinction between hypothetical and categorical imperatives? Why must moral imperatives, in his view, be categorical? How does the notion of an objective principle of morality underlie the idea of a categorical imperative?

5. Kant's second formulation of the categorical imperative (CI$_2$) requires that we treat persons (and by implication rational beings generally) as ends and not means only. Is this realistic? Some would say that much of human progress has resulted from treating people as means only. A greater social good requires it. What examples might such persons appeal to in support of this? Slavery? Sweat shops? Military conscription? Death penalty? Would you agree? Why or why not?

6. If you were Kant, how would you defend your theory against the problems cited in section 8.10?

What is it, let us now ask, that is so compelling about consequentialism? It is, I think, the rather simple thought that it can never be right to prefer a worse state of affairs to a better.[1]
Philippa Foot

Consequentialism

9.1 THE ATTRACTION OF CONSEQUENTIALISM

Everything we do has consequences; every act leaves the world in some ways different from before.

Some of these consequences are unimportant. Whether you put your right shoe on before your left rearranges the molecules in the air a little differently from otherwise, but matters little beyond that. But whether you get married or not, or marry this person rather than that, changes your life in significant respects; as does whether you take drugs, have an abortion, join the Marines, or go to law school. And all these changes alter the world in significant ways.

If all that we do has consequences, this suggests a simple and compelling approach to acting morally. Why not simply always do what has the best consequences? How can such a course of action be improved on?

Consequentialism says it cannot. "Look at how the world will be different if we do this rather than that," says consequentialism. "Then perform the act that will have the best consequences."

There is a sense in which virtually everyone would agree with this, including Kant, who is a paradigm nonconsequentialist. If the claim is only that we should always do what is *morally* best, then indeed that cannot be improved on, at least not from the standpoint of morality. That is just a way of saying we should always do what is morally right (in the sense of mandatory) or obligatory, or, more simply, that we should always do what we should do.[2]

Consequentialism says something more. It says that something about the consequences of acts *makes* them right or wrong. But consequentialists are not agreed about what that is. Their answers divide into two categories.

9.2 DEONTOLOGICAL CONSEQUENTIALISM

Some consequentialist views are deontological. They say certain features of consequences other than—or at least in addition to—their goodness and badness determine rightness.

One such theory appeals to rights. It says that if the consequences of one act involve honoring more rights (or violating fewer rights, as the case may be) than any other alternative, and if the rights honored (or whose violation is minimized) are of the most important kind, then the action is right; otherwise it is wrong. Sometimes such a theory is called a "utilitarianism of rights." It appeals to consequences, yet it is not the goodness of consequences that is important, but their bearing on rights.

Another theory appeals to the distribution of good and bad that results from our actions. It says that the distribution must be of a certain sort to be morally acceptable. An acceptable distribution is just or fair; an unacceptable one, unjust or unfair. Some say that a distribution is an equal distribution; others, a distribution according to merit; still others, a distribution according to need; and so on. This theory, unlike the preceding one, does appeal to the goodness or badness of consequences, but not exclusively. It requires that we consider the *pattern* of distribution.

Still a third says rather than calculating and totaling up the comparative good versus bad of consequences we must ask whether consequences, insofar as they affect others, are such as we would be willing to accept if they happened to us. The consideration of what we regard as good and bad might well enter into that determination; indeed, normally it would. But what makes an act right is not that fact, but the fact that we would be willing to suffer those consequences ourselves. As twentieth-century American philosopher C. I. Lewis puts it, "The basic imperative for individuals in their relations to one another, is simply . . . the dictate to govern one's activities affecting other persons, as one would if these effects of them were to be realized with the poignancy of the immediate—hence, in one's own person."[3] You can see here the similarity between this rule and the Golden Rule, telling us to do unto others as we would have them do unto us.

In each case consequences are held to determine rightness, so each theory is consequentialist. But in the first and the third, not the value of the consequences, but something else is primary; and in the second, the goodness, but not the goodness alone (rather, how that goodness is distributed) is important. So each is deontological in that it either does not appeal to goodness in the determination of rightness or does not do so exclusively. The second of these theories is considered in the next chapter when we examine the problem of justice.

9.3 UTILITARIANISM

We shall limit our present concern to consequentialist theories that are also axiological, holding that the value of consequences determines rightness. This combination of positions, you recall, defines teleological theories (section 2.6). This is the way consequentialism is most often understood (in fact, it is sometimes misleadingly identified with such theories).

This approach best exemplifies the intuitively compelling idea with which we began. It says, in its simplest form: survey the actions open to you, then choose the one that will have the best consequences. That will then be the one that is morally right.

But, as noted earlier (section 2.8), one needs to ask, "Consequences for whom?" We could, of course, be asking about the best consequences for ourselves personally, or for our friends and family, or for our country, race, religion, and so on. Or we could be asking about the best consequences for all people, regardless of who they are and their relationship to us; or, finally, we could be asking about the best consequences overall, considering everyone and everything affected by what we do, including animals and the natural world.

I have already dealt with ethical egoism, which maintains we should be concerned only to produce the best consequences for ourselves. Now I want to look at the other main consequentialist theory of this kind.

Utilitarianism requires not that we ignore our own good but that we extend our concern to include the good of all those people affected by our actions (sometimes it is understood more broadly as including all sentient beings). Its basic directive, stated simply, is

Utilitarianism: Maximize goodness for all people.

This means we should bring about the greatest balance of good over bad that we can for all people. Because the utilitarian believes that for goodness we must look to the consequences of actions, that position, put a little more formally, can be taken to assert that an act is right if and only if it produces at least as great a balance of good over bad in its consequences *for all people affected*—that is, taking into account all its consequences that affect people—as any other alternative.

So to the question regarding what it is about consequences that determines rightness, utilitarianism typically answers that rightness is determined by the good and bad that consequences bring into existence for all people. Thus an important question for the utilitarian is, "What sorts of things are good and bad?"

9.4 INTRINSIC AND EXTRINSIC VALUE

Here, however, I need first to elaborate upon the distinction between intrinsic and extrinsic value noted in the earlier discussion of God's goodness (section 6.11). Utilitarianism makes use of both notions.

Think of some possession you find valuable—a pen, for example. It has some properties or characteristics: a certain size, color, shape, weight, and so on.

These are part of its nature.[4] You don't need to mention other things to understand its possession of these properties (although you would have to mention other things to explain how it acquired them).

But the pen also has other characteristics: it is your pen and not someone else's; it was manufactured by a particular company; it is at this moment in your pocket or purse; it is located on a particular continent. It has these characteristics only by the virtue of its relations to other things. These are relational properties, whereas the first are intrinsic properties.

As noted in section 6.11, when we judge something to have value, we do so on the basis of some properties it has (we cannot even think of or refer to a thing without assuming that it has some properties). If its goodness depends on its intrinsic properties, it has *intrinsic* value. If it depends on its relational properties, we speak of it as having *extrinsic* value.

In the case of your pen, chances are you value it not primarily because of its size, shape, weight, and color, but rather because it writes well (even if its writing well may be a function of some of those other properties). That is, it has extrinsic value for you. Its value can be thoroughly understood only by seeing it in relation to other things. The pen needs a person to hold it, paper to be written on, purposes for which someone wants to write. All these are extrinsic to the pen itself.

Whenever we judge something to be good, therefore, we can ask whether we mean that it is intrinsically good or extrinsically good. Let us characterize these more specifically as follows:

Intrinsic value: Value that depends solely on the intrinsic nature of what possesses it.

Extrinsic value: Value that depends solely on the relationship of what possesses it to other things.

Clearly, most things we value have extrinsic value: cars, telephones, clothing, shoes, television sets, radios, post offices, restaurants, schools, universities, governments. They are valued because of what we can do with them or because of the purposes they serve.

It is less clear, however, which things (if any at all) have intrinsic value. One of the most common candidates for something having intrinsic value is pleasure. From the Epicureans through the nineteenth-century utilitarians to many twentieth-century philosophers, it has been thought that pleasure is the only thing (or, according to some, one of the few things) that is good simply by virtue of what it is, apart from its relationships to other things. This doctrine is called *hedonism*. Pleasure has, moreover, been thought to be the chief or even sole ingredient in happiness. And we recall that happiness has been taken to be the highest good by many philosophers, from Aristotle through the Epicureans and utilitarians; and has been taken to be the highest human good for Augustine and Aquinas, and to be an important element of the highest good for Kant.

But other things have also been thought to have intrinsic value, such as virtue (the Stoics), a good will (Kant), and knowledge (Ross).

If there are things of intrinsic value, chances are they have extrinsic value as well. A Kantian good will is something of intrinsic, unqualified goodness; but if you have a good will, you will be motivated by duty, and may, all other things being equal, succeed in doing what is right much of the time—which would make your will of extrinsic value as well. There is no reason why something with one sort of value cannot also have the other.

Classical utilitarians such as John Stuart Mill and Jeremy Bentham in the nineteenth century, as well as many ethical egoists, have been hedonists in this sense, saying that pleasure is the only thing that is intrinsically good and pain the only thing that is intrinsically bad. In this view, we should bring about as great a balance of pleasure over pain for as many people as possible (or perhaps for all sentient creatures). In so doing, considering that happiness consists of a life of pleasure (including the absence of pain), we'll be promoting their happiness (the egoist, of course, says we should do this ultimately, and as an end, only for ourselves). In addition to hedonistic utilitarianism, there is what is sometimes called "ideal" utilitarianism, which recognizes a plurality of things that are intrinsically good, usually including pleasure, but including also such things as virtue and knowledge.

9.5 PROBLEMS FOR UTILITARIANISM

But two other questions need to be asked of utilitarianism. First, we need to ask how we can realistically be expected to predict the (actual as opposed to intended) consequences of our acts for all the people who may be affected by them, and predict them for all the acts available to us in a given situation. Even the smallest things we do are often carried by the wind, affecting people we do not know in ways we could not have imagined. And even if we could, with enough effort, calculate all the consequences of our actions, to do so might take more time than we can devote to it.

Second, we need to ask what we are to do about those cases in which other kinds of considerations besides the value of consequences seem morally relevant. Should we, for example, be truthful, even if sometimes it does not seem to have the best consequences (the child who confesses to having gotten into the cookie jar may be punished, whereas the child who lies may not)? Should we keep our word only if the consequences can be seen to be better than if we break our promises? Is it, contrary to Kant, all right (or even obligatory) to make a deceitful promise if we can thereby achieve a greater good?

Here I have highlighted two considerations, truth telling and promise keeping. They may not always be decisive when we are trying to decide how to act, but they are surely always relevant.

Notice that these two considerations are of a different *kind* than that of the goodness of consequences. You can know whether you are telling the truth or keeping a promise without knowing what consequences it will have. If these are morally relevant considerations independent of whether they produce better consequences than their alternatives, then utilitarianism has not accounted for some important aspects of morality.

Two other types of consideration are relevant here as well. One type concerns rights, the other justice.

It is sometimes thought that rights may conflict with utility (understood now as the value of consequences). If, for example, there are human rights, then they are possessed by all people simply by virtue of their being human; they are not conferred by anyone; they can't be taken away (although they can be ignored or violated), and having them doesn't depend on the value of the consequences of honoring them. If that is the case, it may sometimes happen—at least in principle—that a greater good can be produced by *violating* some of those rights than by respecting them.[5]

This may well have been the thinking in the former Soviet Union when, after coming to power, Stalin undertook a massive campaign to collectivize agriculture. The campaign deprived countless farmers of their land and eventually resulted in millions of deaths due to starvation. The goal was to implement state socialism as rapidly as possible; and this no doubt was thought to be a greater good for the country as a whole (and eventually for the world, as the Soviet Union led the way to world socialism). But it violated the rights of many individual people, whose preferences, well-being, and even lives, were trampled in the process.

The other consideration pertains to justice. We will discuss justice in detail in the next chapter, but for now let me simply highlight how justice may seem to conflict with utility.

Considerations of justice include those of fairness. And sometimes (arguably) what will promote the greatest good for the greatest number involves being grossly unfair to some one person or group (this could be said as well about the case of Stalin). It has seemed to critics that utilitarianism is committed to saying that in such cases the injustice would be worth it. Because consequences are the only things that are relevant, if they are undeniably better overall, then that is all that counts. But critics charge that, however you weigh considerations such as justice or individual rights in any particular case, if you omit them from your calculations altogether you have not taken account of all the morally relevant considerations.

Thus we have here three kinds of considerations that critics maintain cannot be adequately accounted for by utilitarianism: (1) the moral relevance of such acts as truth telling and promise keeping even when they do not maximize value; (2) rights such as freedom of expression and the right to life, which sometimes seem to conflict with utility; and (3) justice, which may sometimes run counter to what promotes the greatest good.

These considerations highlight the tension between utilitarian and deontological theories of moral rightness. The utilitarian (as a teleologist) insists that the only thing relevant to moral decision making is the value of the consequences; the deontologist insists with Kant that other kinds of considerations are relevant (although most deontologists do not go as far as Kant and deny that consequences are relevant at all).

For the present, let's confine our attention to considerations of the sort mentioned in (1). This leaves us, then, with two basic questions in connection with utilitarianism: first, whether it unrealistically expects us to calculate consequences for all that we do, and second, whether it ignores certain kinds of morally relevant considerations in moral decision making.

One of the most noted of the classical utilitarians, John Stuart Mill (1806–1873), expressly took account of the first problem. In so doing, he pointed out the direction to a way of handling the second as well, a way that has found favor with some more recent defenders of utilitarianism.

Mill makes clear that in defending utilitarianism he is not saying that each and every time we act we must stop and ask how much good (by which he here means happiness) our act will produce worldwide. Clearly this would be an impossible task. What he says is that

> . . . it is a misapprehension of the utilitarian mode of thought to conceive it as im-plying that people should fix their minds upon so wide a generality as the world, or society at large. The great majority of good actions are intended not for the bene-fit of the world, but for that of individuals, of which the good of the world is made up; and the thought of the most virtuous man need not on these occasions travel beyond the particular persons concerned, except so far as is necessary to assure himself that in benefiting them he is not violating the rights, that is, the legitimate and authorized expectations of any one else.[6]

Not only do we need not try to assess consequences for the world at large; Mill also says we need not try always to assess the consequences of particular acts even for all those people most directly affected. Here it is often enough to apply rules, which have come into being as the result of experience showing that cer-tain actions have certain effects on people's happiness. Mill says,

> . . . and the beliefs which have thus come down are the rules of morality for the multitude, and for the philosopher until he has succeeded in finding better. . . . But to consider the rules of morality as improvable is one thing; to pass over the inter-mediate generalization entirely and endeavor to test each individual action directly by the first principle is another. . . . Whatever we adopt as the fundamental princi-ple of morality, we require subordinate principles to apply it by.[7]

These "subordinate principles," as Mills calls them, are secondary rules. It is enough, he is saying, to guide our conduct by those much of the time (maybe even most of the time, although Mill is not clear about this). We need not always appeal directly to the principle of utility itself; need not, that is, always ask how the consequences of *this particular act* will affect the general good; it is enough to ask whether the act accords with a rule—for example, "keep promises"—the general following of which has proven over time to lead to general happiness.

This provides an answer to the first question and suggests a line of reason-ing that may help answer the second as well. It enables the utilitarian to assign an important role to rules in addition to the principle of utility itself. And in so doing it helps answer critics who say that utilitarianism neglects morally rele-vant considerations such as truth telling and promise keeping in situations where it seems to be beneficial to lie or break promises.

Let us focus the issue more sharply, adapting an analysis by W. D. Ross.[8] Suppose we could quantify goodness so that we could measure it in units. And suppose in a particular situation your keeping a promise would produce

1,000 units of good and your breaking it would produce 1,000. Assuming you must either keep the promise or break it (and assuming that any bad produced by the two acts would be the same in quantity), no difference would be made morally by which act you do. You could, if you liked, flip a coin. But the deontological critic of utilitarianism contends that the fact that in the one case you would be keeping a promise and in the other breaking it is itself a morally relevant consideration. If considerations of value balance out in the comparison of the two acts, then this consideration becomes decisive. Because utilitarianism cannot allow that it is decisive—or even relevant—the theory is deficient.

Most deontologists, I might add, would make an even stronger claim. Even if the good produced by breaking the promise outweighed that of keeping it by a small amount—for example, if keeping the promise would bring about 1,000 units of good but breaking it would bring about 1,001—we should forgo the greater good and keep the promise. A promise is important enough that it sometimes outweighs a greater good. Some even maintain that keeping the promise would justify forgoing a substantially greater good.

9.6 ACT UTILITARIANISM AND RULE UTILITARIANISM

The appeal to rules allows utilitarians to concede the force of these objections but to deny that they require giving up utilitarianism. They can allow that we should sometimes forgo a greater good in the consequences of a particular *act* if by so doing we would be acting in accordance with a *rule* the general following of which has good consequences.

That is, even though the consequences of my breaking a promise in this specific situation might be better than the consequences of keeping it, the consequences of people generally following the rule requiring that one keep promises might be better than those of their not following it. If so, then the rule is justified by utilitarian considerations, and the act is justified by the fact that it accords with the rule. The act is not the one in that situation that has the best consequences; rather, it is of a type that generally has better consequences.

Mill comes close to acknowledging this kind of case when he speaks of abstaining from certain kinds of acts (and he might well have had lying or promise breaking in mind here):

> In the case of abstinences indeed—of things which people forbear to do from moral considerations, though the consequences in the particular case might be beneficial—it would be unworthy of an intelligent agent not to be consciously aware that the action is of a class which, if practiced generally, would be generally injurious, and that this is the grounds of the obligation to abstain from it.[9]

It is just that in this passage, rather than emphasizing the good consequences of following a rule (in circumstances in which breaking it might have better consequences), Mill stresses the bad consequences of the *type* of which the act is an instance. Thus, if the act is one of breaking a promise, his point could be put by saying that even though breaking a promise in this particular case would be beneficial, promise breaking in general (the type of act) is injurious.

We see emerging here two kinds of utilitarianism. The formulation we gave initially (section 9.3) may be called act utilitarianism. It says,

> **Act utilitarianism (AU):** An act is right if and only if it produces at least as great a balance of good over bad in its consequences for all people affected as any other act available to the agent.

The other form that we have seen take shape can be expressed as follows:

> **Rule utilitarianism (RU):** An act is right if it accords with a rule the general following of which produces as great a balance of good over bad for all people affected as any alternative rule.[10]

Notice the rule utilitarianism (RU) says only that an act is right *if* it accords with such a rule, leaving open the possibility that where no rule is applicable one can appeal directly to the consequences of the act as act utilitarianism does.

Whereas act utilitarianism (AU) requires that we lie or break promises in cases in which doing so has better consequences, RU may allow that we should tell the truth or keep the promise because following the rules ("One ought to keep promises" and "One ought to tell the truth") has the best consequences. If this works as intended, rule utilitarians can reply to the second question (section 9.5), of whether utilitarianism ignores certain kinds of morally relevant considerations, by conceding that the deontologist has a point in maintaining that we should sometimes consider other factors beside the value of the consequences of acts. But they can at the same time maintain that the proper explanation of this fact is, in the end, still utilitarian.

9.7 ACTUAL RULE UTILITARIANISM AND IDEAL RULE UTILITARIANISM

We need to ask, however, what the rules are to which RU would have us appeal. Are they the actual rules we find in society at the time? Or are they ideal rules that would have the best consequences if they were adopted and that society perhaps would adopt if it could make a wholly rational choice in the matter?

Mill seems to regard the relevant rules as actual rules. So do other rule utilitarians such as G. E. Moore and Stephen Toulmin. But the possibility that we should think, rather, in terms of ideal rules needs to be taken seriously.

The rule utilitarian who appeals to the conventional rules in society that actually exist at the time can be said to be subscribing to **actual rule utilitarianism (ARU)**; those who appeal to ideal rules subscribe to **ideal rule utilitarianism (IRU)**. Let us try to sharpen the difference between the two.

Suppose it is an established rule in society that one ought not to engage in premarital sex (as arguably was the case in U.S. society until fairly recently). Suppose further that for some time the general following of that actual rule had better consequences (for example, by preventing unwanted pregnancies) than would have its violation. Suppose, however, that as scientific advances make it possible to prevent pregnancies through birth control, those bad consequences are avoidable, along with the arguably bad consequences of the frustration caused by abstinence (some people never marry, and they would be prevented by the actual rule from ever having sexual relations). Purely from the standpoint of these consequences (and leaving aside religious and other considerations, such as medical interest in preventing the transmission of diseases like AIDS), it would be better if instead of following the rule, "No premarital sex under any circumstances," everyone were to follow the rule, "Premarital sex only with proper precautions against unwanted pregnancy."

Following the first rule (the actual rule) might have better consequences than simply disregarding it; that is, it might be justified on utilitarian grounds. But it might be better still (that is, people might be happier) if people followed the second rule (an ideal rule). If so, then in this case ARU and IRU would yield different moral judgments. So just as AU and RU can conflict in particular instances, so different versions of RU can conflict with one another.

Strictly speaking, RU of either sort breaks with consequentialism. In either ARU or IRU, it is no longer solely (if at all) the consequences of the act itself that determine its rightness or wrongness. If the act of telling a lie would have better consequences than the act of telling the truth, but I refrain from telling the lie because following the rule, "Do not tell lies," has good consequences, then it is the rule, not the act's consequences that are appealed to. To say that the general following of the rule has the best consequences is to say that, by and large, the individual acts that constitute the general following of the rule have good consequences. It is just that they need not each have the best consequences in the particular situations in which they occur. So, in a sense the ultimate justification for my telling the truth in this case is the fact that most *other* acts of truth telling have good consequences; that is what makes the practice of truth telling a good one. And the value of that practice is the ground of the actual rule, "Always tell the truth."

IRU departs even more obviously from consequentialism. Here the rule need not be generally accepted or followed. It need only be the case that if the rule *were* followed (or accepted), the rule would have the best consequences. For all we know, the best consequences might result if everyone followed the rule, "Turn the other cheek." That would at least eliminate violence that derives from retaliation and revenge, and it would certainly eliminate wars. In any event, such a rule might be an ideal rule, but it is surely not an actual conventional rule, because few people follow it. So if you acted on that rule in a particular case, you would not be basing your judgment about the rightness of nonretaliation on the consequences of the act in that particular case nor on the consequences of a general practice by others.

We may represent the interrelationships of these various forms of utilitarianism schematically as in the diagram:

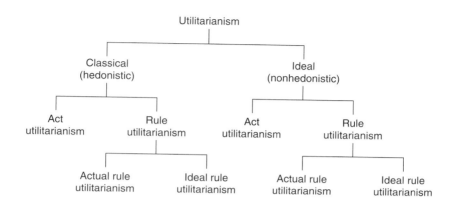

9.8 ARE AU AND IRU EQUIVALENT?

It has sometimes been thought that AU and IRU are equivalent in the sense of yielding exactly the same conclusions when applied to particular cases. If that were so, then IRU could not meet the objection considered earlier by critics of utilitarianism. That objection presupposed that we sometimes ought to act in ways other than those prescribed by AU.

More specifically, a recent defender of utilitarianism has maintained that if we consider what an ideal rule is, clearly there is only one such rule, namely AU itself.[11] Therefore, to adopt IRU is in effect to commit oneself to acting always on AU. In that case, the two cannot yield different conclusions.

This issue is complex, and we cannot go into it in detail. But I want to indicate reasons to think that AU and IRU are distinguishable.

Bear in mind that utilitarians of whatever sort are concerned to maximize value for people; that is the ultimate end of morality. And they believe that focusing on consequences is the way to maximize value. But now, what is the difference between the act utilitarian and the rule utilitarian? We might answer this by saying they have different conceptions of how best to achieve that end. Starting from the basic utilitarian directive, the act utilitarian reasons, in effect, as follows:

1. One ought to maximize goodness for all people.

He then maintains

2. The only (or best) way to do this is for each person to act on AU.

and concludes,

3. Therefore, one ought to act on AU.

In other words, we should each always perform the specific act which in that particular circumstance has the best consequences for all people affected.

The rule utilitarian reasons in an analogous way, starting from the same basic premise but reaching a different conclusion:

1¢. One ought to maximize goodness for all people.
2¢. The only (or best) way to do this is for each person to act on RU.
3¢. Therefore, one ought to act on RU.

Our concern is with RU when it takes the form of IRU. It is clear from the preceding that AU and IRU make incompatible claims. Their respective second premises cannot both be correct, if AU and IRU are indeed distinct theories.

It would seem to be true that many of our actions affect only a few people—friends, family, those around us. A case could be made for saying that what most people do does not affect many people outside of their community. And practically none of our actions affects everyone in our society, much less in other societies.

Suppose now that everyone in one nation, say, the United States, always performs the individual act that has the best consequences for the people affected by it (these being, by and large, other people in that society). They will then be acting as AU directs. Suppose now that everyone in another society, say, that of Japan, does the same for people in that society. They, too, will be acting as AU directs. But if circumstances should be such that the good of the people in one society conflicts with that of people in the other society, the two societies may be on a collision course, each competing for the same natural resources and the same markets or for influence in the same areas of the world. In that case, each person's acting on AU would not maximize goodness for *everyone*.[12] This would be similar to the problem considered earlier (section 5.3) in connection with ethical egoism, in which each person's pursuit of his or her own good might well conflict with that pursuit on the part of others.

On the other hand, suppose everyone in each society acts on rules such as, "Never support aggression against other peoples," or "Never support nationalistic expansionism." It is at least arguable that these rules are ideal; that is, that general conformity to them would have the best consequences. If they are ideal, then everyone's acting on them might very well contribute more to maximizing value for everyone than everyone's acting on AU.[13]

This reasoning contains many assumptions about what constitute consequences, of course, and its assessment would require much more extensive analysis. But it suggests, at least, that AU and IRU may very well not be equivalent in their practical bearings on conduct.

9.9 CAN WE EVER KNOW ALL OF AN ACT'S CONSEQUENCES?

If agreement could be reached about what is good and bad (a problem we have not taken up), and about whose benefit we should primarily be concerned with (that of the individual, or of everyone, or of all living things, and so on), consequentialism would at least in theory be a compelling position.

But morality is concerned ultimately with practice, and as we move from theory to practice we encounter problems with consequentialism.

Not the least of these was detailed by G. E. Moore, himself generally regarded as a utilitarian. He pointed out that if we are talking about the actual consequences of actions (as one is with AU), then in order to know whether an act is right we would have to know *all* the consequences of that act, and *all* the consequences of every other act open to us at the time.[14] In addition, we would have to be able to make a comparative assessment of the goodness and badness of all those consequences.

Now we have assumed that the consequences of most acts affect only a limited number of people, and perhaps that is true in the short run. But may they not affect thousands or even millions in the long run, through the indefinite future?

Consider that at some point Adolf Hitler's mother and father first met, maybe through friends or at church or in a beer hall. They got to know one another and eventually decided to get married. At some point during that marriage she conceived. Had she conceived 15 minutes, or a day, or a week, earlier or later; of if they had not married when they did, or had not met when they did, or had not met at all, Hitler almost certainly would not have come into existence. And if he had not come into existence, World War II almost certainly would not have occurred (not that other conflicts might not have occurred in its place). The more than 50 million people who died in the war, including the 10 million or so exterminated in concentration camps, would not have died as they did; the Holocaust would not have occurred; millions of those people who died would have reproduced and millions of other people who do not now exist would have come into existence, and many of them would have reproduced, and so on. The world, in short, would be radically different from what it is now. And arguably it would be different for all time to come. Whichever of many seemingly insignificant events we single out in the lives of Hitler's mother and father, many of them are such that in their absence the world would be very different from the way it is.

Even without assuming that any of one's progeny will ascend to a position of power, it is clear that many seemingly inconsequential things we do may change the world in dramatic ways. This is true not only of human actions, but of many seemingly inconsequential happenings, as Bentham makes clear in this passage:

> At Rome, 390 years before the Christian era, a goose sets up a cackling: two thousand years afterwards a king of France is murdered. To consider these two events, and nothing more, what can appear more extravagant than the notion that the former of them should have had any influence on the production of the latter? Fill up the gap . . . and nothing can appear more probable. It was the cackling . . . of geese, at the time the Gauls had surprised the Capitol, that saved the Roman commonwealth: had it not been for the ascendancy that commonwealth acquired afterwards over most of the nations of Europe, amongst others over France, the Christian religion . . . could not have established itself in the manner it did in that country. Grant then, that such a man as Henry IV [King of France] would have existed, no man . . . would have had those motives, by which Ravaillac, misled by a mischievous notion concerning the dictates of that religion, was prompted to assassinate him.[15]

If consequences do extend into the indefinite future in this way, the conclusion is inescapable that we can never know what they all are. And if the rightness of our present acts is determined solely by those consequences, then we cannot know whether what we do is right or wrong. At the time we act, the moral status of those acts is indeterminable. And if we cannot know what the consequences of our actions will be, the temptation is strong to convince ourselves they will be what we want them to be. George Eliot caught this idea in her novel *The Mill on the Floss,* when she wrote,

> If we only look far enough off for the consequences of our actions, we can always find some point in the combination of results, by which those actions can be justified: by adopting the point of view of a Providence who arranges results, or of a philosopher who traces them, we shall find it possible to obtain perfect complacency in choosing to do what is most agreeable to us in the present moment.[16]

Some philosophers have proposed a "ripples in the pond" postulate. We should assume, they say, that the consequences of our actions gradually diminish to zero in the distant future, much as the ripples from a pebble dropped in a pond gradually diminish as they radiate outward. But there seems little reason to assume this, other than to enable us to believe with greater confidence that we can predict the consequences of our actions. Rather than diminishing in effect as time goes by, the consequences of many of our actions seem compounded.

This problem is formidable. It is the sort Kant would no doubt emphasize if he were criticizing utilitarianism. It affects both utilitarianism and ethical egoism because both are consequentialist theories.

9.10 WHAT COUNTS AS A CONSEQUENCE OF AN ACT?

The preceding objection presumes that we know how to identify an act's consequences, and deals only with the problem of whether we can predict them into the future.

But there is a more serious, conceptual problem that we must consider. It is that the very concept of a consequence may be too unclear to let us even state once and for all what is to count as a consequence. If we do not know that, even better knowledge of the future would not enable us to assess the comparative value of consequences.

Suppose you throw a stone through a window. Your throwing the stone is an act, and the breaking of the glass is a consequence. But suppose someone comes to your door asking the whereabouts of someone you are hiding (Kant's example). Suppose you tell the truth and reveal where the person is hiding, whereupon the caller then seeks out and kills the person.

Is the person's death a consequence of your act? Many would say it is. But this case surely differs from the stone throwing case. You did not *make* the caller kill the person, in the way you made the stone break the glass. Once you threw the stone, no one else had to do anything in order for the effect (the breaking of the glass) to come about; you threw the stone, and the laws of nature did the rest. In the second case, another person (the caller) had to do many things before the victim died. He had to decide whether to believe you when you told him where the person was; he then had to *get access to* the person; he then had to cause the person's death. There had to be the mediation of rational thought and choice on his part. Without it, the person's death would not have come about (at least not when it did and by the means it did).

Let us call this a mediated consequence (mediated by some thought, choice, action of someone else), and the first consequence (the breaking of the glass) unmediated. There is little question but that we should (if we are consequentialists) always count unmediated consequences among the consequences of actions when it comes to making our moral assessments. But should we always count mediated consequences? I want to suggest that we should not. Rather, sometimes they should be counted and sometimes not.

Suppose another caller simply asks you directions, which you provide without asking why he wants them. He then drives to the street to which you directed him and holds up a bank. During the robbery, a security guard intervenes, shots are fired, people panic. A customer suffers a heart attack and dies.

Is that death a consequence of your giving the caller directions? You did not (directly) cause the person's death; cardiac arrest did that. Nor did you (directly) cause the fear that produced the heart attack; the perception of imminent danger did that. To be sure, the death followed on what you did (as did everything else that happened in the universe after the moment you gave the man directions). But it was mediated by the decisions, actions, and choices of many people, including the bank robber, the security guard, and the heart attack victim (who decided to enter the bank at just the wrong time). These considerations, in this particular case, I suggest, warrant saying that the person's death was *not* a consequence of your act for purposes of assessing what you did in giving the directions.

Why not count all mediated as well as unmediated consequences? To do so would have disturbing implications.

It would mean you could *make* anyone's action wrong provided you did something sufficiently bad in response to it. Mediated consequences include all the things anyone does in response to an act, as well as all those things done independently but that are necessary for the resultant state of affairs to come about.

Suppose you are gay or lesbian and are seen holding hands as you walk down the street. Holding hands with someone you love is an act of affection and normally is morally permissible. But suppose you are seen by a homophobic gang, which then attacks you. Should their attack be considered a consequence of your holding hands? If you say yes and are an ethical egoist, you will almost certainly have to conclude that your holding hands was wrong because it had bad consequences (and, let us assume, no offsetting good ones).

Or suppose you are African-American married to a Caucasian (or vice versa). You move into a neighborhood full of bigots who harass you, damage your property, and threaten your children. After a few months, you move out, frightened and demoralized. For purposes of moral judgment, should their harassment be considered a consequence of your moving into the neighborhood? It clearly was a response to what you did, which makes it a mediated consequence. Generalizing, if interracial marriage elicits such responses, then as a practice it, too, has such consequences, and that would, arguably, according to utilitarianism, make interracial marriage wrong.[17] It would be wrong because bigots respond to it cruelly.

Counting all mediated consequences would empower evil, insensitive, ignorant people to render the actions of others morally right or wrong by their response to those actions. This suggests that we have no clear and acceptable criterion of what to count as consequences for purposes of morally assessing actions. There is no problem with unmediated consequences, so long as there is the appropriate causal connection between the act and the subsequent events. But with mediated consequences there is no morally neutral criterion by which to distinguish what to weigh as a consequence and what not to.

It is, I suggest, a moral question itself what *should be* counted as a consequence. We cannot, as consequentialists would have it, first determine the consequences of actions, assess their value, and then decide whether the act is right or wrong. We first have to make a moral judgment in the very determination of what to count among the consequences.

If correct, this undermines both egoism and utilitarianism; and it seriously compromises principles of distributive justice (see section 10.2) as well because they appeal heavily to consequences. It also compromises those rights-based theories that represent a "utilitarianism" of rights, and that, though they are not thoroughly consequentialist, also rely heavily on the determination of consequences. Only Kantianism and the divine command theory, among legalist theories, are unaffected by this problem.[18]

9.11 CONCLUSION

The intuitive appeal of consequentialism remains strong, and it is plausible to assume that any viable moral theory must make a place for consequences. But if the preceding is correct, consequentialism, as it stands, does not provide us with an adequate account of conduct.

Still, much can be said about those deontological theories that, although they appeal to consequences, do not appeal solely to their value. Theories of distributive justice are of this sort, and they are often taken to provide an alternative to consequentialist theories that are axiological. So I want to examine these theories in the next chapter.

Notes

1. Philippa Foot, "Utilitarianism and the Virtues," in Samuel Scheffler, ed., *Consequentialism and Its Critics* (Oxford, England: Oxford University Press, 1988), p. 227.

2. If there should be more than one action that is right (now in the sense of "permissible"), and one of them was in some way morally better than the others, then to do what is morally best would call for choosing that act from among the group.

3. C. I. Lewis, *The Ground and Nature of the Right* (New York: Columbia University Press, 1955), pp. 90–91.

4. I am speaking now in common-sense terms. From a more critical philosophical perspective, it is questionable whether color is a part of a thing's nature; it has often been designated a *secondary quality* to distinguish it from a thing's *primary qualities*. From an even more critical philosophical perspective, it can be questioned

whether any properties at all can be known to be part of a thing's nature. To the extent that they cannot, then the distinction between intrinsic and extrinsic value cannot be known to apply to things.

5. All this may be true even if rights are ultimately eliminable, as I shall suggest they are in Chapter 13.

6. John Stuart Mill, *Utilitarianism* (New York: Liberal Arts Press, 1953), pp. 19, 20.

7. Ibid., pp. 25, 26.

8. See W. D. Ross, *The Right and the Good* (Oxford, England: Clarendon Press, 1930), pp. 35, 36.

9. John Stuart Mill, *Utilitarianism*, p. 20.

10. An alternative formulation might be in terms of the general *acceptance* of a rule rather than the general following of it, with different implications for the understanding of utilitarianism. The notion of acceptance leaves open the possibility that many who subscribe to the rule might not always do as it prescribes, whereas the notion of following a rule implies compliance.

11. Richard B. Brandt, "Toward a Credible Form of Utilitarianism," in Hector-Neri Castañeda and George Nakhnikian, eds., *Morality and the Language of Conduct* (Detroit: Wayne State University Press, 1965), pp. 107–143.

12. One might question this reasoning, of course, by saying that if each person's acting on AU puts the two societies on a collision course, then they cannot truly be acting on AU at all, since the impending collision then would be among the consequences of the acts of the individual people. This raises the question of what we should count as consequences. I will take that issue up shortly.

13. This would assume, of course, that they are accompanied by other rules as well, because these do not by themselves provide guidance for all conduct.

14. See G. E. Moore, *Principia Ethica* (Cambridge, England: Cambridge University Press, 1956), Ch. 5.

15. Jeremy Bentham, *An Introduction to the Principles of Morals and Legislation* (New York: Hafner Publishing Company, 1948), p. 79, n.1. Originally published in 1789.

16. George Eliot, *The Mill on the Floss* (New York: Harper & Brothers, no date), p. 292. Originally published 1859.

17. Again, assuming there are no offsetting good consequences.

18. Actually, it may be a problem for Kantianism as well, insofar as universalizing maxims requires considering what the consequences would be of everyone's acting on a maxim. It might turn out that whether a maxim could consistently be universalized (or willed to be universally adopted) would sometimes depend on whether certain mediated consequences are counted among the consequences of its universal acceptance.

Discussion Questions

1. Utilitarianism is an axiological version of consequentialism, holding that it is the value of consequences that determine rightness. How do utilitarians answer the question: Value for whom? How do they compare with ethical egoists in this regard?

2. What is the distinction between intrinsic and extrinsic value? What sorts of things (if any) would you call intrinsically good? Do you think pleasure is intrinsically good, as hedonists believe? If so, is it the only thing that is intrinsically good?

3. How may rights and justice be thought to conflict with utility? If they do conflict, which do you think should take precedence? Why?

4. What is the distinction between act-utilitarianism (AU) and rule-utilitarianism (RU)? What are the different versions of RU?

5. What are some of the problems in knowing what the consequences of our actions will be? Does the "ripples in the pond" postulate seem to you plausible? Why?

6. What is the distinction between mediated and unmediated consequences? How do they enter into the analysis of a problem like that (in section 9.10) of the caller asking the whereabouts of a person he intends to murder? Can you think of circumstances in which you are inclined to count mediated consequences among the consequences of an act for purposes of moral assessment—and other circumstances in which you are disinclined to do so? How do you decide whether to do one or the other?

Each person possesses an inviolability founded on justice that even the welfare of society as a whole cannot override.[1]
John Rawls

Justice

10.1 THE IDEA OF JUSTICE

Protagoras, in Plato's dialogue by that name, recounts a myth of creation in which the various animals are equipped with the properties necessary to their preservation. Some have strength, others swiftness, and so on. Only humans are left with no means of defense. This leads Zeus to fear for their survival. So he dispatches Hermes to confer on them a sense of justice, to enable them to exist in community with one another.[2] This is believed to be essential to political wisdom and the art of government, which in turn are necessary to the survival of the species.

Plato hereby underscored the importance of justice for social living, and today it is one of the most pervasive ideas in discussions of social and political issues. If Plato is correct, social organization of the sort that characterizes civilization could not exist without justice.

As Plato apparently thought, the sense of justice arguably resides in all of us to some degree. Psychologist Jean Piaget maintains that it is present in the games and play of children at an early age. And nineteenth-century English philosopher Herbert Spencer found it throughout the interactions of daily life:

> One who has dropped his pocket-book and, turning round, finds that another who has picked it up will not surrender it, is indignant. If the goods sent home by a shopkeeper are not those he purchased, he protests against the fraud. Should his seat at a theatre be usurped during a momentary absence, he feels himself ill-used.

Morning noises from a neighbor's poultry he complains of as grievances. And, meanwhile, he sympathizes with the anger of a friend who has been led by false statements to join a disastrous enterprise, or whose action at law has been rendered futile by a flaw in the procedure. But though, in these cases, his sense of justice is offended, he may fail to distinguish the essential trait which in each case causes the offense. He may have the sentiment of justice in full measure while his idea of justice remains vague.[3]

Although we may all have an intuitive sense of justice, the idea of justice is much less clear. It represents one of the most complex and difficult of the central concepts of ethics.

Let us begin by noting some of the many different uses it has, after which we can narrow our focus to distributive justice, which will be our main concern.

Some have argued that there is a kind of natural justice in the world, one centered around the notion of power. This natural justice is manifested in the fact that throughout nature the strong dominate the weak. This thesis is set forth by Callicles in Plato's dialogue the *Gorgias* (section 13.12), and developed in somewhat different form in Nietzsche's conception of master morality (section 4.4). It is often taken to support the view that, "Might makes right." Others, like Spencer, have understood natural justice differently, taking it to consist of a law in the animal world that each being shall experience the consequences—for better or worse—of its own actions.[4] Accordingly, some do well, and as a consequence survive and prosper. Others do badly, and as a consequence die out. The fittest survive, and there is a kind of justice in this.

Most discussions of justice, however, center around human affairs. Sometimes the focus is legal justice, where the concern is to explain and justify the rules and procedures exemplified in legal systems. But often the concern is with justice understood in moral terms. Here, justice may be thought of as a virtue which people may come to possess (as it was by Plato and Aristotle), or as a moral principle by which to guide conduct. It is with justice as a moral principle that we shall primarily be concerned.

But as Aristotle pointed out, one might think of justice in the moral realm in either of two ways. One might think of it as encompassing the whole of morality, in which case to talk about what is just and unjust is simply another way of talking about what is right and wrong. Or one might think of it as but a part of morality, which would allow the possibility that one could establish that something is just or unjust and still intelligibly inquire whether it is right or wrong. (It is clearly unjust, for example, to execute people for crimes they did not commit; but many people think the practice of capital punishment is right even though it inevitably kills some innocent people.)

In what follows, we shall take justice, as Aristotle does, to be a part but not the whole of morality. Yet even within the topic of justice thus delimited, it is important to distinguish three kinds of justice.

1. **Corrective justice** seeks to restore balance in the wake of disruptive transactions, such as theft or injury; punishment (retributive justice) and the exacting of restitution are among the means to this end.

2. **Procedural (or commutative) justice** governs agreements, contracts, and processes, distinguishing those that are legitimate or fair from those that are not.
3. **Distributive justice** prescribes how benefits and burdens are to be apportioned.

Of these, distributive justice will be our primary concern. In the course of examining it, however, we shall have occasion to ask whether it is reducible ultimately to some form of procedural justice.

10.2 DISTRIBUTIVE JUSTICE

Suppose on your way to class one day someone hands you a basket full of money, explaining that it must be distributed during the class in the fairest way possible. You may share in the distribution, but only if it is part of the fairest distribution. Assume further that the money is not ill-gotten and may not be used for any other purpose.

How would you distribute it? You might think it would be fairest to draw lots and give the whole basket to the winner. Or you might think the money should simply be divided up and distributed equally to everyone. Or you might reason that because some in the class already have more money than others, or are from families that do, it would be fairest to determine the financial situation of each person and then distribute it according to need. Still another possibility would be to give some to everyone, so that everyone is assured a certain minimum, and then draw lots to see who gets the rest. Still another would be to divide it among those with the highest grade-point averages, on the grounds that they have probably worked the hardest. Still other possibilities would be to distribute it to the most talented, or the best athletes, or the best looking, or those of a certain race, sex, or religion, providing you could give some accounting of why that would be fair.

Exactly the same kind of problem could be posed if you were assigning burdensome tasks rather than giving out something everyone wants, such as money. You might think it best to distribute the burdens equally. But just as a certain amount of a good such as money would be of greater benefit to some than to others (to the needy than to the wealthy, for example), so a certain burden might be harder on some than on others (a task that required strength and speed would be easy for the swift and strong but difficult for the weak and ponderous). So you might think it best to distribute tasks according to ability to perform them. A very different approach would be to try to ascertain which people are of questionable moral character, and then assign the burdens to them on the grounds that they are less deserving than others.

The question of distributive justice arises when one has some benefit or burden (or more generally, something good or bad) to distribute and there are two or more people (or groups) among whom you must decide how to distribute it. It is a problem individuals often face (though not in quite as contrived a manner as the preceding example) in the raising of children, and it is a problem societies face in deciding on policies involving the comparative treatment of whole groups of people. Every society, without exception, embodies implicitly or explicitly some conception of distributive justice (or more accurately, some conceptions, because different conceptions may operate in different spheres, as in the economic realm or in the family). What that conception is has much to do with the overall moral character of the society. Here, we want to understand the philosophical underpinnings of the idea of distributive justice as it applies to both interpersonal and social conduct.

10.3 JUSTICE, CONSISTENCY, AND RATIONALITY

The underlying idea in the notion of distributive justice is consistency in the comparative treatment of persons or groups. And inasmuch as consistency, as shown in the discussion of Kant (section 8.4), is an element in rationality, this means that the very idea of justice is linked to rationality.

The rudiments of a principle of consistency were first formulated by Plato in the *Phaedo*, when he said that nothing both has and does not have opposites at the same time and in the same respect. Thus while Mary can be tall relative to Phyllis and short relative to Kim, she cannot be both tall and short relative to the same person at the same time. And although today can be warm compared to yesterday and cool compared to the day before, it cannot be both warm and cool compared to the same day.

Implied is the idea that if anything has a certain property, then it or anything like it must have the same property within the same frame of reference.

Applied to thoughts and beliefs, this idea eventually took form in so-called laws of thought, namely (1) that a belief cannot be both true and false at the same time (cannot have the opposites "true" and "false" at the same time); (2) that if a belief is true, then it is true; and (3) that a belief must be either true or false (must have one or the other of these opposites). Consistency in thought was believed to require conformity to these laws.

But we can ask what constitutes consistency in *judgment* and *conduct* as well as thought. Kant, we recall (section 8.5), captured an important part of the idea of consistency in action in his notion of a maxim—a rule to which we commit ourselves whenever we act, and that commits us to similar acts in similar cases in the future.

This idea has been developed among more recent philosophers in what has come to be called a principle of universalizability. Although the principle admits of different formulations, put simply it says that relevantly similar actions should be judged similarly; or, as we shall understand it:

> **Universalizability (U):** Actions should be judged similarly unless there are morally relevant dissimilarities between them.[5]

Applying this principle to moral judgments, we can say that if I judge it wrong for you to cheat on exams, I must be prepared to say it is wrong for me as well, unless I can explain why my situation is relevantly dissimilar to yours. Or if I say it is permissible for me to lie when applying for a loan, I must be prepared to say it is permissible for you (and others) as well—again, unless I can provide good reasons for exempting myself from the same standards to which I hold you and others. The principle does not by itself tell you whether you should or should not lie and cheat. It just requires that whatever you do, you be consistent.[6]

As formulated, universalizability is a broader notion than we need for purposes of distributive justice because it deals with moral judgments in general, and, therefore, covers cases that may not involve the comparative treatment of persons or groups.

So let us formulate a more specific principle, which we may call the *formal principle of justice* (FJ), which focuses on comparative treatment and requires consistency in conduct:

> **Formal principle of justice (FJ):** Persons (or groups) should be treated similarly unless there are morally relevant dissimilarities among them.

The principle is formal in that it does not tell us how people should be treated. It does not say whether we should lie, cheat, steal, be kind, generous, or compassionate, nor does it even specify what constitutes relevant similarities among people. It has no specific moral content, in other words.

A formal principle of justice may be considered a principle of universalizability formulated expressly for the comparative treatment of people. Accordingly, it may be taken to be derivative ultimately from the basic imperative of rationality, "Be consistent!"

10.4 THREE CONCEPTIONS OF DISTRIBUTIVE JUSTICE

To get from a purely formal principle of distributive justice to a substantive principle requires specifying the criteria by which to make the distributions of benefits and burdens. Here there are many possibilities, depending on which of the following three components in the idea of distributive justice is emphasized:

1. Benefits and burdens to be distributed
2. People among whom the distributions are to be made
3. Process by which the distributions are to be made

The kinds of substantive principles that emerge here can also conveniently be grouped into three categories: mechanical, selective, and procedural. The clearest, and perhaps only remotely plausible, mechanical principle is **egalitarian.** It says simply, "Distribute benefits and burdens equally; to each an identical amount." The principle is mechanical in that once you know how much is to be distributed (assuming it can be quantified), and among how many it is to be distributed, you need only divide the amount to be distributed by the number of distributees. You need know nothing about the people, their character, their needs, or their wants. You simply treat everyone alike. Distributing benefits and burdens equally in this view means treating people identically.

This principle is plausible for some cases, such as the distribution of money from the basket in the example given earlier. But it is problematic for others. For example, few would argue for providing all people with the identical income, irrespective of their needs, or whether they work, or how hard they work, or how well they work (critics of socialism sometimes represent it as egalitarian in this sense). And it becomes even more problematic when the benefits or burdens to be distributed are not quantifiable. You cannot literally divide freedom, health care, education, liberty, child care, and rights in the way you can money, food, or clothing. And, unlike money, which practically everyone wants as much of as possible, some benefits such as education are scarcely valued at all by some people (children are forced to undergo it whether they want to or not); and others, such as political rights, are often not exercised when they are possessed.

In any event, when people speak of egalitarianism they often have in mind a different principle, equalitarianism, which is discussed later.

Selective principles require an assessment of people, judging what each should receive. The ancient Greeks took the basic requirement of justice to be, "Give each his due." In this conception, each person has a certain amount coming, whether of good or bad. In contrast to egalitarianism, such an outlook holds that equal distributions may sometimes be unjust because what is one person's due may not be another's. Consistency, according to selective principles, requires not that everyone be treated equally but only that *equals* be treated equally.

Selective principles are of many sorts, and a general formula for them can be stated as follows:

From each according to _____;

to each according to _____.

The first part specifies the criteria according to which one asks sacrifices (or imposes burdens), the second specifies the criteria according to which one confers benefits. The Marxist principle is a classic example:

From each according to ability;

to each according to need.

For the sake of simplicity, and because many principles of justice do not detail the criteria for imposing burdens, we can state the formula to read merely:

To each according to _____.

understanding this to mean

To each (in benefits and burdens) according to _____.

In that way it can accommodate criteria for distributions of both positive and negative sorts.

Different kinds of justice can be distinguished according to the nature of the benefits and burdens whose distribution the principle governs. Thus if the benefits are economic, such as income or tax advantages, the principle becomes one of **economic justice**; if they are political, such as the right to vote or to run for office, it is one of **political justice;** if they are legal, such as a right to a fair trial or to representation by counsel, it is one of **legal justice,** and so on. All these should be distinguished from retributive justice, which is concerned with the imposition of punishment (when we speak of the justice of the legal system, we often have retributive justice in mind).[7]

The possible criteria for distributing benefits are many. In addition to the Marxist criterion of

1. Needs,

there are

2. Wants (desires),

which might be adequate in circumstances in which goods are so plentiful that all who want them could have them. But, at least with regard to economic benefits, that is never so. This means that criteria must be selected by which to distribute relatively scarce benefits among people, virtually all of whom want more benefits than they can have. Furthermore, even where there is enough to supply people with all they want, some wants are for things that are manifestly harmful. It can hardly be the business of a moral principle to supply those who want it with crack, others who want it with heroin, others with cocaine, and so on.

Another possibility is

3. Desert (deservingness).

According to this criterion, people are to receive in accordance with what they deserve, often as measured by effort, but sometimes measured by such things as commitment, loyalty, dedication, or excellence.

The word *desert* often implies specific actions in performing certain tasks, fulfilling certain responsibilities, or pursuing certain goals. It need not require that people succeed in those efforts (as we acknowledge when we speak of people "deserving credit for trying").

Sometimes, in fact, people who try the hardest do not succeed—often through no fault of their own. The person who has a Kantian good will *deserves* to be happy, in Kant's view, because of the moral excellence he or she has achieved. But life carries no *guarantee* that deserving people will find happiness. The athlete who trains the hardest for the Olympics may slip and fall coming out of the starting blocks. The student who pleads, "But I really studied hard for that exam," may have deserved an "A" as measured by effort but only a "B" as measured by performance.

So we must recognize another criterion by which distributions of benefits are often made:

4. Merit.

This normally implies effort, but it primarily signifies achievement or excellence, either in performing certain tasks, pursuing worthy goals, or developing valued character traits. And this excellence is not always achieved by those who are most deserving from the standpoint of effort. The runner who crosses the finish line first wins even if he or she trained less than the others. And the student who gets all the answers right gets an "A" even if others studied harder.

It may be, however, that distributions of benefits should be based on *moral excellence*—such as that represented by a Kantian good will or by Plato or Aristotle's virtues. One would then have to specify criteria for moral merit that are independent of considerations of justice.[8] But although this might serve as a principle for the comparative treatment of individuals, it would likely be unworkable for social policies because determining who is and who is not a morally good person, and in what degree, would be a formidable task on a large scale.

A related criterion, but one that opens up new areas of consideration from the preceding, is

5. Worth.

By people's worth, we may mean only the measure of what they have achieved or what level of excellence they have attained in some undertakings. In that case, considerations of worth would be covered by what we have said about merit.

But we may think people have *intrinsic* worth, independently of their wants and needs, and independently of anything they have accomplished or even put forth in the way of effort. If such worth were thought to attach only to certain people, or to certain groups of people, defined, say, by race, sex, or intelligence, this conception could readily lead to some of the paradigms of injustice. To say that one group of people is of greater intrinsic worth than another is to say that the first intrinsically superior to the second. Such claims are a central element in racism and sexism as well as anti-Semitism. In *Mein Kampf*, Hitler proclaimed the superiority of so-called Aryan peoples, for example. He accordingly implemented policies that favored them in the distribution of benefits and that disadvantaged Jews, gypsies, homosexuals, and communists (among others) in the imposition of burdens (to the point where he eventually sought their extermination).

Suppose we say instead that *each* person has intrinsic worth, perhaps even equal intrinsic worth, irrespective of race, sex, intelligence, talent, achievement, or effort. This judgment includes the hardened criminal as well as the selfless social worker. One might say this, in the spirit of Kant, on the grounds that all people are rational;[9] or, in the spirit of some religious and philosophical outlooks, on the grounds that all people have a divine spark or light within them, or are, in some ultimate sense, one with reality. What would this judgment mean from the standpoint of distributive justice?

If everyone is equal in intrinsic worth, and if according to selective principles equals should be treated equally, then everyone should be treated equally. What is due to everyone is in some sense the same. This may be called an **equalitarian principle**, as distinguished from the egalitarian. It tells us to *treat* everyone equally, as egalitarianism does. But whereas egalitarianism understands this rule to mean that we should distribute benefits and burdens to all in equal amounts without regard to need, want, desert, merit, worth, or anything else, equalitarianism requires that we assess the *effects* of distributions on people to ensure that the distributions constitute equal treatment. If some have more than they can eat and others are starving, to give each a loaf of bread would satisfy the egalitarian principle but not the equalitarian principle. It would provide some with too much and others with too little; just as, if some are fit and others disabled, to require hard labor of each would ask too much of some and not enough of others. Identical treatment, as called for by egalitarianism, is not necessarily equal treatment as called for by equalitarianism.

But what exactly does the equalitarian principle require of us? What is it to treat everyone equally?[10] Let me suggest a direction in which one might go to try to answer this.

If Plato is correct that everyone desires the good, then we can understand equalitarianism in terms of the satisfaction of this particular want: the desire for as good a life as possible. Desiring the good arguably involves wanting to maximize goodness (and happiness) in one's own life, all other things being equal (such as that one is not harming others in the process).[11] True, some people are self-destructive and seem—at least sometimes knowingly—to want things that are bad for them. So whether or not everyone wants a good life, perhaps we can say that, all things being equal, everyone *deserves* a good life, simply by virtue of being a person and having intrinsic worth. Unlike judgments of desert based on effort or achievement, desert in this sense would not require that anyone have done anything particularly commendable or noteworthy. It would extend the concern of distributive justice to those (such as the severely handicapped) who cannot make the contributions that others can, as well as to those (such as drug addicts or criminals) who could but have chosen not to.

It might be objected that this concern should not be extended to those who have harmed others. Should they not be punished, and is that not incompatible with contributing to a good life for them?

Perhaps, but not necessarily. One might justify punishment on the grounds that it is for the good of the person punished (meaning not that any punishment is *ipso facto* for the good of the person punished, but that each person has a good of which he or she is capable—for example, a state of happiness or moral well-being—and that punishment is legitimate only when it furthers that good). If so, then even though punishment would involve treating certain people differently from others, it would be justified on the grounds that, in their case, contributing to the best life of which they are capable requires holding them accountable for wrongdoing; and that only in this way are we treating them as of equal worth with other people.

This, however, begins to take us into the area of retributive justice, so let us resume our consideration of clearly distributive issues.

10.5 DISTRIBUTIVE JUSTICE AS PURE PROCEDURAL JUSTICE

Suppose we shift away from the quantitative division of the benefits or burdens (as in egalitarianism), and away from the assessment of characteristics of the potential recipients (as in selective principles), to the nature of the *process* by which distributions are made. Such a process may be called one of **procedural justice.** But we may, following John Rawls,[12] distinguish three kinds of procedural justice: imperfect, perfect, and pure.

In **imperfect procedural justice,** we can—at least in principle—specify in advance what the fair or just outcome of a process should be; we have a standard to appeal to that is independent of the procedure. But we lack a foolproof method by which to guarantee that outcome. The criminal court system is a case in point. We may say that people should be found guilty of a crime if and only if they in fact committed the crime.[13] And we have a jury system and extensive safeguards to maximize chances of producing that outcome. Yet the system is imperfect. Sometimes innocent people are convicted, and sometimes the guilty are acquitted.

Perfect procedural justice likewise says that we can specify, in advance of implementing a distributive procedure, what the fair or just distribution should be. But unlike with imperfect procedural justice, here there is a process that if carefully followed virtually guarantees the correct outcome. A simple example makes the point. If you have one piece of cake and two hungry children, the fair outcome (normally) is to see that it is divided equally. How do you accomplish that so that not only is the cake divided equally but both children are satisfied as to the fairness of the procedure? By having one child cut the cake and letting the other have the first choice.

By contrast, in **pure procedural justice** there is no standard to which one can appeal independent of the procedure. Rather, you implement a fair *procedure* for making distributions, then look to see what outcome it produces; and that outcome—whatever it is—will be fair.

Recall the example of the basket of money. If you had chosen to distribute the money on the basis of a lottery, then (assuming various things, such as that everyone agreed to the arrangement and had a fair chance at winning) the outcome would have been fair, no matter what it was.[14] But you could not have specified in advance which person should get the money; you would have had to draw the lots and see who came out the winner. Similarly, you cannot specify in advance of a game of poker how the winnings should be distributed at the end. You have to play the game and see. But so long as it is played fairly (and everyone participates voluntarily and on equal terms), the outcome is fair, whatever it may be.

Now, it has sometimes been thought that distributive justice is a matter of pure procedural justice in this sense. In this view, we not only need not, but in fact should not, concentrate on the division of the goods to be distributed (as mechanical principles do) or on the qualities of people receiving them (as selective principles do). If we can institute a fair *process*—meaning, specifically, a fair socioeconomic-political system—then the resulting distributions, whatever they may be and however much inequality they may involve, are just.

Defenders of capitalism often speak as though they regard it as such a system (at least if it operates as intended in theory). But to be such a system, it must be marked by freedom and equal opportunity. Only in that way will the economic and other transactions among people have a chance of yielding a fair outcome. Then if some people choose to play the stock market and others to write poetry or philosophize, it is perfectly fair if some of the former end up wealthy and some of the latter in poverty. The former sacrifice time they might have devoted to creative activities in order to make money; the latter sacrifice money for time to be creative. That the resultant distributions are unequal is immaterial. That the distributions are not made *by* anyone on the basis of the needs, wants, merit, or worth of the recipients is immaterial. What is important is that they are arrived at by means of a fair system.

This is an attractive approach to distributive justice, although to be able to evaluate it fully you would need to say more about the societal conditions necessary for exemplifying pure procedural justice. In particular, you would want to ask about the likelihood, realistically, of such conditions ever in fact being successfully created.

But one consideration is worth reflecting on. Our judgment that the outcome of such a process is fair seems, in the end, to rest on a further judgment; namely, that in such a process people end up with what they deserve. What they end up with is a function of their free choice, combined with effort, ability, initiative, and hard work. If we did not think this was what they deserved, we might be reluctant to call the resultant distributions just. In fact, to the extent that luck plays a role in determining people's fortunes, we often consider outcomes unfair.

If this is correct, then justice conceived of as pure procedural justice, at least in the economic sphere, would ultimately reduce to a selective principle of just deserts, which might be formulated in the following way:

> To each according to his or her free choices, effort, initiative, intelligence, talent, and so on (that is, according to what he or she deserves), in a fair system that guarantees maximum freedom and equality of opportunity for all.

Although this conception would distribute in part according to natural endowments, such as intelligence or talent, that some would say are not deserved; it would reflect the assumption that, if we do not deserve the benefits resulting from these, at least we are entitled to them.

10.6 THE TRANSITION TO METAETHICS

We have, then, at least some reason to believe that the most plausible principle of distributive justice is a selective one; one that is either equalitarian or stresses deserts. But it is difficult to make a firm judgment after such a brief assessment, and it is best to consider that the whole topic of justice is in need of much further analysis. There is, in any event, more to be said about the idea of pure procedural justice, which we shall take up again in Chapter 12.

For the present, however, we need to take seriously the possibility that the whole approach of moral legalism under consideration in Chapters 5–10 is wrongheaded. That approach, as we have seen (section 2.1), explains the ethics of conduct by appealing to rules and principles. One of the issues of greatest importance with regard to legalism is whether it is possible to provide a justification of principles.

Another is whether more than one basic principle can be justified—for example, one principle in one society, another in a different society. If more than one basic principle can be justified, we seem committed to some form of ethical relativism. But if *no* principle can be justified, we seem committed to moral skepticism. The problem of ethical relativism is one we shall examine shortly; that of justification, in Chapter 12.

These problems require, however, a shift in our orientation. As explained earlier (section 1.8), we have thus far mostly been doing normative ethics: examining different viewpoints about what the correct moral principles are, or, in the case of virtue ethics, about what the true moral virtues are. But, from at least the time of Plato, philosophers have also engaged in **metaethics** (many of whose concerns are sometimes called **moral epistemology**). Rather than trying to set forth and defend normative moral judgments, metaethics seeks to explain the nature of such judgments—whether they are true or false, what the meanings are of the concepts they contain, whether those concepts can be defined. These issues we shall take up in Chapter 13.

Metaethics also tries to explain the logic of moral reasoning and whether we can justify moral judgments, including basic moral principles, if there be such. And it is concerned with whether different moral judgments about the same conduct can both be correct (whether, for example, what is right in one culture can be wrong in another; that is, not merely thought to be wrong, but *actually* wrong). The concern here is whether or not ethics is in some important sense relative to the beliefs and practices of different societies or cultures.

In other words, when we ask what the proper standards are for making moral judgments, we want to know whether there is one set of standards that holds for everyone, or whether standards vary from culture to culture, perhaps even from person to person. This uniformity or variability is important to understanding the nature of morality, because morality represents a point of view for assessing not only one's own conduct but also the conduct of others. So it is important to know whether morality presumes to be able to assess the conduct of all people by the same standards, or only some; and if only some (such as those belonging to one's own community), who they are, and why the scope of morality is thus limited.

To analyze moral relativism requires an approach that is critical and analytical. The question of whether or not morality is relative is a metaethical question. We turn to that question next.

Notes

1. John Rawls, *A Theory of Justice* (Cambridge, Mass.: Harvard University Press, 1971), p. 3.
2. He also confers reverence along with justice for this purpose.
3. Herbert Spencer, *The Principles of Ethics*, vol. 2 (New York: Appleton, 1910), p. 35.
4. *Principles of Ethics*, vol. 2, Pt. IV, Ch. 2.

5. This notion was anticipated by Henry Sidgwick in the nineteenth century, in his *Methods of Ethics* (Chicago: University of Chicago Press, 1962), p. 209, and developed in the twentieth century, notably by R. M. Hare, in his *Freedom and Reason* (Oxford: England: Clarendon Press, 1963).

6. Some have maintained that a judgment's being universalizable is a necessary condition of its being a moral judgment in the first place. See R. M. Hare, *The Language of Morals* (Oxford, England: The Clarendon Press, 1952).

7. Although punishing people is inflicting a burden or something bad and thus might be regarded as a special case of distributive justice, it differs sufficiently enough from other distributive principles that it is best kept separate. (We do not start with a certain amount of punishment and then ask how it is to be distributed, as we might with money, food, or jobs. Rather, we single out certain people to receive punishment in the first place because of their previous wrongful acts.) Among some early biblical peoples, however, all suffering and misfortune in life was thought to be God's retribution for wickedness (and, by implication, prosperity was a reward for righteousness). For someone who holds this view, then—assuming that God rules over the world—distributive justice indeed reduces to divine retributive justice.

8. Note that distributive justice as a principle differs from justice as a virtue as considered by Plato and Aristotle (even though Aristotle deals with distributive justice as part of his overall account of justice).

9. Not that Kant thought that all people are equally rational; he thought women were deficient in the ability to act on principles, one of the marks of rationality.

10. For a discussion of a closely related conception of equalitarianism, see W. K. Frankena, *Ethics,* 2d ed. (Englewood Cliffs, N.J.: Prentice-Hall, 1973), pp. 48–52.

11. Not, as for the ethical egoist, as the ultimate governing end in one's life, but as a legitimate aim along with others.

12. John Rawls, *A Theory of Justice,* Revised Edition (Cambridge, Mass.: Harvard University Press, 1971), pp. 74–78.

13. Ibid., p. 74.

14. This does not, however, mean that this method is the only one that would have been fair. Others might have been fair as well. And other methods might have taken account of other considerations (such as need or merit) that many people would deem morally relevant.

Discussion Questions

1. In what way is the idea of distributive justice linked to the ideas of consistency and rationality?

2. What is the distinction among mechanical, selective, and procedural principles of distributive justice? Which among the possible criteria for a selective principle (section 10.4) do you find most plausible, and why?

3. What is the difference between an egalitarian principle of distributive justice and an equalitarian principle? The egalitarian principle has the advantage of simplicity over the equalitarian principle ("just divide things equally"). Is it more fair? Why?

4. What is the distinction among perfect, imperfect, and pure procedural justice? Pure procedural justice has an advantage over mechanical and selective principles of

distributive justice in that it doesn't require that you know anything either about the individuals who benefit from the procedure or about the quantities of benefits and burdens they receive. Is this advantage offset by any disadvantages?

5. Do you think it is possible for a whole society to embody pure procedural justice as a way of distributing benefits and burdens? Do you think a capitalist economic system succeeds in doing this? If so, are all of the resultant inequalities just? If not, could the capitalist system be improved upon?

6. Do you believe (as section 10.5 suggests) that, in the end, pure procedural justice (as a principle of distributive justice) rests upon a selective principle emphasizing what people deserve?

Society is the school in which we learn to distinguish between right and wrong. The headmaster is Custom, and the lessons are the same for all the members of the Community.[1]
Edward Westermarck

Ethical Relativism | CHAPTER 11

11.1 CULTURAL DIVERSITY

We know from anthropologists and historians that different peoples value different things and in different degrees, and that customs often vary from group to group. Cannibalism and head-hunting are practiced in some societies but frowned upon in others. Having more than one spouse is prohibited by some peoples but permitted by others.

We also know that even within societies customs change. Slavery was once widely accepted in America but is now condemned. Premarital sex was once almost universally condemned but is now widely accepted. And certain groups within societies have their own customs and practices. In our society, Roman Catholic women used to cover their heads before entering church, men did not. Orthodox Jewish men cover their heads at all times, women do not. The Amish ride in horses and buggies, vegetarians eat no meat, and Quakers dress simply. Most people do not.

More specifically still, standards often vary from community to community, even within a society. Obscenity, for example, is understood in the law as what the "average person applying contemporary community standards" would find sexually offensive.[2] But those standards vary from place to place, which means that what is obscene in one community may not be so in another (for example, in 1983 a judge concluded that the community standards in New York were so low that nothing is obscene there,[3] but there might well be many things that by this definition are obscene, say, in Peoria or Salt Lake City).

But does this mean that morality is relative? That what is right for one person or group or culture may not be so for another? This is the problem of ethical relativism. It is one of the most complex and difficult problems in ethics. It is also, arguably, the central problem in ethics, one to which virtually all others eventually lead. Let us begin by trying to understand better what ethical relativism is.

11.2 WHAT IS ETHICAL RELATIVISM?

To understand ethical relativism (or "relativism" for short), it will be helpful to distinguish three theses:

A. Moral beliefs and practices vary from culture to culture.
B. Morality depends on (1) **human nature** (for example, facts about human reason, motivation, emotions, and capacity for pleasure and pain); or (2) the **human condition** (facts about the way human life is constrained by the natural order, such as that all humans are mortal); or (3) specific **social and cultural circumstances** (for example, facts about local traditions and customs); or all three of these.
C. What is morally right or wrong (as opposed to what is merely thought to be right or wrong) may vary fundamentally from person to person or culture to culture.

Thesis A simply affirms cultural diversity, which—as we have seen—is not problematic.[4] It does not mean that every moral belief and practice varies from culture to culture, only that there are such variations, and that in some cases they are pronounced.

Thesis B—what we may call the **dependency thesis**—asserts that morality is determined by, or conditional on, the nature of human beings and/or the world they live in.[5] This is the view of those who believe that morality's function is to guide human conduct and that it has evolved over the centuries in response to practical human needs. As we have seen (section 7.4), it is also the view of many natural law ethicists. If there were no human beings, in this view, there would be no such thing as morality.[6] Any theory that asserts the dependency thesis we may call a form of **ethical conditionalism.**

Thesis C represents **ethical relativism.** It implies both Thesis A and Thesis B but goes beyond them.[7] It is a thesis about what is *actually* right and wrong, not merely about what is thought to be right and wrong. (Even if some relativists believe that what is right reduces in the end to what people, under appropriate conditions, *think* is right.)

Only skeptics seriously question whether some acts are right and others wrong. And only moral nihilists deny such distinctions outright. Most people differ only about *which* acts are right and which are wrong. (Even philosophers rarely question whether these notions apply to conduct; they disagree mainly over how to explain them and how to justify the judgments in which they occur.)

Ethical relativists are neither skeptics nor nihilists. They believe in moral right and wrong. It is just that they contend that what is basically right for one person or culture may be wrong for another.

The qualification "basically" is important here. There are some differences in right and wrong that can be accepted by anyone, relativist or not. No one says, for example, that everyone, of whatever size and nutritional needs, should eat exactly the same food and in the same amounts; or that everyone should wear exactly the same clothing, regardless of climate. And it is clearly permissible to put a child out to play in shorts and T-shirt in the tropics but wrong to do so in the arctic; or to dive into a pool when it is full but not when it is empty. That is, no one denies that some acts are right under some conditions but wrong under others. The question is (1) whether *all* actions similarly depend, and depend exclusively, on variable personal, social, cultural, or environmental conditions; and (2) whether that accounts for variations in what is basically right and wrong for different peoples and cultures. Relativism says yes to both questions.

Relativism does not, however, try to tell us which acts and practices are right and wrong (although to the extent that it characterizes basic cultural diversity, it will in fact be describing what it takes to be right and wrong in various cultures). It says only that however we answer that question, we must acknowledge that an act or practice may be both right and wrong at the *same* time—for example, right in one culture, wrong in another. In other words, differing moral judgments about the same conduct may both be correct at the same time.[8]

Relativism takes different forms depending on how radically right and wrong are thought to vary. If they are thought to be the same for people of the same culture but to vary from culture to culture, this represents **cultural (or social) relativism.** If, however, they are believed to vary from person to person, this represents what we may call **extreme (or individual) relativism.**

11.3 UNIVERSALISM AND ABSOLUTISM

Ethical universalism, on the other hand, holds that what is fundamentally right and wrong is the same for all people. It does not deny Thesis A; it concedes there is variation in what people *think* is right and wrong. And it can acknowledge some variation in what is actually right and wrong of the sort noted earlier. But it says that if two people differ about what is *basically* right and wrong, at least one of them must be mistaken.

Universalism need not even deny Thesis B, although it *may* do so. It can acknowledge that morality is essentially a human creation that has evolved in response to human needs. It simply maintains that, whatever morality's origins, what is prescribed as right and wrong is basically the same for everyone.

Some have thought, for example, that morality is rooted in sympathy, which is a part of human nature. If so, morality obviously does not, and could not, exist apart from human beings (or any other beings with a psychology like ours). If, moreover, humans are the product of evolution, then the sentiment of sympathy must likewise have evolved over time, and morality with it. But if sympathy leads all people to make essentially the same basic moral judgments— that is, leads them to morally approve and disapprove basically the same things (and, of course, if these judgments represent what is actually right and wrong)—then morality will be universalistic, even though it is conditional on human nature.

When universalism does deny Thesis B, it represents **ethical absolutism,** the view that there exists an eternal and unchanging moral law that transcends the physical world and is the same for all people at all times and places. It is valid independently of the thoughts, feelings, and even the existence of humans. If there are extraterrestrial forms of intelligent life, they are bound by it, too. Just as the truth that two plus two equals four would not change if all humans died off tomorrow, so the moral law would remain unchanged as well.

We can represent the interrelationships among these various theories as in the diagram below. This diagram suggests that there are two related but distinguishable issues here: (1) between universalists (whether they be absolutists or conditionalists) and relativists concerning whether right and wrong are the same for all people; and (2) between absolutists and conditionalists over whether morality depends on human nature or the world. In other words, relativists and universalists differ over whether Thesis C is correct, and absolutists and conditionalists differ over whether Thesis B is correct.

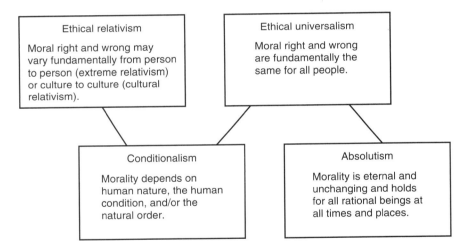

The issue between relativism and universalism is not about what the correct moral judgments are. They are not competing normative theories. Rather, they are metaethical theories. The issue between them concerns what the relationship is among correct judgments, whatever those judgments are; specifically, it is whether those judgments are all consistent with one another. In saying that different judgments about the same kinds of acts may both be true at the same time, relativism is saying that correct (true or valid) moral judgments are not all consistent with one another. Extreme relativists can allow for the coherence of moral beliefs and attitudes within a single individual, and cultural relativists can allow for it within a whole culture. But neither can allow for it among all people.[9] Universalism, in contrast, in holding that the correct basic standards, virtues, or principles are the same for all people, maintains that morality overall is a coherent whole. It may not appear to be a coherent whole, because not all people may agree on what those basic principles or virtues are, much less about what particular judgments they imply for particular cases. But if they all saw things clearly enough, they would agree.

11.4 WHAT DIFFERENCE DOES IT MAKE WHETHER RELATIVISM IS TRUE?

Multiculturalism and the Abuse of Women

Many people oppose relativism because they feel its acceptance would erode moral standards. They believe that if people became convinced that right and wrong are merely relative, they would lose all inhibitions and simply do whatever they want. Universalism, in contrast,—and particularly absolutism—is thought to provide a firm foundation for morality. It is needed to make people toe the moral line.

This view may or may not be correct, but it cannot simply be assumed. To determine its truth would require studying the correlation between such beliefs and actual conduct. But whether relativism is true does not—unless truth itself is relative—depend on how people would behave if they believed it were true, and even less does it depend on what they may *wish* were true. For that reason, we should try to assess relativism on its merits, not on the basis of a predisposition to approve or disapprove of it.[10]

The importance of the issues it raises goes beyond what to us are bizarre practices of other peoples. Head-hunting, cannibalism, and human sacrifice, for example—the kinds of practices typically mentioned in connection with relativism—are not issues that engage us directly. They are matters of curiosity to most of us, unless we are anthropologists.

Other problems of contemporary concern bear much more directly on our lives. One, for example, concerns multiculturalism; another, the abuse of women.

Some people hold that Western culture is superior to others and deserves priority in educating students in our society. Others contend that Western culture is dominated by the values of racism and white male supremacy and so is detrimental to both our society and others. (Many people, it should be added, do not share either of these views; some, for example, think that all cultures are of equal worth.) Both views, which are here oversimplified, acknowledge there are other cultures: those of Africa, Asia, and Latin America, for example. (Some argue that within a culture may exist many subcultures, such as a black culture, female and male cultures, a rock culture, gun culture, drug culture, and so on.)[11] But they differ about the importance that should be attached to them in school and in university curricula.

If cultural relativism is true, the standards and values of Western culture cannot be shown to be more correct (or true or valid) than any other. Hence they cannot be shown to be either of greater worth or more deserving of being taught than any other (at least from the standpoint of truth.)[12] The same with other cultures. People from one culture can, of course, point out that some customs and practices of other cultures are wrong by the standards of their own. But there is no objective standpoint from which they can show theirs to be superior.

If relativism is not true, however, there may be universal standards by which some cultures can be shown to be superior to others, and if this could be shown of Western culture, it would be a reason for giving it priority in education (even if other considerations besides truth, such as a desire to improve understanding among peoples, might argue for other cultures also being taught). The point is that the issue of multiculturalism can be thoroughly understood only by taking seriously the question of relativism.

But relativism bears on issues of greater urgency than merely what is to be taught in schools and colleges. One of these is the abuse of women, particularly wives.

Wife abuse is an extensive problem in our society, and is coming to be recognized as one of the ways in which women have long been systematically mistreated.[13] But among the Masai tribe of Tanzania in Africa, wife beating is the custom, and it is generally accepted even by wives themselves. "If I do wrong, my husband can beat me," one such wife says. Her husband explains, "If the roof leaks, the husband beats his wife" (because care of the home is the wife's responsibility). He adds, "I must, because other men will laugh if I don't."[14]

Are we to say, then, that it is permissible for husbands to beat their wives among the Masai but wrong in America? Would it be presumptuous of us to criticize the Masai for wife beating in the same way it would be presumptuous to fault them for dressing differently from us, listening to different music, or eating different food? Or is there a moral standard that is the same for all people by which we can judge wife beating to be wrong—or right—wherever it occurs, regardless of customs?

These are the sorts of issues at stake in the debate over relativism. Many differences in practices are matters of curiosity but of no particular moral concern. But some are matters of the well-being and happiness—even the life and death—of other human beings.

Let's try to assess relativism, beginning with two objections that relate to the point just made about judging other peoples or cultures.

11.5 RELATIVISM AND MORAL DISAGREEMENTS

I should guard against a possible misunderstanding, however: It is sometimes thought that if relativism is true then we cannot judge the conduct of other people or other cultures. But this is not quite correct. If you disapprove of racial slurs, you can judge that I am wrong to make them even if you are an extreme relativist. In so doing, you simply reflect your disapproval of what I do. And if I come from a Moslem society you may judge that I am wrong to have four wives even if you are a cultural relativist. That simply reflects your society's disapproval of polygamy.[15]

Relativism does not say that you cannot judge the behavior of other people or groups, but it must concede that from a moral standpoint there is not much point in doing so, and indeed that it is even presumptuous to do so. It says only that when different individuals or groups make different judgments about the same conduct, both may be correct.

But if that is the case, then you might object that there is no way to resolve moral disagreements. And this would mean that rational moral discourse has no place in human affairs.

This is a serious objection, but it weighs differently against extreme relativism than it does against cultural relativism. Let us see why.

If two people disagree, say, over the morality of abortion, according to extreme relativism they can both be correct. Abortion is right "for one" and wrong "for the other." The same practice is then, in some sense, both right and wrong at the same time.

According to cultural relativism, on the other hand, both persons cannot be correct—at least not if they are from the same society. Suppose, for purposes of illustration, that the cultural relativist holds the following view:

"X is right" means "My (the speaker's) society approves of X."

and

"X is wrong" means "My (the speaker's) society disapproves of X."

If abortion is an approved practice in a particular society, then in this view anyone from that society who says it is wrong is mistaken. By the same token, if abortion is a prohibited practice, then anyone who says it is permissible is mistaken. Which of the two it is requires a close study of the society in question. But unless the society is so deeply divided that a conclusive judgment cannot be reached, a disagreement between two people from the same society will at least in principle be resolvable. But if the two come from different societies, then for a cultural relativist both may be correct. In ancient India, for example, abortion was condemned; in ancient Greece, it was approved. According to cultural relativism, an Indian and a Greek disputing over abortion could both have been correct, for abortion would have been right in one society and wrong in the other.

So within a society or culture (though not among societies and cultures), cultural relativism allows there may be an objective standard by which to resolve moral disputes. In this it differs from extreme relativism.

Notice the term "objective." It is important to note that relativists need not be **subjectivists** (although they may be, and extreme relativists typically are). That is, they need not say that right and wrong are determined solely by the thoughts, feelings, attitudes, or emotions of the person judging. They may, like cultural relativists, be **objectivists** in maintaining that right and wrong are determined by standards external to, and perhaps independent of, the person judging. It is just that they contend that those standards—usually customs, practices, and associated rules—vary from society to society or culture to culture. Therefore we should not confuse the distinction between relativism and universalism with the distinction between subjectivism and objectivism.

But what of moral disagreements in the extreme relativist's view—does the objection hold here? It certainly carries much greater weight. But there may still be ways to resolve moral disagreements even in the case of subjectivistic extreme relativism.

Suppose you say abortion is wrong and I say it is right. Suppose, further, that we are both extreme relativists. Must we simply agree to disagree and be content to acknowledge that what is right for one is wrong for the other?

Not necessarily. If I can get you to change your beliefs or attitudes, I can *make* abortion right for you. And I might succeed in doing so if I know enough about you and why you feel as you do—because then I can call your attention to facts of which you may have been unaware or to which you may have been inattentive. And that might cause you to feel differently. I might, for example, document the effects of unwanted children on people living in poverty, or explain the burden it imposes on women to have the state interfere in their control over their own bodies, or detail the hazards of "back-alley" abortions when abortion is illegal. You, by the same token, might just as easily try to change my outlook. You might try to convince me that the fetus is a person, or show me gruesome pictures of aborted fetuses, or call my attention to interviews with women who considered abortion but are now glad they bore the child. There is no guarantee that either of us will succeed, of course. But then there is also no guarantee that either of us will succeed if there is a standard according to which abortion is universally right or wrong.

What we cannot do, however, if relativism is true (and can do if universalism is true) is profitably try to change one another's beliefs by producing moral reasons for our respective positions. If we are extreme relativists, we both *know* that abortion is wrong for you and right for me. And we both know why. There will be little to discuss on that issue. We can, then, profitably pursue only *non*moral ways of trying to change one another's beliefs or attitudes.

So, in the cultural relativist's view, there may be an objective, rational way to resolve disagreements within a society, but there will be none for disagreements between societies (or members thereof). And there will be no way to solve disagreements in the extreme relativist's view, whether within a society or between societies, though there may still be nonmoral ways.[16]

11.6 CAN THERE EVEN BE GENUINE MORAL DISAGREEMENTS ACCORDING TO RELATIVISM?

To discuss whether it is possible to resolve moral disagreements presupposes that there are moral disagreements to resolve. An even more serious objection is that if relativism is correct there can be no genuine moral disagreements in the first place. There can only be the appearance of such disagreements. Because, according to this objection, there obviously are moral disagreements, the objection concludes that relativism is mistaken. Let's try to understand why a critic might argue this.

Suppose an extreme relativist were to defend the following definitions:

"X is right" means "I (the speaker) approve of X."

and

"X is wrong" means "I (the speaker) disapprove of X."

According to such an account,[17] if Kim and Michelle disagree over the morality of abortion, then when Kim says, "Abortion is right," she is saying only, in effect, "I approve of abortion," and when Michelle says "Abortion is wrong," she is saying only, "I disapprove of abortion."

Now obviously, the statements, "I approve of abortion" and "I disapprove of abortion," when spoken by Kim and Michelle respectively, can both be correct at the same time. People approve and disapprove different things all the time. But if they are both correct, what are Kim and Michelle disagreeing about? How can there be any genuine moral disagreement between them?

There can't, if moral disagreements concern only matters of fact. The only facts relevant to the truth of their respective claims concern their respective approval and disapproval. And each knows she approves (or disapproves) and that the other does the opposite. The same objection, appropriately modified, applies to cultural relativism. If the cultural relativist held the definitions discussed in the previous section, then when two people from different cultures seem to disagree, each is saying only that his or her society approves (or disapproves) of the practice in question. And both can obviously be correct.

But relativists might deny that moral disagreements must be only about matters of fact. They might distinguish, as some philosophers have, between disagreements in belief (over matters of fact) and disagreements in attitude (over how one feels about the facts).[18] If so, they might maintain that moral disagreements are, in the end, basically disagreements in attitude; or at least, that attitudes are the central element in such disagreements, determining when they terminate and by what means.

In this view, Kim and Michelle may agree completely on the facts about abortion. And they may understand perfectly well that when each makes the judgment she does she is describing only her own approval or disapproval. Still, they *feel* differently about abortion. One woman's emotions are engaged for it; the other's, against. And each may want the other to feel as she does. Their disagreement is in feeling and attitude, not belief.

If feelings, attitudes, and emotions are at the heart of moral disagreements, then the relativist may say that there is a genuine disagreement here, and that the objection reflects a misunderstanding of the nature of such disagreement. The two objections just mentioned, then, are not fatal to relativism, although they pose serious problems for it.

11.7 IS THERE CULTURAL DIVERSITY IN BASIC MORAL BELIEFS?

Relativists typically attach considerable importance to cultural diversity, and the existence of such diversity is indisputable. What is not so obvious is that there is also diversity in *basic* moral beliefs. A simple example may help explain why.

The British drive on the left-hand side of the road, Americans on the right. These practices are legally enforced, and British and American laws differ in this regard. But these differing practices do not necessarily establish differences in basic beliefs. Formulators of the laws in the two countries may have been acting on the same principle, such as that it is for the good of everyone alike that people in the same society abide by the same rules of the road (so as to minimize confusion and accidents). It probably does not matter much whether people drive on the left or on the right. But it matters a great deal whether everyone (at least in the same society) does the *same* as everyone else. So, although U.S. and British practices differ, the same principle may well underlie both practices.

In less legalistic examples, anthropologists report that the peoples of British New Guinea used to practice infanticide. In so doing, they tended to spare girls because of the price they would eventually bring as brides. But in Tahiti, boys were spared because they were considered of more use in war.[19] Despite the fact that their practices differed in this regard, both peoples may well have acted on the same principle: preserve those children of greatest value. They clearly valued boys or girls differently,[20] but they may have held the same belief regarding how those deemed to be of greatest value are to be treated.

Similarly, the Incas are said to have looked after the aged even when they were unfit for work, whereas some Eskimo groups and the people of West Victoria (Australia) killed the elderly. These practices are radically different, but they do not by themselves establish differing underlying values or moral beliefs. The Eskimos killed the elderly in the conviction that only those who died violently were happy in the afterlife, and the West Victorians killed them to spare them the risk of being tortured and killed by enemies. So they, no less than the Incas, may have both been acting out of concern for what is best for the aged. It is just that they differed in their beliefs about what that was.

Thus even if moral practices diverge widely in the world, there might yet be underlying agreement on basic values and principles. This pair of examples, of course, does not show that there *is* such agreement; to show that would require extensive inquiry. But it does show that considerable cultural diversity is compatible with universality in basic values and principles.

11.8 CULTURAL DIVERSITY IN BASIC MORAL BELIEFS WOULD NOT ESTABLISH RELATIVISM

Relativists can concede that *some* values and practices are common to all people; indeed, they could hardly do otherwise. All peoples value food, practice at least some heterosexual relations, and care for at least some of their offspring; otherwise they would not have survived. And some practices, such as truth telling and restraint in taking human life, seem necessary for the very existence of society (if people killed one another as readily as they swat flies or slap mosquitoes, social life would be impossible). It is just that many relativists believe there are differences in moral beliefs and practices among peoples that cannot be explained away as due to different applications of the same principle.

Suppose the belief stated in the preceding sentence is true. Would it be enough to establish relativism? I want to suggest some reasons for thinking it would not.

Shortly before his death Socrates (469–399 B.C.E) emphasized that some people might be in the right even if they went against the opinions of the multitude. As he awaited execution, his friend Crito tried to persuade him to escape, citing, among other things, what people would think if he (Crito) let his friend go to his death. There followed this exchange between them:

> SOCRATES: . . . Reflect, then, do you not think it reasonable to say that we should not respect all the opinions of men but only some, nor the opinions of all men but only of some men? What do you think? Is not this true?

> CRITO: It is.

> SOCRATES: And we should respect the good opinions, and not the worthless ones?

> CRITO: Yes.

> SOCRATES: But the good opinions are those of the wise, and the worthless ones those of the foolish?

> CRITO: Of course.

> SOCRATES: . . . And, Crito, to be brief, is it not the same in everything? and, therefore, in questions of justice and injustice, and of the base and the honorable, and of good and evil, which we are now examining, ought we to follow the opinion of the many and fear that, or the opinion of the one man who understands these matters (if we can find him), and feel more shame and fear before him than before all other men?[21]

Socrates' point is that the mere fact that the multitude of people in society hold a certain opinion (and he was thinking of those in Athenian society at the time[22]) does not make the opinion correct; what is just or unjust, or good or evil, is not a function of the views of the majority. In this he was going against the views of the Sophists (professional teachers in ancient Greece), who were ethical relativists. In moral matters, he was saying, we must pay attention only to the opinions of the wise.

This suggests that even if one could establish that a particular society held basic moral beliefs that differed from those of other societies, that fact alone would not show that those beliefs were correct, even for that society.[23] Isn't it possible that a few people—or even just one—could be right on a moral issue even if the rest of society thought otherwise?

Like Socrates, Thoreau thought it *was* possible. We have noted that slavery was once generally accepted by whites in our society. But a small minority of abolitionists like Thoreau argued that it was wrong. And he spoke passionately of the force of example on the issue:

> I know this well, that if one thousand, if one hundred, if ten men whom I could name—if ten *honest* men only—ay, if *one* HONEST man, in this State of Massachusetts, *ceasing to hold slaves,* were actually to withdraw from this copartnership [with the government], and be locked up in the county jail therefor, it would be the abolition of slavery in America. For it matters not how small the beginning may seem to be: what is once well done is done forever.[24]

Throughout history there are examples of people like Socrates—Jesus, Thoreau, Susan B. Anthony, Emma Goldman, Mohandas Gandhi, and Martin

Luther King, Jr.—who set themselves against deeply entrenched beliefs and practices in their societies. Whether or not one agrees with everything they stood for, we should consider whether it is possible that they were right and the majority who opposed them wrong. That possibility alone should make us cautious about unquestioningly assuming that conventional beliefs and practices, however deeply entrenched, are right.[25]

So even if cultural diversity in basic moral beliefs and practices could be conclusively established, that would not by itself establish relativism. It *would* establish some important facts to try to understand and explain. But those facts alone would not show that the beliefs in question were correct or that the accepted practices ought to be engaged in.

Establishing such diversity would not even establish the dependency thesis, because such diversity is compatible with absolutism, which denies the dependency thesis. If, as absolutists believe, there is an absolute moral law, it does not follow that everyone knows what that law is, or even believes that there is one. (The very existence of relativists confirms that some people do not believe there is an absolute moral law, and the existence of missionaries who try to enlighten other peoples about what the missionaries take to be absolute moral truths confirms that some people who believe there is an absolute moral law do not think that everyone knows what it is.) If absolutism is compatible with cultural diversity, then such diversity is not enough to establish the dependency thesis.[26]

So establishing Thesis A does not establish either Thesis B or Thesis C.

11.9 UNIVERSALISM AND THE GROUND OF MORALITY

But if the truth of Thesis A (see section 11.2) would not be enough to establish relativism, the truth of Thesis B would not do so, either. It is possible that morality depends on human beings or the world and yet that basically the same things are right and wrong for all people.

To be a universalist, one need not be an absolutist; one need not say there is an eternal and unchanging moral law. One need say only there is a *ground* of morality that is the same for all people and according to which the same acts are *in general* right or wrong for everyone. This ground may be a sentiment like sympathy (as discussed in section 11.3), a feeling such as compassion, a capacity such as conscience, or a faculty such as intuition. Its salient feature is that, if properly attended to, it reveals certain actions to be right or wrong wherever they occur (it might either identify properties that *make* acts right or identify properties associated with right acts). It is universal because it characterizes everyone alike, whatever the culture to which someone belongs. But it need not be eternal or even unchanging; it may have come into existence with human beings and evolved over time.

But if relativism would not follow from the truth of either Thesis A or Thesis B (or the combination of the two), the burden is on relativists to show what it is about the fact that different cultures have different beliefs and practices that *makes* those beliefs correct and those practices right. And relativists must do so in a way that does not presuppose standards that may be tacitly shared by other cultures and that explain their different beliefs and practices.

11.10 ARE LOGIC AND TRUTH THEMSELVES RELATIVE?

Perhaps the most ambitious way to try to do this philosophically would be to argue that logical reasoning and/or truth itself is relative. This would require a sophisticated argument, one that would call into question widely held assumptions about language, knowledge, and even philosophy itself. I cannot do justice to such an argument here, but I can sketch its general outlines.

In this view, the very criteria of what is good and bad or valid and invalid in the way of reasoning—like the notions of right and wrong—grow out of the practices of communities and cannot be extended beyond them. To criticize relativism on the grounds that one cannot go from the fact that there are certain practices in a particular culture to the conclusion that those practices are right is—in effect, to impose one's own conception of good reasoning (which some say is a Western, masculine conception) on the assessment of other cultures. And that conception may have no force in other cultures. Furthermore, it might be claimed that the very notion of truth itself is similarly relative to communal practices as they evolve in particular cultures and has no meaning in the abstract. So the idea of a moral standard that purports to be true for everyone alike makes no sense. There simply is no Olympian standpoint from which to render it intelligible.

Although this argument raises more questions than can be evaluated here, I can give two responses to it. The first is to point out that the same reasoning that shows that cultural diversity in basic moral beliefs would not establish relativism also shows that cultural *uniformity* in such beliefs would not establish universalism.

If a belief's being held by the majority in a society does not make it right, simply multiplying the number of societies in which majorities hold that belief would not make it right either. The same with established practices. Again, men have dominated women in nearly all cultures, but it does not follow that they ought to do so. War has traditionally been used to settle disputes by nearly all cultures, but it does not follow that it ought to be. If someone supports war or the domination of women, he or she must find other reasons than these for doing so. Pointing out their near-universal acceptance is not enough.

So even if the question of whether there is cultural diversity in basic moral beliefs could be conclusively settled one way or the other, that would not resolve the issue between relativism and universalism. And that means, in turn, that the reasoning by which that is shown to be the case is neutral between relativism and universalism. This conclusion does not rebut the claim that the validity of such reasoning is itself relative; that would take extensive argument. But it does show that this application of the reasoning, and the use of the conception of logic it embodies, does not bias the case against relativism.

Second, to argue for the relativity of truth does not actually support relativism; in fact, it scuttles relativism along with universalism. To be important, relativism must account for the nature of morality wherever it is found, not just in this or that culture. If one cannot make sense of the possible truth of such an account—which would mean that we can use the concept of truth cross-culturally—then relativism as well as universalism is not a viable theory. Rather than salvaging relativism, then, if such an argument were successful it would undermine the whole dispute between relativism and universalism.

11.11 RELATIVISM AND MORAL TOLERANCE

We should consider one further defense of relativism: the idea that if people think relativism is true, they will be more tolerant of moral differences than they would otherwise be.[27] If you believe the moral opinions of your culture have no greater authority than those of any other, perhaps you will be more accepting of people from other cultures who disagree with you. And if you are an extreme relativist and believe that the moral opinions of other individuals are equally as valid as your own, perhaps you will better tolerate behavior of which you disapprove. (Relativists who are offended by polygamy and homosexuality, for example, might become more tolerant of those practices.)

But just as the alleged bad consequences of accepting relativism (see section 11.4) would be hard to establish, this good consequence would also be hard to establish. One would have to study relativists and see whether they are in fact more tolerant than universalists.

On the face of it, there is about as much reason to think people would *not* be more tolerant if they were relativists than if they were not relativists. It is clear, for example, that many cultures are intolerant in religious, racial, or sexual matters. Many practice discrimination rooted in centuries of custom and tradition. So it is hard to avoid concluding that, according to relativism, intolerance is permissible in those cultures, and thus that anyone living in those cultures who wants to do right will have to cooperate with the intolerance.[28]

In any event, even if there might be more tolerance if relativism is true and everyone knows it is true, there might well be less tolerance if relativism is true but most people think it is false. If people think relativism is false—and, moreover, mistakenly think there *is* a standard of right and wrong for everyone alike[29]—they are likely to argue for the correctness of their own views against their adversaries' views in cross-cultural disagreements. But if relativism is true, no such arguments will succeed. They will not succeed because there won't be any objective standard by which the correctness of either side's position can be demonstrated. This will make it easy for each to dismiss the other's arguments—indeed, they will have good grounds for doing so—and can readily lead each side to conclude that the other is not only wrong, but culpably so. When that happens, particularly among nations, the temptation is to try to resolve differences by threats, violence, and war.[30]

11.12 CONCLUSION

If the preceding is correct, formidable problems confront relativism. This does not mean that it has been refuted; but it suggests that unless relativists can find ways around these problems—or unless alternative theories prove to have even greater difficulties—the theory cannot claim our assent.[31]

In any event, most of Western moral philosophy has been nonrelativistic, sometimes absolutistic, but at least generally universalistic. Whether or not it has been right to adopt that orientation depends in part on the plausibility of the theories it has produced. Most of the theories considered in the preceding chapters are normative. In this they differ from relativism and universalism, which, once again, are metaethical theories—they are *about* morality but do not, as such, seek to provide us with the content of morality—the rules, principles, values, or virtues of which it is composed. For this content, we need normative ethics.

Notes

1. Edward Westermarck, *Ethical Relativity* (Paterson, N.J.: Littlefield, Adams, 1960), p. 50.

2. The definition is more complex than this, and depends on whether such a person would find that the material, as a whole, appealed "to the prurient interest in sex," portrayed sexual conduct "in a patently offensive way," and lacked "serious literary, artistic, political or scientific value." This material, including the quotation from the judge in the text, is quoted from *The New York Times*, 19 January 1992.

3. Ibid.

4. Cultural diversity, it should be noted, is sometimes—and somewhat misleadingly—called *cultural relativism*. It is also sometimes called *descriptive relativism*. See, for example, W. K. Frankena, *Ethics,* 2d ed. (Englewood Cliffs, N.J.: Prentice-Hall, 1973), p. 109.

5. I borrow the term "dependency thesis" from John Ladd. See John Ladd, ed., *Ethical Relativism* (Lanham, Md.: University Press of America, 1985), p. 3. The thesis affirms that morality is relative to human beings; hence it represents ethical *relativity*. But it does not of itself establish ethical *relativism* in the sense I define. To avoid confusion, I speak of "ethical conditionalism" rather than "ethical relativity," and distinguish it from "ethical relativism." As I am using it, the dependency thesis holds that what *makes* some acts right and others wrong are certain facts about human nature, and so forth—not merely that such facts are presupposed by calling specific acts right or wrong, which can be granted even by absolutism. (If there should be an eternal law that says, "Eat no junk food," the wrongness of my eating junk food presupposes certain facts about me and the world, even though, given those facts, what makes my act wrong is that it violates the eternal law.)

6. I should note that B1 and B2 could be understood broadly enough to include the possibility that human nature or the human condition is defined partly in religious terms. Thus (as we saw in section 7.7) St. Thomas Aquinas holds that the natural law, which is an important part of the moral law, is impressed on human nature in the form of natural inclinations to good. But the whole of this order of which humans and the physical world are a part is ultimately the creation of God. Similarly,

some people think that original sin as understood by Christianity is a defining feature of the human condition. If B1 and B2 are understood this broadly, then it would not necessarily be true that—but for human beings—there would be no morality, because there might be thought to be a moral law that is applicable to nonhumans, like angels.

7. By saying that Thesis C implies both Thesis A and B, I mean that those who hold C normally hold A and B as well, not that those who hold C *must* hold A and B.

8. Just as cultural diversity is sometimes called "cultural relativism," ethical relativism is also sometimes called "cultural relativism."

9. Unless by some strange coincidence it just happened that all peoples arrived at the same judgments.

10. A relativist *might* concede that this assessment is true for people or groups judging that relativism is bad. It is just that for the relativist the judgment that relativism is good might also be true.

11. It might be argued that right and wrong vary among these more loosely defined cultures as well, but that is a controversial claim I cannot go into here, except to say that most of what I say about relativism can also, with appropriate qualifications, be applied to this claim.

12. There are actually two issues here: first, whether the moral standards and values of Western culture are superior to others (presumably in the sense of being more nearly correct or valid); and second, whether Western culture is superior in the sense of being more valuable than others. To maintain the superiority of Western culture in the first sense might be grounds for maintaining it in the second as well; but one might maintain superiority in the second sense (say, on grounds of artistic and scientific achievement) without maintaining it in the first. Even then, however, one would be saying that there are some standards of value that are cross-cultural, and according to which Western culture stands out.

13. Estimates are that as many as two million women each year may suffer such abuse. This figure, a federal estimate, includes domestic violence against women by male companions as well as by husbands, according to a *Washington Post* report ("Exposing the War at Home—A Photographer Takes a Close-Up Look at the Face of Domestic Violence," by Marjorie Williams) carried in the Rochester, New York, *Times-Union*, 23 January 1992, p. C1.

14. *The New York Times*, 2 December 1991.

15. I am assuming for the purposes of these examples that the approval of individuals or societies is the relevant right-making characteristic for the relativist.

16. The view that there is no objectively valid, rational way of conclusively resolving disagreements over basic moral judgments is sometimes called "metaethical relativism." See W. K. Frankena, *Ethics,* 2d ed. (Englewood Cliffs, N.J.: Prentice-Hall, 1973), p. 109.

17. It might be thought that a theory such as this would not actually be relativistic because it would imply that whatever the speaker approves is right (and so on), and this would be a universal standard. But while it is true that this theory would have that implication, it is not clear that the implied statement would represent a universal moral principle. The statement, "Whatever any speaker approves is right" would then be true by definition, hence analytic; and it is arguable that no analytic statement can function as a normative moral principle. Any relativistic account of

what constitutes the right-making characteristics of acts or practices (such as that they are approved by the appropriate people or societies) will be committed to some general statements affirming that all acts having these characteristics are right. If being committed to such a general statement were considered incompatible with relativism, it is doubtful that there could be any relativistic account of morality in general.

18. See Charles L. Stevenson, *Ethics and Language* (New Haven, Conn.: Yale University Press, 1944).

19. William Graham Sumner, *Folkways* (New York: Dover, 1959), p. 317.

20. At least, they differed over the value of the ends of profitability in marriage and effectiveness in war—ends that girls and boys respectively served.

21. Plato, *Euthyphro, Apology, Crito*, tr. F. J. Church (New York: Macmillan, 1948), pp. 55–56.

22. More specifically, he was most likely thinking of males who were not slaves.

23. Although there are differences between a society and a culture, I am using the two terms interchangeably here.

24. Henry David Thoreau, "Civil Disobedience," Carl Bode, ed., *The Portable Thoreau* (New York: Viking Press, 1964), p. 121. Originally published 1849.

25. Not that the belief in slavery was necessarily a basic moral belief; for many it was derivative from other beliefs, some moral, some religious. We should note also that the views of a majority on a given issue do not necessarily reflect established customs and practices, and hence are not necessarily right on all relativistic theories. It is one thing to take current majority opinion as a right-making characteristic, another to take established customs and practices and traditions as right-making. Both positions are relativistic but they represent different theories.

26. Not that all missionaries are necessarily absolutists, but most of them are almost certainly universalists.

27. See for example, Edward Westermarck, *Ethical Relativity* (Paterson, N.J.: Littlefield, Adams, 1960), p. 59.

28. On this subject, see Paul F. Schmidt, "Some Criticisms of Cultural Relativism," *Journal of Philosophy* 52, No. 25 (December 1955): 780–791.

29. I am assuming, for the sake of argument, that to reject relativism is to endorse universalism. Strictly speaking, that assumption is not necessarily true because one might reject relativism and still be a skeptic about whether there even *is* a right and a wrong, or be a nihilist and deny outright that there is.

30. This issue is considerably more complex than we have space for. If relativism is true but most people think it is not, they will be unable to resolve their differences by rational moral argument. So when they resort to moral argument and find it of no avail (because none of the arguments on either side—intended to show that the position of the other is mistaken—will ultimately be good ones), intolerance may very well be the result.

31. An admirable attempt to deal with many of these issues is found in Alan Goldman, *Moral Knowledge* (New York: Routledge, 1988). See also Michael Krausz and Jack W. Meiland (eds.), *Relativism: Cognitive and Moral* (Notre Dame: University of Notre Dame Press, 1982); and David Copp, *Morality, Normativity, and Society* (Oxford: Oxford University Press, 1995), Ch. 11.

Discussion Questions

1. What is ethical relativism? How is it distinguished from both universalism and absolutism? What is the difference between cultural ethical relativism and extreme ethical relativism?

2. So-called "honor killings" of women are practiced in some societies (killing a woman believed to have dishonored the family, say, through adultery). While based partly on religious grounds, the practice is often deeply rooted in the customs of a particular village or tribe. Are such practices justified because they are so rooted? Or are they wrong, whenever and wherever they occur?

3. If relativism is true, does it follow that moral disagreements cannot be resolved? Is there a difference between cultural relativism and extreme relativism in this regard?

4. Need an ethical relativist be a subjectivist?

5. Why does cultural diversity—a documentable fact—not suffice to establish ethical relativism?

6. Do you believe that ethical relativism, if generally accepted, would lead to greater tolerance among peoples? If so, why? If not, why not?

The idea that the basic principles of morality are known, and that the problems all come in their interpretation and application, is one of the most fantastic conceits to which our conceited species has been drawn.[1]

Thomas Nagel

Can Moral Principles Be Justified?

CHAPTER **12**

12.1 DIVERSITY AT THE LEVEL OF PRINCIPLES

We saw in Chapter 11 that the diversity of moral beliefs and practices often prompts people to think ethical relativism is true. We have seen further that a common approach to conduct is to appeal to moral principles. But just as there is a plurality of beliefs and practices at the level of conduct, so there is a plurality of principles at the level of theory. If the former points in the direction of relativism, does not the latter as well?

Notice that if any of the principles we have examined—such as the categorical imperative or the principle of utility—could be shown to be true (correct, valid), that would refute relativism because it would show that the principle held for everyone. We could then say that whatever people *think* about right and wrong, this principle is what in fact determines right and wrong. Thus moral legalism, in the forms we have considered it, provides an alternative to relativism.

But for it to be convincing as an alternative, we must have some way of choosing among the various proposed principles. Otherwise we have simply avoided the problem of relativism at the level of practice by transferring it to the level of theory. Is there a way to make such a choice, and can any of the principles we have considered be justified?

I will examine three attempts to justify principles. They are called, respectively, intuitionism, ethical naturalism, and contractarianism. These are not the only approaches to justifying principles, but they are three of the most influential ones.

12.2 MORAL FOUNDATIONALISM: INTUITIONISM AND NATURALISM

The term **intuitionism** stands for different things. With regard to principles, it may mean only that a principle is incapable of proof. This is what G. E. Moore, a leading twentieth-century intuitionist (whom we will consider further in Chapter 13), says he means by calling a proposition an "intuition."[2] Mill before him had observed "[t]o be incapable of proof by reasoning is common to all first principles, to the first premises of our knowledge, as well as to those of our conduct."[3] Although Mill did not consider himself an intuitionist, he took his observation to apply to the principle of utility as well as to other principles.

The point is that if by "proof" we mean producing other propositions from which we can deduce a principle, then of course there can be no such proof of basic (or, as Mill calls them, "first") principles. Basic principles are those from which we derive other propositions and which are themselves not derived from others.

Thus the principle of utility can be used as the major premise in an argument to justify a rule, such as that one ought to keep promises:

1. One ought to promote the greatest general happiness (utility).
2. Keeping promises promotes the greatest general happiness.
3. Therefore one ought to keep promises.

From such a rule, one can then deduce particular moral judgments about what to do in specific situations:

4. One ought to keep promises.
5. To return this loan would be to keep a promise.
6. Therefore, I ought to return this loan.

But in this view, premise 1 itself cannot be justified by appeal to any more basic principle because there is none that is more basic.

However, if this is what is meant by calling a principle an intuition, that doesn't help much with our problem because each of the principles previously mentioned could be considered intuitive in this sense. This view would provide no way of distinguishing among them.

A second meaning of intuitionism is more promising. In this sense, to call a principle (or for that matter any proposition) an "intuition" is to say it is self-evident. Its truth or falsity is grasped immediately upon understanding it.

Thus Aquinas concluded that the propositions that a whole is greater than its parts, or that two things equal to a third are equal to one another, are self-evident. In the sphere of morality, he thought it self-evident that good is to be done and evil avoided, which he took to be the basic principle of natural law (see section 7.7).

Are any rules or principles in fact self-evident in this way?

Some philosophers have thought so. W. D. Ross, for example, contends that some rules are known intuitively, such as (1) that we ought to tell the truth, (2) that we ought to keep promises, (3) that we ought to make reparation for wrongs we have done, (4) that we ought to seek the distribution of happiness in accordance with merit, (5) that we ought to do good for others, (6) that we ought to do good for ourselves, and (7) that we ought not to injure others.[4]

These rules, however, represent only what Ross calls *prima facie* duties; that is, they tell us what we should do only if there are no other, overriding moral considerations. They do not tell us whether there *are* such considerations; hence they never tell us what we actually should do or what our *actual* duties are in any particular situation. *Prima facie* duties are self-evident, but actual duties are not. Moreover, various rules can conflict with one another. Thus we have a *prima facie* duty to tell the truth. But we also have a *prima facie* duty to do good. If the wolf asks which way Little Red Riding Hood went, do you tell the truth and let her get eaten, or lie and save her? You cannot do both (although you could do neither by not answering).

As interesting as Ross's theory is, it fails to solve our problem for two reasons: First, even if we assume that the various principles considered earlier (throughout Part III) express only *prima facie* obligations, this theory provides no way to choose among them. It would, in fact, expand the number of alternatives among which to choose by adding itself to them. It represents morality as based on many rules rather than on just one principle; that is, it is pluralistic where the other approaches are monistic. Rather than enabling us to choose among various theories—each of which bases morality on *one* basic principle—this theory would itself base morality on a plurality of principles. Second, in this view (unlike Aquinas's), it is not quite enough to simply understand self-evident propositions in order to apprehend their truth. To understand how rules can be self-evident, we must first see (intuit) the rightness of particular *acts,* then by a kind of intuitive generalization (induction, as Ross calls it) come to see that all acts of that type are *prima facie* right. So in the end, this theory is a blend of particularism and legalism.

You might, however, think that the truth of some basic principle is self-evident but deny that it comes to be self-evident in the way just described. You might think we can just apprehend the truth of the principle without having first judged the rightness of particular acts it prescribes. A utilitarian might maintain that the principle of utility is self-evident in this way.

But then we need to ask, "Self-evident for whom?" The principle of utility is not self-evident to everyone—certainly not to Kantians, divine command theorists, or ethical egoists. Are we to say, then, that its being self-evident to certain people but not to others warrants our saying it *is* self-evident? Why those particular people? If some Kantians also think that the categorical imperative is self-evident, how do we decide between the two? And how do we make a distinction between a principle's being self-evident to some people and its merely *seeming* self-evident to them?

These represent two of the most difficult problems for intuitionism: first, how to choose among conflicting intuitions; and second, how to distinguish genuine from merely apparent intuitions. Unless plausible resolutions to these problems can be found, it is doubtful that principles can be justified in this way.

12.3 ETHICAL NATURALISM

Another possibility is that a principle is justified by certain facts about the world and the nature of language.

Suppose, for example, that pleasure is the only thing intrinsically good. Suppose further, as traditional utilitarians and ethical egoists hold, that happiness consists of a life of pleasure (one with as great a balance of pleasure over pain as possible). This would mean that whether something is good is purely a factual matter because you would need only to determine whether it is an instance of pleasure. And what conduces to happiness would likewise be a factual matter because you would simply need to know what will maximize the balance of pleasure over pain in your life.

Suppose further that "right" simply *means* "conduces to as great a balance of pleasure over pain as any other alternative." Then to say,

This act is right.

is, in effect, to say,

This act conduces to as great a balance of pleasure over pain as any other.

If further, "ought" could be defined as meaning "promotes a greater balance of good over bad than any other alternative," then the principle of utility, which states that one ought to promote the greatest general happiness, would be true by definition. Given that pleasure alone is good, and that happiness consists of a balance of pleasure over pain; and given the meanings of "right" and "ought," we could see that the principle of utility is the correct principle of morality. Showing this would justify the principle.

A theory that maintains that facts about the world (including facts about language) suffice to warrant a basic moral principle is a form of **ethical naturalism**. (Ethical naturalism is also a theory about the nature of specific moral judgments as well, as we shall consider in the next chapter.)

One could try to justify any of the principles considered in Part III of this book in essentially the same way, by defining the moral concepts they contain in such a way as to make the principles true by definition. It is just that not all of them could appropriately be called ethical "naturalism" because the facts to which some of them appeal would not be facts about the world of nature, at least as understood and studied by science. (God's willing something is not a fact of the natural world, for example, but of the supernatural world.) Still, the basic strategy involved in trying to defend them would be the same.

Let me simply note one serious problem with naturalism. It is a problem that parallels the problem with intuitionism. If we maintain that an ethical term such as "right" or "ought" is definable in a way that would justify some specific moral principle, we must ask, "Definable by whom?" And here again we encounter conflicting views. Just as advocates of different principles might have conflicting intuitions about which of those principles is true, so they might (if they approach justification in this way) have conflicting convictions about the correct definitions of the ethical terms those principles contain. And if they do, it is not easy to see how to resolve that conflict.

It will not do to consult a dictionary, as we can with most disputes about the meanings of words. Philosophers can be presumed to know the dictionary definitions of ethical words. So the competing definitions must be taken to express meanings of a somewhat different sort from those conveyed by the dictionary. The burden is then on adherents of the various principles to explain both what sense of meaning is captured by the definitions they propose and why it is the relevant one for purposes of understanding morality.

This is a tall order, and one may seriously question whether it has been filled by defenders of any of the preceding principles (or for that matter, by defenders of other principles, such as that one ought to do what is approved by society). And until it is filled, this approach can probably not enable us to justify one principle and discard the others.

12.4 CONTRACTARIANISM

Suppose the people of the world assemble to discuss which principle or principles are to govern them. Suppose they reach agreement and contract, so to speak, to accept and abide by a certain principle. Would that justify the principle?

Surely not, you might say. Just as society's approving a certain practice does not make it right, so everyone's approving a certain principle would not make it correct. In any event, people never have agreed on moral principles; the plurality of principles proposed by philosophers attests to this. Perhaps they never will. As the cultural relativist points out, beliefs and practices on moral matters differ radically among peoples. If such a gathering of people ever took place, and if, miraculously, they did reach agreement, one might suspect it was because some people—those with wealth, power, and influence—manipulated the proceedings so as to win acceptance of the principle most advantageous to them.

These points are all well taken. But contractarians believe the core idea in contractarianism is sound and that when developed properly it can provide a justification for moral principles.

The idea is that there is something validating about agreement freely reached by people regarding the principles to govern them. Because they are the ones affected by the principles, they should decide what those principles shall be. The principles should not be imposed externally—either by God or by some political authority. Nor should they be presumed to exist eternally.

To be plausible, this idea needs to be developed. No such contract has ever been made or probably ever will be made, so we must talk only of hypothetical agreement. In so doing, we are free to specify whatever we want about the people who enter into the contract, and about the conditions under which they enter. Both points are important.

12.5 RAWLS AND THE ORIGINAL POSITION

Consider the contractarian theory of John Rawls in his *Theory of Justice*. He defends certain principles of social justice intended to govern the way society distributes rights and responsibilities and the advantages of social cooperation.

But his procedure illustrates a possible approach to justifying any moral principle. Let us highlight its main features.

It is important to specify certain things about the people who enter into the hypothetical contract and about the conditions under which they operate. Rawls says this. It is assumed that people (that is, not everyone in the world, but those of a particular society) are assembled in what he calls the "original position," for the purpose of choosing principles to govern them in a well-ordered society. A well-ordered society is one (1) designed to advance the good of its members, (2) effectively regulated by a public conception of justice that the basic institutions of society satisfy and are known to satisfy, (3) in which everyone accepts and knows that others accept the same principles of justice, and (4) that is stable.[5] The people in the original position are not choosing principles to govern them in relation to other peoples or societies. They are only choosing principles to govern relations among themselves. They are presumed, moreover, to be rational and self-interested.

If people are self-interested, they may be expected to favor principles that would promote their interests. Because different people are differently situated in society (some wealthy, some poor; some educated, some not, and so on), the principles they would favor would likely differ—if not from person to person, at least from group to group, or class to class.

This variance could be an obstacle to reaching agreement. To avoid this obstacle, Rawls imposes a condition on the original position: that the people make their choice under a "veil of ignorance."

> First of all, no one knows his place in society, his class position or social status; nor does he know his fortune in the distribution of natural assets and abilities, his intelligence and strength, and the like. Nor, again, does anyone know his conception of the good, the particulars of his rational plan of life, or even the special features of his psychology such as his aversion to risk or liability to optimism or pessimism. More than this, I assume that the parties do not know the particular circumstances of their own society. That is, they do not know its economic or political situation, or the level of civilization and culture it has been able to achieve. The persons in the original position have no information as to which generation they belong. These broader restrictions on knowledge are appropriate in part because questions of social justice arise between generations as well as within them, for example, the question of the appropriate rate of capital saving and of the conservation of natural resources and the environment of nature.[6]

This deprives people of any advantage based on knowledge of their particular circumstances in society. If you are wealthy, you might support a principle favoring the wealthy (such as "To each according to status"). But under the veil of ignorance, you would not know you are wealthy in the actual society the principles are to govern, and so could not be influenced by such a bias. By the same token, if you are poor you likely would choose a principle that would favor the poor (such as "To each according to need"). But you, too, would be deprived of the knowledge that you are poor, hence could not allow your particular circumstances to affect your choice.[7]

Moreover, each can participate fully and equally in the process leading to a choice, with no one having more say in the matter than anyone else, and no one holding power over others. As Rawls says, "If the original position is to yield agreements that are just, the parties must be fairly situated and treated equally as moral persons."[8] They are all moral persons with a capacity for a sense of justice, ensuring that they "can rely on each other to understand and to act in accordance with whatever principles are finally agreed to."[9]

Under these conditions, Rawls believes, rational people will choose in accordance with what is called the **maximin rule.**[10] It says that alternatives should be ranked in order of preference according to the superiority of their worst outcomes. Thus given the choice of two principles in circumstances in which you do not know what your position will be in society, if you can foresee that the worst off you could be according to one principle is less bad than the worst off you could be according to the other, you would choose the first.

Rawls believes that people in the original position, so described, would choose two principles:

> First: each person is to have an equal right to the most extensive basic liberty compatible with a similar liberty for others.

> Second: social and economic inequalities are to be arranged so that they are both (a) reasonably expected to be to everyone's advantage, and (b) attached to positions and offices open to all.[11]

Our concern, however, is not with these principles *per se* (a matter for normative ethics), but with the question of whether or not they have been shown to be justified (a matter for metaethics).

Rawls believes they have. He believes the fact of their being the outcome of choice in the original position *makes* them correct.

To see why requires returning to the idea of pure procedural justice discussed in section 10.5, where we distinguished among three kinds of procedural justice. In perfect procedural justice, it is possible to specify in advance of the procedure what is a fair outcome and to devise a procedure that, if followed, virtually guarantees that outcome. According to imperfect procedural justice, however, it is possible to specify what the correct outcome should be, but there is no foolproof procedure by which to produce that outcome. According to pure procedural justice, the outcome is fair, no matter what it is, provided the procedure producing the outcome is fair. It is not possible to specify in advance what the fair outcome is; one must implement the procedure and then see.

The process of rational people deciding and agreeing on principles in the original position is, according to Rawls, a case of pure procedural justice.[12] Whatever principles are agreed to will be just (and presumably, correct or justified). The original position has been designed to ensure that. It is the fact that these principles have been chosen under these conditions that justifies them.

Let us consider exactly what this means. If the principles are correct by virtue of having been chosen in the original position, then the distributions that will result from following them (when the people in the original position resume their place in actual society) will be just. Remember, the people in the original position are choosing principles for a well-ordered society. That, again, is a stable society designed to advance the good of its members; one that is effectively regulated by a public conception of justice and in which everyone accepts and knows that others accept the same principles of justice. This virtually guarantees that agreed-on principles of justice will be followed (as does the capacity for a sense of justice that Rawls attributes to people in the original position). That, in turn, virtually guarantees that the resultant distributions will be just. Indeed, Rawls specifies that part of the second principle (what he calls the "principle of fair opportunity") ensures that the resulting system is one of pure procedural justice.[13]

But, remember, we are talking about hypothetical people in a hypothetical situation. This means that even if pure procedural justice is designed into the original position, all it shows is that if there were such people, and if they went through such a process, the principles agreed on *would* be justified; and if those principles were implemented by those people in a well-ordered society, the resultant distributions *would* be just. It does not yet show that those principles are justified.[14] Even if we agree (as many philosophers do not) that people in the original position would select the particular principles Rawls thinks, we must ask what relevance that has to us.

The answer to this question is not altogether clear. You might contend that the conditions of pure procedural justice in the original position simply justify the resultant principles for anyone. Rawls does say, "We shall want to say that certain principles of justice are justified because they would be agreed to in an initial situation of equality."[15] But this would seem to overextend the notion of pure procedural justice, which requires that the process in question actually be carried out. It is not enough that the process *could* be carried out or would be carried out under certain circumstances.

Suppose that before the cards are dealt in a poker game one player claims the lion's share of the money on the grounds that if the cards were dealt and played fairly (with appropriate assumptions about the rationality and self-interest of the players), he would win. Even if he were correct in that judgment, we couldn't know that he was correct, and no one would concede him the money until the hand had in fact been played. The problem is to establish the bearing of that hypothetical outcome on our interactions in the actual world.

This is not to say that this bearing cannot be established. You might argue, for example, that Rawls's procedure ensures that the chosen principles are impartial, a desirable feature of moral principles; and that for that reason we should seriously consider that they may be the correct principles for the world we live in. This argument can be granted. And perhaps, with further argument, a persuasive case can be made for those principles. But the further argument is needed, and the bridge from the hypothetical world to the actual world must be constructed.

12.6 MORAL COHERENTISM

Another possibility is that the principles are justified because they match certain judgments we hold about justice—not as we held them before examining the conceptions of justice as set forth in Rawls's investigation, but after duly reflecting on them in the light of that examination. Indeed, Rawls says that part of what determines what conditions to build into the original position is whether or not it yields principles that cohere with our considered judgments about justice.[16]

There will be a process of adjusting those conditions, and perhaps of adjusting our initial judgments about justice as well, until a kind of stability and coherence is achieved, which Rawls calls **"reflective equilibrium."** This notion of reflective equilibrium is an important and complex one and has received considerable attention by contemporary philosophers. Appropriately qualified, it can be applied to particular judgments and principles of any sort. It does not, however, provide a justification of principles of a sort that would establish the correctness of moral legalism as opposed to particularism. The justification it provides requires that we weigh our assessment of particular cases (or at any rate, particular judgments) in justifying principles. The principles and the particular judgments are justified together, so to speak, as part of the process of arriving at reflective equilibrium.

More than that, unless virtually all peoples would achieve reflective equilibrium with the same principles, this would not provide an answer to ethical relativism. Indeed, if peoples from different cultures had different considered judgments, and if after arriving at reflective equilibrium those differences persisted (along with presumably different principles), it would seem to substantiate relativism. The coherence achieved in one society might differ from that achieved in another. Then conflicting principles espoused by people of different cultures could be equally justified, in which case those conflicting principles could not all accord with the principles chosen in the original position. If, even beyond that, it turned out that different individuals within the same culture found that different principles characterized their considered judgments, then this fact would support the more radical extreme relativism. Rawls acknowledges, "I shall not even ask whether the principles that characterize one person's considered judgments are the same as those that characterize another's."[17]

12.7 PROBLEMS IN THE APPLICATION OF RULES AND PRINCIPLES

The preceding discussion does not exhaust the possible lines of argument by which someone might attempt to justify moral principles, but it represents some of the main attempts. Suppose, however, that one of those approaches proved successful, and that some principle and/or set of rules could be shown to be justified. There would remain the practical problems of knowing both when they apply to a particular situation and precisely what they prescribe for that situation. The first is a problem primarily for rules, the second for both rules and principles.

Most rules, for example, purport to regulate only some conduct, not all. Such is the case with rules regarding honesty, truth telling, promise keeping, murder, rape, sexual harassment, incest, fidelity, and the like. To apply them, we must know that the particular situations are ones to which they are relevant.

Often this is no problem. If you are speaking with someone, you can be expected to know that the rule (we shall assume there is one) prescribing truth telling is relevant to the situation. The same holds with regard to honesty. If you are taking an exam, you can be expected to know that the rule stating that cheating is wrong is relevant to the situation. But consider a rule such as this:

One ought to respect the right to life of all people.

If you are considering an abortion, you will not know whether this rule applies to your situation unless you know whether the fetus is a person. And if you cannot decide that, you cannot decide whether respecting life constrains you in this case. The same is true if you are deliberating whether to turn off the respirator hooked up to someone in a persistent vegetative state. People in that state are still human beings, but it is an open question whether they are still persons. They lack the qualities of consciousness, purpose, and an ability to communicate that are normally associated with personhood.

For a dramatic illustration of the problem, recall the case of Oedipus. He presumably knew that parricide (killing one's parents) and incest are wrong. Yet through a bizarre turn of events, he ended up both killing a man who turned out to be his father and marrying a woman who turned out to be his mother. He did not know that the rules prohibiting parricide and incest applied to what he was doing at the time he performed the relevant actions. In Aristotelian terms, in order to apply rules, we always need to know the minor premise of the practical syllogism appropriate to our immediate situation (see section 3.9), and however justified certain rules might be, we sometimes do not know that.

If morality contains only one principle (rather than a set of rules or a principle plus secondary rules), this problem will not arise because the principle will apply to *everything* we do and will therefore be relevant in every situation. But then we encounter the second problem, that of knowing exactly what the principle requires of us. We have already seen the seriousness of this problem in the case of consequentialist principles (see section 9.9). But it affects deontological principles as well. Take the case of the following principle:

One ought always to obey God.

If you subscribe to the divine command theory, you will believe you should do as God commands. But you may not be sure what is commanded. If one day the heavens part and a voice tells you to build a church on a particular site, is that God speaking, or are you just hearing things? How would you be able to tell? This just symbolizes a broader problem. Few people think that God speaks to them directly. Rather, they rely on what they believe God has communicated to others, either directly or by way of inspiration, as traditionally represented in holy books such as the Bible or the Koran. But people often do not agree on what has been conveyed. Among Christians alone there is disagreement about God's will on a wide range of issues, from abortion, premarital sex, and homosexuality to interracial marriage, capital punishment, and war. Add to this the differences between Christians and followers of other monotheistic religions such as Judaism and Islam, and the extent of the problem can be perceived as enormous—resulting in intolerance, persecution, killing, and war.

In theory, at least, Kantianism fares well in this regard. The categorical imperative purports to govern all conduct, and presumably it is not difficult to determine what that imperative prescribes. But we have already seen reason to question that presumption (section 8.10). It is hard to be certain what the correct maxim is for testing universalization. And if you are unsure of that maxim, then you are uncertain as to whether or not you have accurately determined your duty.

Combined with the difficulties encountered in previous chapters, these considerations suggest that, as deeply entrenched as it is in Western moral philosophy, moral legalism is deficient as an approach to the ethics of conduct. This does not mean that moral legalism has been disproven; I do not believe it to be possible to convincingly disprove an approach to ethics that embraces so many different kinds of positions. I suggest, rather, that, whatever we may decide theoretically, from the practical standpoint of making actual moral decisions in concrete situations, legalism does not serve us well.

Notes

1. Thomas Nagel, "Autonomy and Deontology," in Samuel Scheffler, ed., *Consequentialism and Its Critics* (Oxford, England: Oxford University Press, 1988), p. 168.

2. G. E. Moore, *Principia Ethica* (Cambridge, England: Cambridge University Press, 1903), p. x.

3. John Stuart Mill, *Utilitarianism* (New York: Liberal Arts Press, 1953), p. 37.

4. W. D. Ross, *The Right and the Good*, Ch. 2.

5. John Rawls, *A Theory of Justice,* Revised Edition, (Cambridge, Mass.: Harvard University Press, 1971), pp. 397–405.

6. Ibid., p. 118f.

7. However, it has been pointed out that this does not preclude your knowing your sex in society, which would (at least in a society anything like ours) give a decided advantage to males. Although Rawls did not explicitly list sex as one of the facts behind the veil, he could have done so without any significant change to his theory. See Susan Moller Okin, *Justice, Gender and the Family* (New York: Basic Books, 1989), p. 91, who says of the Rawlsian theory that a feminist reader finds it difficult not to keep asking, "Does this theory of justice apply to women?"

8. *Theory of Justice*, p. 122.

9. Ibid., p. 125.

10. Ibid., p. 133.

11. Ibid., p. 53. As principles of justice, these belong with the fuller treatment of justice we undertook in Chapter 10. That is, they belong to normative ethics. But rather than specifying the proper distribution of benefits and burdens as principles of distributive justice typically do, the first principle specifies an equal distribution of *rights*, and the second simply places some constraints on the distribution of benefits and burdens, whatever that distribution might be. So there are important differences between Rawls's conception of justice and the principles of distributive justice

already considered. In any event, Rawls elaborates the principles throughout the remainder of his book.

12. Ibid., p. 118.

13. Ibid., p. 76.

14. Although the Kantian character of Rawls's position is often stressed, the hypothetical well-ordered society for whose governance the people in the original position have chosen principles is a little like the ideal state Plato describes in the *Republic*, in which everyone acts justly and upholds just institutions.

15. Ibid., p. 19.

16. Ibid., p. 18.

17. Ibid., p. 44.

Discussion Questions

1. Do you think the diversity of moral principles discussed in Part III leads to a kind of relativism at the level of theory in the same way in which the diversity of moral practices is sometimes thought to support relativism at the level of particular moral judgments?

2. Do you believe that there are some basic principles of morality that are incapable of proof? If so, how is their truth to be known? If not, how do we avoid moral skepticism?

3. What is Ross's distinction between *prima facie* and actual duties? Do you find the distinction useful? Would you agree with Ross that *prima facie* duties are known intuitively but actual duties are not?

4. What are two of the main problems for an intuitionistic theory of the justification of moral principles?

5. Does ethical naturalism seem to you a more plausible approach to justifying principles than intuitionism? Why?

6. Does a contractarian approach to justification, as represented by Rawls's analysis of the so-called "original position," seem to you a more promising approach than intuitionism or naturalism? Does the idea of trying to achieve "reflective equilibrium" seem to you a plausible approach? Do you find yourself ever adjusting principles and judgments in this way?

. . . this question, how "good" is to be defined,
is the most fundamental question in all ethics.[1]
G. E. Moore

The Nature of Moral Judgments

13.1 ETHICAL LANGUAGE

We have seen that two concerns of metaethics are ethical relativism and the problem of justifying moral principles. A third concern—one that underlies the others—has to do with the nature of moral judgments. A central part of that concern is to understand the meanings of moral terms.

Concerns of this sort have a long history. As far back as Plato, Socrates asks Meno (in Plato's dialogue by that name): "What, according to you and your friend, Gorgias, is the definition of virtue?" Plato and Socrates thought that to make headway with any philosophical problem you had to be clear about the meanings of the central concepts you were using. And this, they thought, required providing definitions.

Plato didn't call such questions metaethical. Distinctions among metaethics, normative ethics, and applied ethics didn't become current until the twentieth century. But such questions are a part of the traditional attempt to understand morality philosophically.

As a simple example, suppose you're discussing the abortion issue with someone and that person asks you:

1. Is abortion wrong?

If you're thinking philosophically, you might ask in return:

2. What do you mean by "wrong"?

You might want to know whether "wrong" is meant in a moral sense or a legal sense (or some other sense defined, say, by a religious or medical perspective). Often the context makes this clear. But sometimes it doesn't. As a result, people may be at cross-purposes because they're actually discussing different questions.

If "wrong" is meant in a moral sense, you might want to know what it means to say that something is morally wrong. Question (2) understood in this way is a metaethical question. It isn't about *what* is wrong. It is, rather, about the language used in asking (and answering) questions about what is wrong. It's a question *about* morality rather than a question within morality.

13.2 CATEGORIES OF ETHICAL TERMS

Our language contains distinctively ethical terms. They are part of our ethical vocabulary,[2] which breaks down into three types:

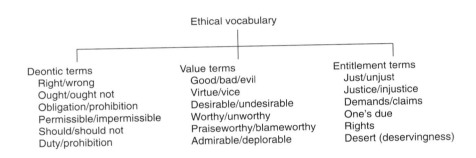

The above aren't exhaustive of our ethical vocabulary. But they include the terms that are of primary interest for understanding moral discourse.

Philosophical theories about the moral issues arising within these categories can then be called:

Deontic Theory: 1. Theory of rightness.
                 2. Theory of obligation.

Value Theory: 1. Theory of goodness.
                 2. Virtue ethics.

Entitlement Theory: 1. Theory of justice.
                    2. Theory of rights.

There are normative theories within each of these categories. They attempt to explain and justify propositions about is fundamentally right and wrong, good and bad, etc. The main theories dealt with in Part III are normative in this sense (thus, for example, Kantianism and utilitarianism are normative deontic theories, hedonism a normative value theory, and Rawls's theory of justice a normative entitlement theory).

Our concern at present is with the metaethical dimensions of these theories, specifically with the question of the proper understanding of the key terms. We can thus formulate one of the main questions of metaethics:

I. What is the proper understanding of ethical terms?

This question has often been taken to ask specifically about the *meanings* of ethical terms. So it yields a subsidiary question:

A1. What are the meanings of ethical terms?

When we want to know the meaning of a word, we often look it up in a dictionary. There we find its definition. Philosophers also often provide definitions, but they often have in mind a different sense of "definition" than do compilers of dictionaries who are trying to report accurately on current usage. Philosophers propose definitions which, at minimum, are specifically designed to clarify certain philosophical issues. At other times they are meant to constitute a philosophical analysis of a particular concept. In any event, question A1 yields a subsidiary question:

A2. What are the definitions of ethical terms?

The assumption behind A2 is that meanings of ethical terms are best captured by definitions. But A2 presupposes an answer to a prior question:

A3: Are ethical terms definable?

If ethical terms aren't definable in the first place (or if some are definable and others not), then some other way will have to be found to understand them. So let us begin with question A3.

13.3 CATEGORIAL AND CROSS-CATEGORIAL DEFINITIONS

In asking question A3, we might be asking one or the other of several different questions. For example, we might be asking:

A3': Are ethical terms definable by other ethical words in the same category (for example, deontic terms by other deontic terms)?

or

A3": Are ethical terms definable by ethical words in other categories (for example, deontic terms by value terms)?

Definitions of the first sort are **categorial definitions;** those of the second sort, **cross-categorial definitions.**

Most philosophers agree that ethical words are definable by (or at least can be used interchangeably with) other words within the same category. Most would say that "right" is generally interchangeable with "permissible";

"wrong" with "ought not to be done"; and "good" with "desirable." If such terms can be used interchangeably, they would seem to be synonymous, hence (at least in some sense) interdefinable.

The fact that ethical terms are definable in that way is not by itself of great philosophical interest, for it does not preclude their also being definable cross-categorially—by reference to terms in other categories. It also (as we shall see in section 13.6) doesn't preclude their being definable **extra-categorially**—by terms that are outside of the ethical vocabulary altogether. Only if ethical terms were definable exclusively by reference to other ethical terms within their category would that fact be of philosophical interest.

The more interesting question at the moment is whether ethical terms are definable cross-categorially, as A3″ asks. And this question is controversial.

Some, for example, have thought that deontic terms are definable by value terms. Others have thought that value terms are definable by deontic terms. Consider the following:

Def 1: Right = def. Cause of a good result.[3]

Here, the deontic term, "right," is defined by reference to the value term, "good." Now consider:

Def 2: Good = def. What ought to be the object of a pro attitude (i.e., any favorable attitude).[4]

Here the value term, "good," is defined by reference to the deontic term, "ought." Next, consider

Def 3: Rights = def. What it is right for persons to do or to abstain from doing.[5]

Here the entitlement term, "rights," is defined by reference to the deontic term, "right." Although they have the same spelling but for the "s" on the end of the first word, these words have different meanings: the first signifies entitlements that people (and perhaps animals) *have*; the second signifies that actions *are* right, that is, not wrong.

We can now see why question A3″ is important. If you define "right" in terms of "good," as Def 1 does, then you are committed to an axiological theory of right or obligation (see Chapter 2). To determine what is morally right will require determining first what is good. Deontic Theory (specifically the theory of rightness) will then presuppose Value Theory (as Epicurus, Bentham, and Mill thought). Sometimes virtue ethics is understood in such a way that deontic notions are derivable from value notions, particularly those related to virtues.[6]

On the other hand, if "good" is definable in terms of "ought," as in Def 2, then determining what is good will not be sufficient for determining what we ought to do. One will have to look to other kinds of considerations, such as conformity with rules and principles. Deontic Theory will then be at least partly independent of Value Theory (as it was for Aristotle, the Stoics, and Kant). If Def 3 should be correct, then rights theory (that aspect of Entitlement Theory dealing with specifically with rights) will presuppose Deontic Theory.

13.4 ARE RIGHTS REDUCIBLE TO DEONTIC AND VALUE TERMS?

Just as we can ask whether either value or deontic terms are basic relative to the other, so we can ask whether entitlement terms are basic relative to either value terms or deontic terms. This question, too, is complex. To answer it fully would require close examination of both the Theory of Justice and Rights Theory. I shall comment only on Rights Theory.

Many people believe in human rights. They think that the basic questions of how we ought to treat people—that is, questions about right and wrong—are answerable ultimately in terms of such rights. If this should be correct, then deontic terms would ultimately be understood (and perhaps definable) in terms of entitlement terms.

This, of course, leaves questions such as (1) how it is that people have human rights (unless one believes that people are endowed by their Creator with such rights, as the Declaration of Independence states, a question such as this one may be difficult to answer), (2) whether human rights are inalienable (cannot be surrendered, transferred, or forfeited), (3) whether they are imprescriptible (do not depend on being set forth by someone or some governmental body), and (4) whether they can ever be justifiably overridden, infringed upon, or violated. Although they speak freely of rights, other philosophers (such as Mill) hold that rights are ultimately explainable by reference to other moral notions, such as that of utility (a value term).

There is no consensus among contemporary philosophers as to what a correct account of human rights might be. However, I want to suggest a reason for supposing that the language of rights, useful as it is, can be eliminated, and hence, that rights are not basic to morality. The reason is this: that we can say everything we want to say with regard to moral judgments by using deontic and value terms alone.

Specifically, there doesn't seem to be anything to say about the rights of people (or animals, for that matter) that cannot be said in terms of good and bad or right and wrong (and their correlative concepts). If we say people have certain rights against interference (as in the case of free speech), we can take that to mean that it's wrong to interfere with them in those ways. If we say they have rights to have certain things provided for them (as in the case of food, jobs, or medical care), we can say that it's wrong not to provide them with those goods. It's doubtful, however, that all deontic judgments (such as "You ought to visit your sick grandmother") can easily be understood in terms of rights. It's even more doubtful that value judgments as such as "She is a good person" can be rendered in terms of rights.

So while cautioning that this is a controversial topic, I shall assume that the language of rights is translatable into deontic and value language. This doesn't mean we shouldn't speak of people as having rights. The language of rights is a useful and established part of our moral discourse and plays a central role in the discussion of most contemporary issues. It means only that, in the end, we don't need the notion of rights to understand morality.

Notice, however, that if deontic terms (e.g., terms such as "right") are definable by value terms (e.g., terms such as "good"), then both entitlement language and deontic language would in principle be eliminable. We could say everything we need to say about ethics by means of the concept of goodness. Even if we didn't change our actual way of speaking about ethics, we would have achieved theoretical simplicity by reducing our number of ethical concepts to one; namely, to the concept of goodness. Just as science seeks a unified theory to explain the natural order (as noted earlier in section 2.1), so some philosophers seek a unified theory to explain the moral order.

Whether deontic language is ultimately translatable into value language (or vice versa) we won't try to decide. In what follows, we shall concentrate on both value and deontic terms.

13.5 ARE ETHICAL TERMS DEFINABLE BY NON-ETHICAL TERMS?

If all the ethical words in a given category were definable in terms of one another, then there would be a circularity in those definitions (if you defined "good" as "the opposite of evil" and then "evil" as "the opposite of good," the circularity would be obvious; it would be only slightly less obvious if you defined "right" as "permissible," and "permissible" as "not wrong," and then "not wrong" as "right."). The definitions would show us something about the possible interrelationship of terms within the category but wouldn't otherwise deepen our understanding of the meanings of the terms.

If, however, some terms in one category were definable cross-categorially—for example, "right" in terms of "good"—then (provided "good" is not in turn definedas "right" or some other deontic term) our understanding would have been advanced.

But just as it is important to avoid circularity of definitions *within* a category, it is equally important to avoid circularity generally within the broader domain of ethical words.

If, for example, "right" were defined cross-categorially as "good," "good" as "the opposite of evil," and finally "evil" as "the opposite of good," we wouldn't know how to go about determining what is right. The quest to understand "right" would lead us from the deontic category to the value category, but we would then encounter a circularity in the definition of "good" within the value category.

There is a possible way out of this problem. If some ethical words are *basic*, in the sense that they cannot be defined (or defined exclusively) in terms of other ethical terms (even though other ethical terms may be defined in terms of them), then there need be no circularity.

This would be true, for example, if some ethical words were definable **extra-categorially**, that is, in terms of *non–ethical* words. So this gives us a third way of understanding question A3:

A3‴ Are ethical words definable by reference to non-ethical words?

If "good" were definable as "pleasure," it would be definable in terms of a non-ethical word. Even if other value terms were definable in terms of "good," there would be no circularity because "good" would be definable by a word outside of that category. And if all deontic terms were definable in terms of "right," and "right" was definable in terms of "good," then there would be no dead-end. The definitions would lead us eventually out of the ethical realm and connect, so to speak, with the rest of the world. The ethical world would be grounded in the non-ethical world.

Is this an accurate representation of the relationship between the ethical and the non-ethical realms? This question defines one of the central issues in metaethics.

13.6 IS ETHICS AUTONOMOUS?

The central issue is whether ethics is autonomous (an issue raised in section 7.10 in connection with Kant). Does ethics stand by itself or is it, in the end, reducible to the non-ethical world?

Suppose, again, that "right" is defined as "what maximizes good," and "good" is defined as "pleasure." Since "pleasure" is a non-ethical term, ethics is reduced, in the end, to the non-ethical realm. What is or isn't pleasant is an empirical question, and what maximizes pleasure is an empirical question. Empirical questions are in principle answerable by scientific means. Thus such a definition would reduce ethics to a kind of empirical science.

Some philosophers have thought this to be correct. They believe that we should disabuse ourselves of the notion that ethics belongs to a transcendent realm (as Plato thought in connection with the Idea of the Good, and as Divine Command Theorists believe with respect to God). Ethics needs to be explained in terms of the world we live in and can know by scientific means.

Many (though not all) of those who hold this view are **metaphysical naturalists.** They believe that the natural order that can be studied by science is all there is. If they believe, further, that morality must be understood in terms of the natural order—as would be true if basic ethical terms were definable by non-ethical terms referring to characteristics of that order—then in addition to being metaphysical naturalists, they are also **ethical naturalists.**[7] Unless indicated otherwise, by naturalism we shall henceforth mean ethical naturalism.[8]

Others have thought that such an attempted reduction of ethics to the natural order distorts the true nature of morality. A. C. Ewing, for example, says, ". . . if all ethical concepts are analyzable completely in terms of non-ethical, this will reduce ethics to something else and destroy its distinctive nature altogether."[9] Ewing directs the objection against the definability (he uses the term "analyzability") of *all* ethical terms by reference to non-ethical terms. But his point, if correct, holds equally against the definability of only *some* ethical terms by non-ethical terms, namely, those that are basic.

If morality is reducible to the natural world (as is entailed by the definability of ethical words in terms of non-ethical words), then morality, in this view, is destroyed.

13.7 AUTONOMY AND REDUCTIONISM

The problem, however, is more complicated than this. What troubles **ethical autonomists** (as we may call those who affirm the autonomy of ethics) is not just that ethical naturalists try to define ethical terms by non-ethical terms that stand for natural properties (that is, those characterizing the natural order); they are troubled by *any* attempt to define ethical terms by reference to non-ethical terms, even if the non-ethical terms refer to a supernatural realm.

For example, if "right" should be defined as "What is commanded by God," (see Chapter 6) then, in this view, morality would have no reality of its own. In being reduced to the commandments of God, morality is reduced to something it is not just as surely as if it were reduced to facts about the natural order. The fact that God is presumed to exist in a supernatural order doesn't change things. It is the *reduction* of ethics to something else that destroys its autonomy, not the precise nature of what it is reduced to.

It is, in this view, as much a mistake to reduce morality to non-ethical facts about a transcendent supernatural realm as it is to reduce it to non-ethical facts about the natural realm. The error is the same in each case. Critics of such reductionism have called this mistake **the naturalistic fallacy** (to be discussed further in section 13.12), even though its commission isn't restricted to ethical or metaphysical naturalists.

According to ethical autonomists, each of the following definitions would be equally reductionistic:

Right = def. What I approve.
Right = def. What my society approves.
Right = def. What God approves (or commands).
Good = def. Desired.
Good = def. Any object of any interest.
Good = def. The pleasurable.

Insofar as ethics is thought to deal first and foremost with right conduct, the first definition would reduce ethics to what each speaker approves, the second, to what each speaker's society approves, the third, to what God approves. The definitions of good reduce value respectively to desire, interest, or pleasure.

We have seen that ethics is circular if ethical terms are definable only in terms of one another. We have also seen that there is a way out of this circularity if some ethical terms can be defined in terms of non-ethical terms.

But there is another solution to the problem. This solution is to say that some ethical terms are *indefinable*. The reasoning here is captured in the following passage:

> If ... ethical terms are not all to be defined (analyzed) in terms of non-ethical, since they cannot all be defined in terms of each other, at least one ethical concept must be indefinable. This does not imply that its nature cannot be known— it may be very distinctly known—only that it cannot be reduced to anything else.[10]

This doesn't mean that these terms may not be defined categorically ("good," for example, might still be used interchangeably with "desirable in itself"). It means, rather, that they are not definable cross-categorically. More importantly for our present purposes, it also means that they are not definable extra-categorially—by terms outside the ethical vocabulary altogether (that is, by non-ethical words).

The assumption here is that words don't have to be definable to be meaningful. They have meaning if they refer to properties. If there are ethical words that are indefinable but property-referring, the circle stops with them.

13.8 IS "GOOD" INDEFINABLE?

We cannot discuss whether all ethical terms are definable, so we shall focus upon "good." This is a term around which much controversy has swirled (note that Moore, in the epigraph at the beginning of this chapter, takes this to be the fundamental question of ethics).

In a common-sense view, things can be defined only if they have parts. A triangle can be defined because it is made up of lines and angles. Water can be defined because it is composed of hydrogen and oxygen. If there is an actual property of goodness and it is simple (has no parts), then there is nothing to explain by means of a definition. If it has no parts, goodness can't be defined.[11]

But some natural properties are simple in this sense as well. Pleasantness is an example. Experiences that are pleasant can be explained and perhaps defined. But the property of pleasantness that characterizes them doesn't have parts. If "good" stood for a property like pleasantness, then even though it would be indefinable, it would make value a feature of the natural world. Hence (given a few other assumptions) it would violate the autonomy of ethics.

Some autonomists, specifically intuitionists, deal with this problem by maintaining that goodness is a **non-natural property.** For this reason, ethical intuitionism (which we shall discuss at greater length shortly) is sometimes called **non-naturalism.** And intuitionists believe that this property is unique, in the sense that it is unlike, and irreducible to, any other property.[12]

The idea here is that there is a dimension to reality beyond the natural order. Key ethical terms refer to properties belonging to that dimension. Most religious people believe there is a reality that transcends the natural order, too. They believe in God and, perhaps, souls, angels, ghosts, and spirits. But this supernatural realm differs from the non-natural realm intuitionists think moral properties belong to.

To explain the distinction between **supernatural** and **non-natural** realms in depth would take us far afield into metaphysics. For our purposes, the following account will do. Supernatural things **exist;** they are temporal and can have natural properties even if they aren't spatial. Ghosts, for example, are supernatural beings. If there are such things, they're said to exist. Yet Marley's ghost appeared to Scrooge at a particular *time* and possessed the natural property of being a speaker of English. Even though science cannot locate, examine, and analyze them, ghosts (if they exist) have some temporal and natural characteristics. Non-natural entities, on the other hand, are eternal and unchangeable. Like Plato's Idea of the Good, or the number Two, they're outside of space and time. They have **being** (rather than existence) and can be exemplified in natural objects (that are good or that are two in number). But they themselves are non-natural, atemporal, and have no natural properties.[13]

Some ethical intuitionists have thought that "good" stands for just such a non-natural property as this, and hence that ethics (which some ethical intuitionists see as based upon goodness) is autonomous and irreducible to anything else.

13.9 MORAL REALISM

Notice the shift that has taken place here. We began by talking about ethical language and the definability of ethical words. Now, however, we are talking about properties or characteristics—things presumed to have some sort of reality outside of the linguistic realm.

Whether ethical terms are definable is a linguistic question. Whether there are moral properties is a metaphysical question. Those who contend there are moral properties and/or moral facts are **moral realists.** Those who deny this are **anti-realists.**

If there are moral properties, then there will be moral facts, since it will be a fact that certain things possess those properties. But there might be moral facts without there being moral properties, if those facts are irreducible or have no constituents which include moral properties. For simplicity, we shall focus upon moral properties in what follows.

Bearing in mind the distinction among natural, supernatural, and non-natural realms, let us define moral realism as follows:

MORAL REALISM = def. The assertion of the proposition:

1. There are moral properties.

and the assertion of one or more of the following propositions:

2. Moral properties are natural properties.
3. Moral properties are supernatural properties.
4. Moral properties are non-natural properties.

Sometimes moral realism is restricted to the claim that moral properties are objective, in the sense that they don't depend upon feelings, attitudes, and emotions (see section 11.5). At other times it is understood to include subjective as well as objective properties. We won't try to decide between these theories but will retain a conception of moral realism that is broad enough to accommodate either the assertion *or the denial* of the following:

5. Moral properties are objective.

While the assertion of (1) suffices for a **minimal moral realism,** a fuller account requires specifying what sorts of properties moral properties are. So we may say that **complete moral realism** is the assertion of (1) and either (2), (3), or (4) (or some combination thereof), *and* either the assertion or denial of (5).

Moral realism, so understood, is a metaphysical view; that is, part of the ontology of morals.

13.10 COGNITIVISM

We can now characterize one of the two main metaethical theories about the nature of moral judgments. It's called cognitivism, a term that stands for a family of theories which typically consist of a blend of linguistic, epistemological and metaphysical elements.

COGNITIVISM. An ethical theory is cognitivistic if and only if it asserts one or both of the following:

1. Ethical terms, when used morally, (a) have conceptual meaning and (b) are property-referring.[14]
2. Moral judgments are (a) true or false and (b) essentially convey information.[15]

The main versions of cognitivism are ethical naturalism and ethical intuitionism. We may define these as follows:

A. ETHICAL NATURALISM
    1. Ethical terms (a) refer to natural properties, and/or (b) are definable by non-ethical terms that refer to natural properties.
    2. Moral judgments are (a) true or false and (b) essentially convey information about the natural world.
    3. The truth or falsity of moral judgments can be known empirically.

Ethical naturalists typically subscribe to view (1a) and (1b). We may call this view **definitional naturalism** (sometimes called analytical naturalism). In this view, ethical terms are property-referring by virtue of being definable by non-ethical words that are property-referring.

But naturalists may hold that words like "good" stand for a natural property like pleasantness, which, because it is simple, is indefinable. In that case, they will hold view (1a) but not (1b). Ethical words will be property-referring but indefinable. They may also say that moral judgments symbolize moral facts. Naturalism, construed in either of these ways, becomes essentially an ontological theory rather than a linguistic one. To distinguish it from definitional naturalism, we may call it **ontological naturalism** (it is also sometimes called synthetic naturalism). Bear in mind that both definitional naturalism and ontological naturalism, as we are using those terms, are forms of ethical naturalism and as such are to be distinguished from metaphysical naturalism as defined in section 13.6. Condition (1b) covers both possibilities. Both definitional naturalists and ontological naturalists hold (2) and (3).

B. ETHICAL INTUITIONISM
    1. Some ethical terms (a) refer to non-natural properties and (b) are indefinable by non-ethical terms.

2. Moral judgments are (a) true or false and (b) essentially convey information about the natural, supernatural, or non-natural realms.
3. The truth or falsity of moral judgments can be known (partially or wholly) a priori.

That moral judgments may convey information about the natural, supernatural, and non-natural realms needs some explaining.

Consider "good." If it stands for a non-natural property, that property will nonetheless characterize things in the natural realm; namely, things that are good, such as pleasure, knowledge, virtue, and some persons. Similarly, there is no reason why it could not characterize things in the supernatural or metaphysical realms as well. If there are angels, they are presumably good. If so, supernatural beings would possess a non-natural property, and the judgment "Angels are good" would then convey information of both a supernatural and non-natural sort. Regarding (3), the truth or falsity of a judgment such as, "Pleasure is intrinsically good" would require both experience (hence empirical knowledge) of pleasure and a priori knowledge that it has the non-natural property of goodness; hence its truth or falsity would be knowable partially empirically and partially a priori.

C. THEOLOGICAL ETHICS
1. Ethical terms (a) refer to supernatural or metaphysical properties and/or (b) are definable by non-ethical terms that refer to supernatural or metaphysical properties.
2. Moral judgments are (a) true or false and (b) essentially convey information about the natural, supernatural, or metaphysical realm.
3. The truth or falsity of moral judgments can be known (partially or wholly) a priori.

If "right" is definable as "commanded by God" (as in the divine command theory; see Chapter 6), then an ethical term is definable by a non-ethical term referring to a supernatural property. If "right" isn't so defined, but simply stands for the property of being commanded by God, then it refers to a supernatural property as in (1a). In either event, judgments about rightness will be true or false and essentially convey information about the natural, supernatural, or metaphysical realm. Their truth or falsity will then be known wholly or partially a priori, depending upon one's theology (that is, depending upon whether you believe that God imprints on our souls the knowledge of right and wrong—or whether you believe we need some empirical knowledge, say by reading the Bible or Koran, to come by that knowledge).

13.11 ETHICAL NATURALISM AND INTUITIONISM

A prototype of modern ethical naturalism is the following theory of R. B. Perry (1876–1957), who defines "good" as follows:

Good = def. Any object of any interest.[16]

Interest is understood broadly to include: liking/disliking, loving/hating, hoping/fearing, desiring/avoiding, etc.[17] Being an object of interest in this sense is a natural property, verifiable empirically. To say that something is good conveys information. It is to make an empirical assertion that is either true or false.

While the value term "good" is thus defined by non-ethical terms (being an object of interest), the deontic term "right" is defined cross-categorially by "good."

Right = def. Conduciveness to moral good (harmonious happiness).[18]

The definition of "right" in terms of "good" grounds this version of ethical naturalism in Value Theory. Judgments of moral rightness, no less than judgments of value, will then be cognitive assertions whose truth or falsity can be established empirically. The way is then open to making ethics a form of empirical science.

A prototype of modern ethical intuitionism is the theory (already mentioned in Chapter 12 section 13.9) of G. E. Moore (1875–1958). Moore distinguishes intrinsic value from extrinsic value ("value" covers both good and bad here; we shall focus upon good). Let us revisit the distinction discussed earlier in section 9.4.

Intrinsic value: value that depends solely on the intrinsic nature of what possesses it.

Extrinsic value: value that depends solely on the relationship of what possesses it to other things.

The value of happiness is intrinsic. It's what happiness is—its very nature—that makes it good. The value of a hammer, on the other hand, is extrinsic; its value consists in what you can do with it (drive nails, build and repair things), and hence in its relationship to other things.

Although indefinable, "good" (in the sense of intrinsic goodness) stands for an actual property, that of being intrinsically good. Unlike being an object of interest, which is a natural property, this property is non-natural. Though goodness characterizes natural objects (as we represent when we say that various things are intrinsically good), it itself is not a natural property.[19] It can't be studied by empirical science.

Intrinsic goodness, furthermore, is a quality as opposed to a relation. A single thing by itself may possess a quality (say, redness). But a single thing in isolation can't possess a relation (say, being a parent of); the idea of a relation typically implies at least one other thing to which the first is related.[20] As a quality, intrinsic goodness supposedly has the following characteristics:

Intrinsic goodness: 1. Simple.
2. Indefinable.
3. Unique.
4. Non-natural.

Judgments of intrinsic value are cognitive assertions: they have truth value and convey information. But the assertions they make aren't empirical. They're a priori, known by reason. These judgments are intuitive. By calling these judgments intuitions, Moore says he means only that they're incapable of proof; but in fact his treatment of them suggests he thinks they are known a priori.

Like Perry, Moore also thinks that "duty" and "right" (deontic terms) are definable by "good" (a value term).[21]

Duty = def. "[T]hat action, which will cause more good to exist in the Universe than any possible alternative. And what is 'right'... only differs from this, as what will *not* cause *less* good than any possible alternative."[22]

So for Moore and Perry both, judgments of moral rightness reduce, in the end, to judgments of value. They are judgments of extrinsic value, about what things lead to good. In this sense, the deontic realm reduces to the value realm. But then Perry thinks that the value realm is reducible further, to the natural order (that is, to natural properties), whereas Moore thinks that it is not. For Moore (as for Plato) the value realm is autonomous, independent of the natural order.

13.12 THE NATURALISTIC FALLACY

As noted earlier (section 13.7), some philosophers think that ethical naturalism is guilty of a basic error, what Moore calls the naturalistic fallacy. In broadest terms, the supposed fallacy is the denial of the autonomy of ethics by trying to reduce it to something it is not. More narrowly (as we shall consider it), it is the supposed fallacy of reducing ethics specifically to the natural order.

As this issue defines much of metaethical debate, it is important to understand it. The basis for the issue is found in a famous passage from David Hume (1711–1776):

In every system of morality, which I have hitherto met with, I have always remark'd, that the author proceeds for some time in the ordinary way of reasoning, and establishes the being of a God, or makes observations concerning human affairs; when of a sudden I am surpriz'd to find, that instead of the usual copulations of propositions, *is,* and *is not,* I meet with no proposition that is not connected with an *ought* or an *ought not.* This change is imperceptible; but is, however, of the last consequence. For as this *ought,* or *ought not,* expresses some new relation or affirmation, 'tis necessary that it shou'd be observ'd and explain'd; and at the same time that reason should be given, for what seems altogether inconceivable, how this new relation can be a deduction from others, which are entirely different from it.[23]

Hume's point is that from descriptive, nonmoral statements about the world—statements stating what is or is not the case—we cannot deduce moral judgments about what *ought* or *ought not* to be the case (a problem we saw in connection with natural law in section 7.8). To derive such conclusions, further reasons must be given. These reasons must contain, at least implicitly, the notion of "ought." Otherwise we commit the **naturalistic fallacy** (violating the distinction between "is" and "ought").[24]

Consider an example from Plato's dialogue, the *Gorgias.* Callicles argues that if we look at the behavior of animals and the conduct of humans when that conduct is unconstrained by conventional laws, nature shows "among men as well as among animals, and indeed among whole cities and races, that justice consists in the superior ruling over and having more than the inferior."[25] It is clear from the discussion that by the "superior" he means the strong and by the "inferior" the weak. So Callicles is asserting:

1. The strong naturally dominate the weak.

This states what supposedly is the case, that is, what can be observed in nature and human behavior. But from this he concludes that it is just (or right) that the strong dominate the weak—or (if we substitute "ought" for "just") that

2. The strong *ought* to dominate the weak.

In other words, from the alleged fact that the strong dominate the weak in the natural order, Callicles concludes that they ought to do so; he draws a moral conclusion from a statement of fact. This is the kind of shift of which Hume speaks in the above passage.

What is wrong with this? In purely logical terms, the inference from statement 1 to judgment 2 is invalid. An argument (understood here not in its usual sense, but simply as reasons and the conclusion supposedly supported by them) is valid if and only if it is impossible for the premises (or reasons) to be true and the conclusion false.

We can see that 2 doesn't follow validly from 1 because 1 is not an adequate reason by itself for asserting 2; it could be true and yet 2 be false. One cannot derive a conclusion about what *ought* to be from a premise that doesn't contain an "ought."[26] In practical terms, you might acknowledge the truth of 1 and yet quite reasonably question 2 or even deny it outright.

For example, historically men have dominated women. But it doesn't follow that they ought to do so. The Romans fed Christians to lions. But it doesn't follow that they should have done so. Some governments torture political prisoners. But that doesn't make it right. Drugs are desired by many people. But that doesn't make them good. Simply describing the behavior of animals or the conduct of people and practices of societies doesn't tell us how we should act. How the world *is* may not always be the way it *ought* to be. And no description of nonmoral facts about the world entails that they are good.

There are actually two distinctions here. If we take Is to stand for non-moral statements of fact and Ought to stand for judgments of right, duty or obligation, one distinction is between **Is/Ought.** If we take Fact to stand also for non-evaluative statements of fact and Value to stand for judgments of what is good or bad, the other distinction is between **Fact/Value.** Violation of either of these distinctions is thought to commit the naturalistic fallacy.

The complaint against definitional naturalism is that it defines ethical terms in such a way that ethical judgments follow, as a matter of definition, from nonmoral facts about the world, and hence violates either or both of these distinctions. Thus in Perry's theory,

1. X is an object of desire,

would entail (by virtue of the definition of "good" as "any object of any interest")

2. X is good.

Anti-naturalists sometimes allege that the error of such theories can be shown by means of a simple test, the open-question argument.

13.13 THE OPEN-QUESTION ARGUMENT

The open-question argument (OQA) is directed against definitional natural-ism.[27] But it can, with modification, be used against ontological naturalism as well.

A. Consider first definitional naturalism. Suppose it is proposed that "good" can properly be defined by reference to some non-ethical term ("NET") referring to a natural property "N" (e.g., "being pleasurable," "being desired," "being approved," etc.).

Good = def. NET.

Suppose that some thing, X, has N.

1. X has N.

Suppose then that someone asks,

2. But is X good?

If the definition (listed above) were correct, according to the anti-naturalist, 2 would be equivalent to asking

3. But does X have N?

which we would already know (by virtue of 1). If X has N, then it obviously isn't an open question whether it has N. But, says the critic, it is *always* an open question whether something that has any natural property is good (e.g., drugs have the property of being desired, but it doesn't follow that they're good). This shows that any naturalistic definition is incorrect.

Similarly, if the definition were correct, the statement

4. X is good,

should (given [1]) amount to nothing more than the assertion

5. X is N,

which would be redundant (if X has N then obviously X has N). And the statement

6. X is not good,

should (again given [1]) be equivalent to saying

7. X doesn't have N,

which would be contradictory (it can't be the case that X has N and X doesn't have N). The point is that if the naturalistic definition were correct, we should expect that questions like 2 aren't open questions, and statements like 4 and 6 are respectively redundant and contradictory. But they aren't. For any natural property, according to the critic, if something has that natural property, it still makes sense to ask whether it is good. And if something has that property, we can assert that it is good without redundancy or deny that it is good without contradiction.

So the results we should expect if the naturalistic definition were correct aren't forthcoming. Hence the definition is incorrect. "Good" cannot properly be defined by reference to any non-ethical term.

The naturalist has a possible reply, however. It is to say that even if it could be shown that the words "good" and "N" have different meanings (hence can't be defined in terms of one another), that wouldn't necessarily show that they can't refer to the same property. In the first case we're talking about identity of meaning between two linguistic items (words), in the second we're talking about absolute identity between two ontological entities (properties). Just as the property of being a horse differs from the word "horse," so the property of being good differs from the word "good."[28] The words "good" and "NET" might differ in meaning (as the OQA purports to show) but still refer to the same natural property.[29]

This reply on the part of the naturalist would, however, require giving up definitional naturalism in favor of ontological naturalism.

B. To refute the ontological naturalist, one must show that the following claim is incorrect: **Goodness (the property) is identical with N (the property).** So consider this modification of the OQA: Suppose now we ask the following question (and make the following assertions), not now about some X which has the property N, but about the property N itself:
    1. Is N good?
    2. N is good.
    3. N is not good.

If these are significant in the same ways ([1] being an open question, [2] non-redundant, and [3] non-self-contradictory), then again it may be supposed that the naturalist account is incorrect.

Whether we ask about *what* has N, as in A, or about N *itself*, as in B, the outcomes are supposed to show that naturalism is incorrect.

In A and B the assertions (and questions) are about the property N, not words referring to N. On the face of it, it would seem that *if* the OQA works against definitional naturalism (i.e., against naturalistic definitions of "good" in terms of NETs), it should work equally against ontological naturalism (the identification of the property goodness with the property N). That is, it should refute equally the following two theses:

A. The proper definition of "good" is as "NET."
B. Goodness (the property) is identical to N (the property).

In A, the claim is that there is an equivalence of meaning between the definiendum "good"(that which is defined), and the definiens "NET"(that which constitutes the definition). These are *linguistic expressions*. In the case of B, the claim is that there is an identity between the property goodness and the property N. These are *ontological entities*. The OQA, if sound, presumably refutes both claims. According to the anti-naturalist, ethical naturalism in both its definitional and ontological forms is mistaken.

There is, however, a third possible form of ethical naturalism, a variant of ontological naturalism. The naturalist might claim, not that "good" (or "right" or whatever) refers to the same natural property as some non-ethical word, "N," but that "good" refers to a *unique* moral property. It's just that this property is a natural property. If a naturalist were to maintain this, his position would be strikingly similar in one respect to that of the intuitionists. The word "good" would stand for a real property of goodness. But that property would be unique in the sense that it couldn't be defined, or properly referred to, by any other term or identified with any other property. The difference from intuitionism would be that the property would be a *natural* property, not, as intuitionists think, a non-natural property. The question then would be how we know such a property, whether empirically (as the naturalist maintains) or a priori (as the intuitionist maintains).

13.14 THE ERROR THEORY

One theory that exploits the problems in dealing with that question is called the error theory. It maintains, in short, that ethical words are *putatively* property-referring. Indeed, there is a striking grammatical similarity between the sentences

1. X is red.
2. X is good.

"Red" is a paradigm property-referring word. When we say that a rose is red, we believe that we are saying something about that particular rose (or about roses in general). We believe that we are making a cognitive assertion and saying something about the actual world.

When we say "X is good" (or "right," "wrong," "obligatory," etc.) we have these same beliefs. We *think* we are attributing a property of goodness to things. But in fact we are not. There is no such property. We are systematically mistaken when we make moral judgments, consistently in error. This would be a variation on the views considered in section 11.12 in connection with the possibility that ethical relativists and universalists might be mistaken about the truth of their theories.

In its more extreme form, this theory would say that our moral judgments are in fact all false. It's not merely that we believe we're making objective assertions about the world but are mistaken (which is consistent with our moral judgments actually serving a different function from what we believe them to serve); it's that our moral judgments do actually ascribe properties to things but those properties don't exist. Hence our moral judgments are false.

Some philosophers concede to the error theorist that we do in fact believe that moral terms refer to objective properties They say we do in fact believe that we're making objective assertions about the world, which are true or false, when we make moral judgments. Indeed, some philosophers make this fact a central one—one that ethical theory must deal with—as does contemporary ethicist, Stephen Darwall:

> Our normative ethical thought and feeling seems to commit us to something like objectivity, correctness, and truth in ethics. The philosophy of ethics, therefore,

must explain how ethics can admit of objectivity and truth, explain how ethical thought and discourse can justifiably proceed without these, or, somehow explain ethics away.[30]

Some, however, are skeptical of this psychological claim about what we believe (college freshmen, for example, are stereotypically alleged to be subjectivists and relativists in their thinking about ethics). Others—whether they accept this claim or not—deny flatly that moral judgments *in fact* function to ascribe objective properties to and make assertions about the world. So we must distinguish three questions:

1. Do we believe that moral terms are property-referring?
2. Are moral terms in fact property-referring?
3. If moral terms are in fact property-referring, do the properties to which they refer actually exist?

The first is a factual question that should be answerable by sufficiently careful empirical investigation, perhaps of a psychological sort questions (2) and (3) are distinctively philosophical. Question (2) is at least in part a linguistic question, about the role of ethical terms in our language, and whether those terms can fail to be property-referring even if we believe they are, or be property-referring even if we believe they aren't; (3) is an ontological question, about whether moral properties (and facts) are real.

Some philosophers think that it is not the job of metaethics (or of philosophical ethics generally) to try to answer empirical questions like (1). But they do think it is the job of metaethics to answer question (2), and they answer it No. Because question (3) doesn't arise unless one answers (2) Yes, question (3) doesn't arise for those philosophers. Those who hold these views are noncognitivists in ethics.

13.15 NONCOGNITIVISM

Noncognitivists tend to agree with intuitionists that naturalists commit the naturalistic fallacy as demonstrated by the OQA. But they disagree with both intuitionists and naturalists that moral terms refer to properties and that moral judgments are cognitive assertions. Rather, in the simpler versions to which we will limit ourselves, they hold that ethical terms express feelings and emotions. Accordingly, the moral judgments in which ethical terms occur aren't true or false and don't convey information about the world.

For both ethical naturalists and intuitionists there is such a thing as *moral knowledge*. For noncognitivists there is not. For them (to oversimplify), moral judgments, rather than conveying knowledge, function to show how we feel about things and to try to get others to feel the same way. Ethics can't be a science, in the sense of a systematic body of knowledge (as, in various ways, intuitionists and naturalists believe), because there is no such knowledge to be had.

Thus, in this view, the judgment "Abortion is wrong" wouldn't attribute a property of wrongness to abortion. Rather, it would express the speaker's disapproval of abortion and would function to try to get the hearer to share that disapproval (contrast this with the discussion in section 11.6, which deals with what we can now see to be forms of ethical naturalism, theories according to which such sentences do make statements).

This isn't simply abstract theorizing. It represents a way of understanding some genuine differences among people making moral judgments. If, for example, you believe that God prohibits abortion (and that God's prohibitions determine what is wrong), then in saying that abortion is wrong, you would, in effect, be saying that abortion possesses the property of being prohibited by God. That would be a supernatural or metaphysical property. In making that claim, you would be siding with both the metaphysical ethicist and the realist. You would believe that there is an actual, objective property possessed by the practice of abortion that renders it wrong. On the other hand, if you think that moral language simply expresses how people feel about practices like abortion, then in saying that abortion is wrong you would understand yourself to be merely expressing your disapproval of it, not to be stating any objective fact about the world.

Noncognitivism, like cognitivism, stands for a family of theories, some very complex. We can't do justice to their differences here, but we may define a prototypical type of noncognitivism called **emotivism,** as follows:

> Emotivism = def. Any theory according to which
> 1. Moral terms don't refer to properties, either natural, supernatural or non-natural.
> 2. Moral judgments are neither true nor false and don't convey information.
> 3. Moral language functions primarily to express the feelings and emotions of the speaker and to redirect the feelings and emotions of others.

In fact, some emotivists don't hold thesis (1) in as bald a form as this. They allow that, in some of their uses, moral terms do refer to properties (that is, have conceptual or descriptive meaning); it's just that such meaning is secondary to their "emotive" meaning—the expression of feelings and attitudes. Likewise, regarding (2), emotivists concede that there are senses in which it is perfectly intelligible to speak of moral judgments as true or false. It is just that these senses aren't important philosophically and do not alter the fact that, in their primary uses, moral judgments are not literally true or false and do not report information.

Exploration of all of these permutations of noncognitivism would take us too far afield, however; so we shall confine ourselves to the rudimentary theory characterized by (1), (2), and (3), above.

If moral terms are not property-referring, then of course they can't be defined, since any definition will make reference to properties possessed by things to which the term applies. Thus, naturalistic definitions will, according to noncognitivists, all be, in some fundamental way, mistaken. Noncognitivists tend to agree with intuitionists in this assessment. They sometimes allege that the naturalist has committed the naturalistic fallacy, and therefore often use the OQA, as intuitionists do, to try to show the error of ethical naturalism.

13.16 FROM MEANING TO USE

But noncognitivists also object to intuitionism as well. Their main objection is that cognitivist theories (principally intuitionism and naturalism, but metaphysical ethics as well) cannot explain how moral judgments guide conduct—and the guidance of conduct is their main function.

Philosophically, this marks a major shift. Recall that in section 13.2 we posed the question:

I. What is the proper understanding of moral terms?

and then we said that many think the best way to answer this question is by answering the subsidiary questions:

A1: What are the meanings of ethical terms?

A2: What are the definitions of ethical terms?

which require answering the prior question:

A3: Are ethical terms definable?

It is these questions that frame much of the metaethical debate we have been considering thus far. But many noncognitivists, though they think question I is important, take a different route to answering it. Instead of asking about the meanings of ethical terms, as A1 does, they ask:

B1: What are the *uses* (or functions) of ethical terms?

They recognize that language may have a variety of functions. To describe and report facts (as cognitivists emphasize) is only one of them. To guide conduct, to express emotions, to influence attitudes are others. And it is within these other uses that the proper understanding of moral language is to be found. Accordingly, they tend to say either that ethical terms are not definable—or that they are not definable in any philosophically important way.

Such noncognitivsts break with the tradition (going back to Socrates and Plato) that approaches philosophical issues by asking for definitions and trying to clarify meaning by way of them.

Predictably, things aren't quite this simple, however. Noncognitivsts sometimes preserve the term "meaning"—but distinguish between cognitive and "noncognitive meaning,"—subsuming under "noncognitive meaning" the uses of language alluded to in B1. Whether they speak of "noncognitive" as opposed to "noncognitive meaning" (in which case question A1 for them is tantamount to asking question B1), or distinguish sharply between meaning and use (in which case, at the outset, they bypass question A1 in favor of B1), their approach marks a major philosophical shift in emphasis. Let us try to understand the implications of this shift.

13.17 THE NONCOGNITIVIST OBJECTION TO COGNITIVISM

Philosophers since the time of Aristotle have recognized a distinction between theoretical reason and practical reason—between the use of reason for gaining knowledge and understanding the world—and the use of reason for making practical (including moral) decisions. Any plausible account of the nature of moral judgments, most philosophers now agree, must reflect this.

Moral judgments, in other words, are action-guiding. Purely cognitive statements (for example, "Water boils at 212 degrees") are not. Although they are needed to make practical decisions, they do not themselves tell us what to do or not to do. Moral language, in short, simply functions differently from purely descriptive or informative (some would say "scientific") language.

Put simply, then, the objection to cognitivism is as follows:

A. If cognitivism is correct, moral judgments do not guide conduct.
B. Moral judgments do guide conduct.
C. Therefore, cognitivism is false.

We guide conduct by making evaluations and prescribing what people ought or ought not to do or by telling them what is right and wrong. No collection of purely descriptive statements does this.

Consider a Rembrandt painting. Suppose you describe the painting in detail, identifying the type of paint, its manner of application, the colors used, the dimensions of the canvas, its weight, and so on. You could subject the painting to microscopic examination as well, compiling a list of finely-detailed statements describing the painting. No such collection of descriptive (or cognitive) statements would add up to the judgment that the painting is beautiful. That's a value judgment. And, noncognitivists would say, it's a different *kind* of judgment from the factual statements describing the painting.

The same is true of actions. We could describe them in as fine a detail as we like. But such descriptive statements, though informative, wouldn't tell us whether the actions were right or wrong, or whether anyone ought or ought not to perform them. Nor would a mere description of an object tell us whether it is good. Deontic and value language simply function differently from purely cognitive language.

Why do noncognitivists think that premise A (above) is true? That is (assuming—what is relatively uncontroversial—that B is true, and that moral judgments guide conduct), why suppose that cognitivists cannot account for this?

The implicit reasoning goes as follows:

1. If cognitivism is correct, then moral terms are either (a) property-referring or (b) definable, or both.
2. If moral terms are either (a) property-referring or (b) definable, or both, then they are terms used only (or primarily) for the process of describing.
3. If moral terms are used only (or primarily) for the process of describing, then moral judgments are used only (or primarily) for the process of describing.

4. If moral judgments are used only (or primarily) for the process of describing, then they don't guide conduct.
5. Therefore, if cognitivism is correct, moral judgments do not guide conduct.

The point is that critics of cognitivism focus upon the standard cognitivist account of moral terms and moral judgments, arguing that it precludes moral judgments from performing the distinctive function they have in morality; and hence, that cognitivism is defective.

13.18 POSSIBLE COGNITIVIST REPLIES

The cognitivist might challenge premises (2) and (3), contending that being descriptive doesn't prevent language from also guiding conduct. To illustrate this contention, the cognitivist might cite the functions of a clearly nonmoral, descriptive term like "yellow," which refers to a natural property. In the following sentences, the term is used to perform the functions identified in the parentheses:

1. This magic maker is yellow. (to describe)
2. Is that your yellow marker? (to inquire)
3. He's yellow [i.e., cowardly]. (to defame)
4. Go Yellowjackets! (to cheer something on, for example, an athletic team)
5. That's a nice yellow sweater you're wearing. (to compliment)

The word "yellow" is a paradigm property-referring, descriptive term.[31] Yet in these possible uses, only (1) is used to describe something. This suggests that there is no necessary connection between a term's being property-referring and its being used only to describe. It's questionable whether property-referring terms are used even *primarily* to describe. It's easy to conclude that they are so used because we often speak of property-referring words as descriptive words, and this facilitates a transition to the assumption that they're used only or primarily for descriptive purposes.

Consider further the possible uses of the following descriptive sentences:

6. That ice is thin.
7. That road is mined.
8. The water from that faucet is polluted.
9. There's a tarantula crawling up your sleeve.
10. There are man-eating tigers in that forest.

None of these sentences contain ethical words. The language is descriptive. Yet each sentence, in the appropriate context, might be action-guiding.

If descriptive terms and the cognitive sentences in which they occur may (in addition to, and indeed by way of conveying information) be action-guiding, then cognitivists may argue that there is no reason why moral judgments, understood as cognitive, may not also be action-guiding. In other words, property-referring terms, even if used for describing, may at the same time guide conduct; and some of them may even be used primarily for guiding conduct.

Language may be sufficiently flexible, and its ontological implications insufficiently clear, that we cannot rule out the possibility that moral judgments are both cognitive and action-guiding.

A second possible cognitivist response is to deny that language has anything to do with the proper understanding of morality; and hence to challenge the whole linguistic orientation of much of metaethics. The following passage, from contemporary ethicist Nicholas Sturgeon, is illustrative:

> So, most generally, I think of ethical naturalism as I have said as a metaphysical thesis, just as it appears to be. It holds that there are ethical properties and facts, and that they belong to a certain category, that of natural properties and facts. It is not in the first instance a doctrine about language at all.[32]

This approach associates ethical naturalism (a form of cognitivism) essentially with moral realism rather than with any particular linguistic theory. In the definition of cognitivism above, it stresses the fact that moral terms are property-referring (a metaphysical thesis) rather than that they are definable (a linguistic thesis). For them, the central issue isn't to understand ethical language; it is to answer the question:

II.   What is the proper understanding of ethical properties and/or facts?

Understanding morality, and the nature of moral judgment, which is the topic of this chapter, would require launching an inquiry directly into the ontology of morals rather than approaching it by a linguistic route.

We cannot go into the particulars of such a theory here, or evaluate the philosophical issues raised by the tension between the linguistic and metaphysical approaches. The point, however, is that much of recent metaethical debate has to do with the answer to the question of what is the best approach for understanding moral judgments (see question A in section 13.2). Is it, as question A1, A2, and A3 presume, by trying to understand ethical language? Or is it by trying to understand the metaphysics of morality?

There are, in contemporary metaethics, resurgent forms of intuitionism, naturalism, and cognitivism that try to answer the long-standing objections to each type of theory and to demonstrate the superiority of one over the others.

Notes

1. G. E. Moore, *Principia Ethica* (Cambridge: Cambridge University Press, 1903), p. 5.

2. Since all of these terms can be used in both moral and nonmoral senses, they could with equal plausibility be called normative terms. Since our concern is with their moral uses, we shall call them "ethical" terms.

3. G. E. Moore, *Principia Ethica* (Cambridge: Cambridge University Press, 1903), p. 89.

4. A. C. Ewing, *The Definition of Good* (London: Routledge & Kegan Paul Ltd, 1948), p. 148f.

5. A. I. Melden, *Rights and Right Conduct* (London: Basil Blackwell, 1959), p. 20. Melden is here paraphrasing A. C. Ewing.

6. See Michael Slote, "Virtue Ethics," in Marcia W. Baron, Philip Pettit, and Michael Slote, eds., *Three Methods of Ethics* (Malden, MA: Blackwell Publishers, 1997), p. 177.

7. Natural Law Ethics, as we saw (section 7.1), also holds that morality is part of the natural order, but it tends to interpret "natural order" more broadly than contemporary naturalists—and natural law ethicists aren't usually considered ethical naturalists. They are, however, moral realists in a sense that will be defined in section 13.9.

8. Although ethical naturalists are also typically metaphysical naturalists, they needn't be. A naturalistic account of ethics doesn't commit one to a naturalistic account of all there is.

9. A. C. Ewing, *The Definition of Good*, p. 78.

10. A. C. Ewing, *The Definition of Good*, p. 78.

11. Here I am following the reasoning of Moore in *Principia Ethica*.

12. Notice that intuitionists maintain that "good" stands for a simple, indefinable, non-natural property only insofar as we are talking about intrinsic goodness (see section 13.11). Insofar as "good" is used in the sense of extrinsic goodness, it is a complex notion and, in principle, definable.

13. The concept of God poses special problems, since God (if there is one) is said to exist and yet to be eternal.

14. In this context, the definition of the term "conceptual meaning" is that moral terms express or symbolize intelligible concepts, to the degree that the concepts are capable of conveying information when properly used. If concepts are understood as properties, then condition (b) is unnecessary. If, however, concepts are understood as ideas or mental representations, then they are distinguishable from properties.

15. By "essentially" conveying information, the moral judgments don't merely suggest or call information to mind but convey it as part of their proper function.

16. See Ralph Barton Perry, *General Theory of Value* (Cambridge: Harvard University Press, 1954), Ch. 5, and *Realms of Value* (Cambridge: Harvard University Press, 1954), Ch. 1.

17. Ralph Barton Perry, *Realms of Value*, Ch. 7.

18. Ralph Barton Perry, *Realms of Value*, p. 106.

19. Precisely what the relationship is between intrinsic value (a non-natural property) and the intrinsic nature of possesses it (which will consist of natural properties), Moore, in the end, is unable to say—other than that the intrinsic value depends upon those natural properties. In contemporary parlance, the relationship is said to be one of supervenience.

20. We're ignoring a host of philosophical issues here, such as whether supposedly secondary qualities like color can in fact characterize things in isolation from a perceiver, and whether things in isolation might possess the putatively relational property of being identical with themselves.

21. For the record, Moore changes this view in his later book, *Ethics* (1912), in which he maintains that "right" as well as "good" is indefinable.

21. G. E. Moore, *Principia Ethica* (Cambridge: Cambridge University Press, 1903), p. 148.

23. David Hume, *A Treatise of Human Nature*, Bk. III, Pt. I, Sect. I. Reprinted from the original edition (1739) in three volumes, ed. L. A. Selby-Bigge (Oxford, England: At the Clarendon Press, 1958), p. 469. Claren edition originally published in 1888.

24. While the naturalistic fallacy is often understood in terms of the distinction between "is" and "ought," it applies also to attempts to deduce any moral judgments about right and wrong, or about good and bad, exclusively from nonmoral descriptive statements.

25. *Gorgias* 484, in *The Dialogues of Plato*, vol. 1, tr. B. Jowett (New York: Random House, 1937), p. 544.

26. There are some trivial counterexamples to this in logic which need not concern us. We should also note that a premise's containing an "ought" isn't sufficient for allowing us to draw a conclusion about what ought to be. In discussions of cultural diversity one finds statements such as, "Some fundamentalist Moslems believe adulterers ought to be stoned to death." These statements contain an "ought"—but one from which one cannot validly conclude anything about morality. Such statements are still basically "is" statements (descriptive, nonmoral, and factual) about the beliefs of some people, rather than prescriptive moral judgments about what ought to be the case.

27. The Open Question Argument can also be used against theological and metaphysical theories. We considered a variation of it against the Divine Command Theory in section 6.13.

28. And, depending upon how we understand concepts, both the word and the object may differ from the concept of goodness.

29. In support of this, it's sometimes pointed out that words with different meanings can have the same referent. Thus "Mark Twain" and "Samuel Clemens" refer to the same person, "The Morning Star" and "The Evening Star" to the same planet, and "Water" and "H20" to the same substance. Differences of meaning at the linguistic level don't preclude identity of the referents at the ontological level. But in each of these cases the referent is an *object* (or substance), something which has properties but is not itself a property. Whether the same holds of words referring to properties is less clear. That is what one would have to show to establish that "Good" and "N" can have different meanings and yet refer to the same property.

30. Stephen Darwall, *Philosophical Ethics* (Boulder, Colo.: Westview Press, 1998), p. 26.

31. "Yellow" isn't, however, definable, so we would need examples of definable property-referring words that are action-guiding in order to fully cover the cognitivist position as characterized above.

32. Nicholas Sturgeon, "Moore on Ethical Naturalism," *Ethics*, Vol. 113, No. 3, April 2003, p. 537.

Discussion Questions

1. It is sometimes said that philosophical questions are simply a more comprehensive and systematic treatment of the questions an ordinary person asks in the course of moral thinking and discussion. Do you think this is true of metaethical questions of the sort examined in this chapter? Have you encountered concerns or questions, in your own thinking or in discussion with others, that could easily lead to metaethical questions? What are they?

2. Much of the discussion in this chapter presupposes a fairly sharp distinction between ethical terms (our Ethical Vocabulary) and non-ethical terms. Some philosophers have questioned whether there is such a sharp distinction. What do you think? Can you think of any words that appear to be non-ethical but that in fact conceal evaluations or moral judgments? How about "courageous," "patriotic," "democratic"?

3. Ethical autonomists say it is a mistake to reduce ethics to something it is not. But a reductionist (e.g., an ethical naturalist) might say that if ethical terms can properly be defined in terms of non-ethical terms, or moral facts be reduced to natural facts, then that is simply the correct account of what morality is, and morality, therefore, isn't being reduced to anything it isn't. How would you evaluate this reply?

4. On the basis of your reading, do you think the naturalistic fallacy is actually an error committed by naturalists? Or can one derive an Ought from an Is, a Value from a Fact? Does it follow from the fact that you're speaking to someone that you ought to speak the truth? Or, from the fact that you've promised to do something, that you ought to do it?

5. Do you believe (as the Error Theory surmises) that when you make moral judgments you're making objective assertions about the actual world? Do you think most people believe this? If so, should philosophers take that into account in their development of ethical theories? If not, how should that belief be reflected in ethical theory?

6. Does cognitivism or noncognitivism seem to you the most plausible approach to understanding the nature of moral judgments? Why? How would you defend your answer against objections by those who believe otherwise?

. . . only feminist moral theory can adequately understand the alternatives to traditional moral theory that the experience of women requires.[1]
Virginia Held

14 CHAPTER | Feminist Ethics

14.1 QUESTIONING TRADITIONAL ETHICS

We have seen grounds for skepticism about the possibility of justifying moral principles. This skepticism does not mean that none of the theories we have considered may not yet be correct. But it at least provides reason to look seriously at other alternatives.

Considerations such as those examined in the previous chapter have led recent writers increasingly to emphasize the uniqueness of particular situations and what they see as the inadequacy of a rule-oriented approach to morality. They have not all agreed about what a more satisfactory approach would be. But all see themselves as departing radically from traditional ethical theories—particularly, in many cases, those with a Kantian or contractarian orientation. As Annette Baier writes from a feminist perspective:

> The recent research of Carol Gilligan has shown us how intelligent and reflective twentieth-century women see morality, and how different their picture of it is from that of men, particularly the men who eagerly assent to the claims of currently orthodox contractarian-Kantian moral theories. Women cannot now, any more than they could when oppressed, ignore that part of morality and those forms of trust which cannot easily be forced into the liberal and particularly the contractarian mold. Men may but women cannot see morality as essentially a matter of keeping to the minimal moral traffic rules, designed to restrict close encounters between autonomous persons to self-chosen ones.[2]

In the remainder of this chapter we shall consider feminist ethics, which in most of its contemporary forms shares this questioning of traditional ethics and seeks to understand morality in a way that emphasizes concrete situations of choice.

14.2 WHAT IS FEMINIST ETHICS?

In most general terms, feminist ethics may be characterized as any ethics espoused by feminists *qua* feminists. Much of such ethics consists of factual claims about the treatment of women and judgments about the wrongness of that treatment; as such, it belongs properly to substantive ethics. Our concern, however, will be with *feminist ethical theory* (and by "feminist ethics" we shall henceforth mean feminist ethical theory), which itself is an umbrella term for a range of theories of considerable diversity. These theories are still evolving as thinking about women's issues advances. Although their diversity is so great as to make it difficult to define feminist ethics in more specific terms, it is nonetheless possible to distinguish three general categories of feminist ethics according to the judgments they express and the types to which those judgments belong. Among those judgments (though by no means exhaustive of them) are the following:

A.   **Substantive Ethics**
1. Women are inherently equal to men.
2. Women and men have the same human rights.
3. Women ought to be treated as equal to men, in worth, respect, and rights.
4. Women are superior (inherently and/or morally) to men.
5. Women ought to dominate men.

B.   **Metaethics**
6. Women's experience should weigh equally with men's in ethical theorizing.
7. Feminist ethics must be grounded in a proper understanding of gender.
8. Feminism must construct a new ethics.
9. Men and women have different moralities.
10. Masculine ethics appeals to principles, feminine ethics to particulars.
11. Masculine ethics is individualistic, feminist ethics relational.
12. Male ethics is rights-oriented, feminist ethics caring-oriented.
13. Feminism makes a fundamental shift in the valuation of good and evil.
14. Feminist ethics must move beyond justice to the alleviation of suffering.

C.   **History of Ethics**
15. Traditional ethical theory has a male bias.
16. Traditional ethics is misogynistic.
17. The male agent is the model for Anglo-European ethics.
18. Western ethics is androcentric.
19. Western ethics is meant for the public market place, not the private realm.
20. Standard moral theory is male-dominated.
21. Traditional ethics ignores questions of importance to women.

D. **Epistemology and Metaphysics**
   22. Moral reasoning differs in males and females.
   23. Male and female thinking differ on the nature of truth.
   24. Male and female thinking differ on relations between:
       a. mind/body
       b. reason/emotion
       c. public/private
       d. absolute/concrete
       e. self/other
       f. culture/nature
   25. Masculine thinking distorts reality.
   26. Western science, epistemology, and metaphysics have distinctively male patterns.
   27. Women have a special moral vision.
   28. All knowledge is constructed.
E. **Sociology and Psychology**
   29. Society is patriarchal, with male domination of females.
   30. Patriarchy falsely distinguishes public from private.
   31. Women in patriarchy are considered evil.
   32. Conventional scholarship supports patriarchy.
   33. Western philosophy, ethics, and social thought are androcentric.
   34. Liberalism has a male bias.
   35. Males control language.
   36. Grammar is used by men to deceive.
   37. Women are "moronized" by being led to accept "male" texts as true.
   38. Femininity traps women in heteronomy.
   39. The intent of gynecology is to control women.
   40. The Anglo-European model of male moral agency emphasizes isolation, egoism, and competitiveness.
   41. Lesbianism threatens male supremacy.
   42. Heterosexuality helps maintain male supremacy.
   43. There is a men's culture and a women's culture.
   44. The person is socially constituted.
F. **Theology**
   45. God is conceived in a masculine image.
   46. Woman is held responsible for original sin.
G. **Biology**
   47. Sexuality is at the root of women's oppression.
   48. Sexuality maintains and defines male supremacy as a political system.

We may take **minimalist feminist ethics** to be any theory that holds one or more of (1), (2), and (3) *and* claims that the moral considerations contained therein define a central (even *the* central) concern of ethics.[3]

We may take **standard feminist ethics** to be any theory that holds what is maintained by minimalist feminist ethics *and* typically holds at least (6), (7), and (8) from Category B and one or more propositions from each of categories C, D, and E.

Finally we may take **radical feminist ethics** to be any theory that holds:

(a) Either (4) or (5) from Category A; at least (7) and (8) from Category B; and one or more propositions from categories C, D, and E; *and claims*

(b) that traditional ethical theory, conventional scholarship, and society as a whole (culturally, educationally, politically, and economically) are part of a system of subordination of women that needs to be overthrown in favor of radical feminist values and norms.

So understood, each of these types of feminist ethics can encompass many different theories varying in points of detail. Some feminists suggest the need to move beyond ethics altogether, but we shall not consider that position here. And some maintain that substantive ethics and metaethics (and perhaps metaphysics and epistemology as well), are all of a piece, and that to compartmentalize them as we have above is to obscure their interconnections. Whether that is true or not, the above should not be taken to foreclose that possibility. It may be, finally, that much of feminist ethics should be thought of as an undifferentiated blend of substantive ethics, applied ethics, and ethical theory (both normative and metaethical) in varying proportions.[4] If that should be true, then attention to theory would capture only one dimension of such ethics.

Because of limitations of space we shall confine ourselves to aspects of feminist ethics that relate most directly to the sorts of issues discussed throughout the rest of the book. That, of course, uses a principle of selection that gives priority to mainstream moral philosophy (by which I shall mean Anglo-American ethics). As that is part of what comes in for criticism in much of standard feminist ethics and virtually all of radical feminist ethics, some may consider this approach suspect from the start. Be that as it may, if, as some feminist ethicists also maintain, there is no wholly neutral ground from which to discuss these issues, then we have no choice but to start from some non-neutral standpoint or the other; so we shall proceed in this way, acknowledging at the outset its possible limitations.

Let us begin by exploring in a little more detail each of the types of feminist ethical theory just characterized.

14.3 MINIMALIST FEMINIST ETHICS: WOLLSTONECRAFT'S RIGHTS-BASED THEORY

Mary Wollstonecraft (1759–1797), in her *Vindication of the Rights of Woman*,[5] maintains that there is one morality for men and women and that it is universalistic. There is, likewise, one truth for men and women. But because of the historical subjugation of women, only men have been accorded full human rights. Not only have women been subjugated by men, they have also been taught to be subservient and thereby to participate in their own oppression. Obedience has been among the cardinal virtues fostered in women. Having been led to accept their inferior status, women have cultivated ways to exercise what limited power they can from their position of disadvantage. Thus Wollstonecraft says, "What arts have I not seen silly women use to interrupt by *flirtation*—a very significant word to describe such a maneuver—a rational conversation, which made the men forget they were pretty women."(p. 181) Women, she believes, need to become aware of the nature and extent of their oppression and of the ways they have been beguiled into helping perpetuate it.

As measured by historical achievement, women indeed appear inferior to men, Wollstonecraft says. But that is because they have been denied their full rights. Their "inferiority" is socially determined, not inherent to their sex. The remedy is full equality of rights with men and education that empowers women to think and act for themselves. The cultivation of reason is the key. "I love man as my fellow"; she says in a passage of which Kant would have approved, "but his sceptre, real or usurped, extends not to me, unless the reason of an individual demands my homage; and even then the submission is to reason, and not to man. In fact, the conduct of an accountable being must be regulated by the operations of its own reason; or on what foundation rests the throne of God?"(p. 29) Autonomy—the capacity to live your life as you choose—thus becomes a central notion for Wollstonecraft. In speaking of "accountability," she implies that moral agency—the capacity to act freely according to standards of right and wrong—requires that people be able to act in accordance with the dictates of their own reason (much as Kant maintained). Thus Wollstonecraft's critique is rights-based, rooted in entitlement concepts.

The oppression of women, she contends, undermines morality both in theory and in practice. With regard to theory:

1. If reason is subverted in women through their being taught to be subordinate, and if reason is essential to the flourishing of morality, then morality itself is undermined by the oppression of women.
2. If women have no rights, they also have no duties; and if they have no duties, then morality is truncated, applying only to half of humanity.
3. Even if women were inherently inferior to men, their virtues would be the same in quality, if not in degree; "consequently their conduct should be founded on the same principles, and have the same aim."(p. 18)

With regard to practice Wollstonecraft says, "It has long since occurred to me that advice respecting behaviour, and all the various modes of preserving a good reputation, which have been so strenuously inculcated on the female world, were specious poisons, that encrusting morality eat away the substance. (p. 131) . . . It was natural for women then to endeavour to preserve what once lost—was lost for ever, till this care swallowing up every other care, *reputation for chastity, became the one thing needful to the sex.*"[italics added] (p. 133) So we may say that from the standpoint of the practice of morality:

4. Rules to preserve reputation in women have come to supercede those regarding moral obligation. Accordingly,
5. Women's reason [as devoted to the preservation of reputation] is used to strengthen rather than break the chains of their repression.

Finally, with regard to the practical cultivation of virtue, those qualities are fostered in women that ensure their subordination to men:

Gentleness, docility, and a spaniel-like affection are, on this ground, consistently recommended as the cardinal virtues of [women] . . . and, disregarding the arbitrary economy of nature, one writer has declared that it is masculine for a woman to be melancholy. She was created to be the toy of man, his rattle, and it must jingle in his ears whenever, dismissing reason, he chooses to be amused. (p. 26)

6. Female "virtues" ensure women's submission to men.

Thus, with regard to rules, virtues, and the use of reason, ". . . morality is very insidiously undermined, in the female world, by the attention being turned to the show instead of the substance."(p. 135)

It is part of classical liberal political thought that citizenship depends upon equal rights. This suggests that if women are not accorded equal rights,[6] then not only morality, but also citizenship is undermined as well. Therefore, there is a clear sense in which men as well as women are harmed by the oppression of women. It is in everyone's interest to have a flourishing society, and that is possible only if morality and citizenship are allowed to develop to their full potential. And that requires full equality for women.

The preceding concern with rights would apply to any oppressed group. But Wollstonecraft cites a kind of wrong that, in the form it takes, arguably distinguishes the plight of women from other oppressed groups. It is a wrong that is distinguishable from the infliction of pain and suffering. Paradoxically, it can be committed even while those suffering it are treated with special consideration, such as by being spared hard physical labor or sheltered from unpleasantness. The wrong is that of *degradation*. Women might be loved and cherished, but if they are not also treated with respect, then they are degraded. As Wollstonecraft says:

Fragile in every sense of the word, [women] . . . are obliged to look up to man for every comfort. In the most trifling danger they cling to their support, with parasitical tenacity, piteously demanding succor; and their *natural* protector extends his arm, or lifts up his voice. To guard the lovely trembler—from what? Perhaps the frown of an old cow, or the jump of a mouse; a rat would be a serious danger. In the name of reason, and even common sense, what can save such beings from contempt; even though they be soft and fair.

These fears, when not affected, may produce some pretty attitudes; but they show a degree of imbecility which degrades a rational creature in a way women are not aware of—for love and esteem are very distinct things. (p. 57)

Simone de Beauvoir, feminist and existentialist philosopher in the twentieth century, sees a similarity here between slavery and sexism:

The southern planters were not altogether in the wrong in considering the negroes who docilely submitted to their paternalism as "grown-up children." To the extent that they respected the world of the whites the situation of the black slaves was exactly an infantile situation. This is also the situation of women in many civilizations; they can only submit to the laws, the gods, the customs, and the truths created by the males. Even today in western countries, among women who have not had in their work an apprenticeship of freedom, there are still many who take shelter in the shadow of men; they adopt without discussion the opinions and values recognized by their husband or their lover, and that allows them to develop childish qualities which are forbidden to adults because they are based on a feeling of irresponsibility.[7]

Wollstonecraft subscribes to propositions (1)–(3) above, and these represent the central concern of her theory. It is this that makes hers a minimalist feminist ethics. But for her, feminist ethics (though she doesn't use this term) operates within the general framework of traditional ethical theory, specifically a rights-based theory. She proceeds as though there is nothing wrong with traditional ethics *per se*, but only with the judgments it has supported and the treatment of women it has justified. She makes her case for equal treatment of women by arguing that, properly undertaken, ethical inquiry leads to radically different conclusions than has traditionally been supposed.

14.4 A STANDARD FEMINIST ETHICS: THE ETHICS OF CARING

Various ideas, some ancient, some modern, converge in the notion of an ethics of caring. The ethics is rooted in a certain way of understanding the world and our place in it. It takes caring to be central to the human condition:

> The more deeply I understand the central role of caring in my own life, the more I realize it to be central to the human condition. My world becomes intelligible for me through caring and being cared for. . . . In the sense in which intelligibility means being at home in the world, we are ultimately at home not through dominating or explaining or appreciating things, but through caring and being cared for.[8]

The point here is that there are many ways that we can relate to the world. We can dominate and exploit other people and animals and manipulate the environment. We can try to explain all things rationally, as science and much of philosophy do. We can take an appreciative interest in things, as students of art or music do, and so on.

But we can also engage others by caring. When we care for others and for other things (and we can care for animals, ideas, ideals, and projects, such as writing books or composing music, as well as people), we view them as having worth in themselves, apart from their value to us in giving us pleasure or entertainment. We can commit ourselves to helping the other grow and flourish without trying to mold it to what we want to see it become. This requires consistency, patience, honesty, trust, humility, hope, and courage. We must be willing to nurture other people in the hope and faith that they will grow in ways that are best for them and that in the process they, too, will become caring people and thereby find fulfillment. We ourselves may find fulfillment in the process, although that is not the aim. As long as we act for ourselves, as the ethical egoist does, we are not genuinely caring for others.

Thus far the ethics of caring has antecedents as far back as the ancient Chinese philosopher Lao Tzu (around the sixth century B.C.E.), who wrote,

> Giving birth and nourishing,
> having without possessing,
> acting with no expectations,
> leading and not trying to control:
> this is the supreme virtue.[9]

It also has antecedents in Buddha's conception of compassion and in Jesus' conception of love. But it has more recent antecedents in Hume's rooting of morality in sympathy in the eighteenth century and in Schopenhauer's doing the same with compassion in the nineteenth century.

Thus the father who cares for his child will nurture its growth, guiding without seeking to control. He will have faith that as it develops (in ways that may be unpredictable by him) it will achieve self-fulfillment in caring and being cared for by others. The writer who cares for the book she is writing will nurture its ideas, allowing them to acquire a life of their own, guiding but not forcing—seeming at times even to follow it, as writers often say of their novels once they have begun to develop.

Some feminists contend that caring plays a more central role in the lives of women than of men. They say this reflects a difference between an **ethics of caring** and principle-oriented theories. As Nell Noddings writes,

> . . . when we approach moral matters through the study of moral reasoning, we are led quite naturally to suppose that ethics is necessarily a subject that must be cast in the language of principle and demonstration. This, I shall argue, is a mistake.
>
> Many persons who live moral lives do not approach moral problems formally. Women . . . define themselves in terms of *caring*. . . . An ethic built upon caring is, I think, characteristically and essentially feminine—which is not to say, of course, that it cannot be shared by men any more than we should care to say that traditional moral systems cannot be embraced by women. But an ethic of caring arises, I believe, out of our experience as women, just as the traditional logical approach to ethical problems arises more obviously from masculine experience.[10]

It is sometimes claimed that this perceived role of caring in the lives of women gives rise to different ways of moral thinking, with women tending to reason in a contextualistic, particularistic fashion and men in a more abstract, rule-governed way. Associated with these different ways of thinking are two different "moralities"—a masculine morality of rights and a feminine morality of caring.

Contemporary philosopher Sara Ruddick, in her book *Maternal Thinking*, focuses more specifically upon one dimension of caring, namely, mothering. This, she believes, provides a standpoint for feminist thought, particularly as it connects with nonviolence and peacemaking. Contending that ways of thinking grow out of practical activities, she argues that "maternal thinking" grows out of the activity of mothering. Further, she seems to agree with some feminists that there is a superior feminist epistemological "standpoint." A standpoint, she says, "is an engaged vision of the world opposed and superior to dominant ways of thinking."[11] Comparing Marxism and feminism, she says:

> As a proletarian standpoint is a superior vision produced by the experience and oppressive conditions of labor, a feminist standpoint is a superior vision produced by the political conditions and distinctive work of women. (p. 129) . . . Standpoint thinkers are ready . . . to declare that dominant values are destructive and perverse and that the feminist standpoint represents the "real" appropriately human order of life. One might say that the standpoint theorists, including the maternal thinkers among them, have seen the Truth—and, indeed, many of the standpoint theorists whose invigorating work I have found indispensable seem to say just that.

> Although I count myself among standpoint theorists, I do not take the final step that some appear to take of claiming for one standpoint a Truth that is exhaustive and absolute. Epistemologically, I continue to believe that all reasons are tested by the practices from which they arise; hence justifications end in the commitments with which they begin. Although I envision a world organized by the values of caring labor, I cannot identify the grounds, reason, or god that would legitimate that vision. (pp. 134f)

Ruddick appears to hold here not only that the feminist epistemological standpoint is superior to dominant standpoints, but also that it is true, though the truth presumably is not absolute.

Ruddick's approach involves some redefinition. Typically, we think of mothers as female, fathers as male. But Ruddick understands a mother to be anyone who takes on the work of mothering. Most of such work can be done by either males or females. But not all of it. Males cannot become pregnant, give birth, or breastfeed. (p. 48) So most mothers are in fact female. Moreover, whereas to be a mother is to take on work "determined by children's needs," fatherhood is determined by cultural demands—the need to be providers and defenders. The authority of fathers, Ruddick says, "is not earned by care and indeed undermines the maternal authority that is so earned." (p. 42) Males can thus dominate and exploit the work of the mothers of their children. To transcend this genderization of roles—so that men and women can equally engage in mothering, and hence (almost) equally qualify as mothers—is a central goal of an ethics rooted in maternal thinking. The work of mothering, according to Ruddick, reflects the nonviolent ideals of renunciation (of violence), resistance, reconciliation, and peacemaking. (p. 176) Not all mothers exhibit these traits or do so all of the time, but there is a tendency in mothering to try to approximate these ideas, a "*struggle* toward nonviolence." (p. 57)

Nodding sees a male bias, not only in society and in the judgments about the worth of women's thinking, but in the very approach to ethics typical of traditional ethics. As she says:

> One might say that ethics has been discussed largely in the language of the father: in principles and propositions, in terms such as justification, fairness, justice. The Mother's voice has been silent. Human caring and the memory of caring and being cared for, which I shall argue form the foundation of ethical response, have not received attention except as outcomes of ethical behavior.[12]

In this view, traditional ethical theory is grounded in principles and preoccupied with questions of justification, fairness, and justice (presumed by this analysis to be preeminently male concerns). As such it diminishes the importance of caring, the true foundation of ethics, realized most fully in women's experiences. Criticizing what they see as Western philosophy's perpetuation of an anti-female bias, some contemporary feminists argue that: "Feminism by contrast, rejecting *a priori* the premise of male superiority, has argued that if women perceive the normative structures of ethical theory as inadequately grounded in their own experience, then the fault lies with the theory and not with women."[13] As this claim is probably supported by most standard and radical feminists ethics, let us examine it more closely. Let us use the alleged difference in men's and women's moral thinking as an example.

Kant, in an oft-quoted passage, alleges that women do not think in as abstract and rational a way about moral matters as men: "Nothing of duty, nothing of compulsion, nothing of obligation. . . . I hardly believe that the fair sex is capable of principles, and I hope by that not to offend, for these are extremely rare in the male. But in the place of it Providence has put in their breast kind and benevolent sensations, a fine feeling for propriety, and a complaisant soul."[14] Given this alleged difference, Kant's theory—because it holds abstract, rational thinking to be the ideal for moral thinking—implies that women's moral thinking is deficient. Some feminists, on the other hand, agree that men and women think differently. But rather than conclude that this shows that women's thinking is deficient, they reject as inadequate any theory that would dictate that conclusion. Rather than begin with a predetermined, male-oriented theory and then accept the judgments to which it leads, they *begin* with a judgment of the equal (and perhaps even superior) worth of women's thinking and then reject any theory that would deny that judgment. Only in this way, they contend, is women's experience given its due in a male-dominated world.

Whether women and men do think differently—either in general or more specifically about moral issues—is, of course, a factual, psychological question, and one that is controversial. And if they do engage in different moral thinking, one would have to be confident about what those differences were. But if they did give decidedly different importance to different moral concepts (women to caring, for example, and men to justice and rights), this would need to be reflected in any ethical theory that pretended to completeness.

Unlike Wollstonecraft, such feminists call into question the very foundations of what they see as traditional ethical theory. Added to the general moral judgments of minimalist feminist ethics (regarding the equality and worth of women) is a critique of the very approach to ethical theory represented by tradition.

14.5 RADICAL FEMINIST ETHICS

Radical feminist ethics typically proceeds from a broad set of socio-historical-value judgments that locate the problems, not only of women, but of society and civilization at large, in male supremacy. For example:

> We identify the agents of our oppression as men. Male supremacy is the oldest, most basic form of domination. All other forms of exploitation and oppression (racism, capitalism, imperialism, etc.) are extensions of male supremacy: men dominate women, a few men dominate the rest. All power structures throughout history have been male-dominated and male-oriented. Men have controlled all political, economic and cultural institutions and backed up this control with physical force. They have used their power to keep women in an inferior position. *All men* receive economic, sexual, and psychological benefits from male supremacy. *All men* have oppressed women.[15]

As part of this outlook, it is often claimed that the whole of Western philosophy and the ethical theory associated with it is actually part of the system of oppression designed to subjugate women. It is a mistake, for that reason, to try to operate within the confines, say, of traditional ethics (as minimalist feminist ethics and some standard feminist ethics do), to explain the plight of women and to establish the basis for reform. The whole way of thinking characteristic of traditional ethics needs to be transcended. The problem extends to all of the academic fields as well:

> Patriarchal expropriation of "the past" and of memory is accomplished by many means in addition to the media. Not only "history" but all Academic fields erase and reverse women's history. The constant erosion/erasure/distortion of our past is accomplished also through art, through religious feasts and the ceremonies of civil religion, through music/muzak, through the repetitive rituals of family, school, and "social life."[16]

A small percentage of radical feminist ethics takes things one step further, and argues, not that women are equal to men, but that they are in fact superior (whether innately or morally), and in some cases advocates hatred of men (misandry, the counterpart of misogyny):

> Incapable of a positive state of happiness, which is the only thing that can justify one's existence, the male is, at best, relaxed, comfortable, neutral, and this condition is extremely short-lived, as boredom, a negative state, soon sets in; he is therefore doomed to an existence of suffering relieved only by occasional, fleeting stretches of restfulness, which state he can achieve only at the expense of some female. The male is, by his very nature, a leech, an emotional parasite and, therefore, not ethically entitled to live, as no one has the right to live at someone else's expense.
>
> Just as humans have a prior right to existence over dogs by virtue of being more highly evolved and having a superior consciousness, so women have a prior right to existence over men. . . . If all women simply left men, refused to have anything to do with any of them—ever, all men, the government, and the national economy would collapse completely. Even without leaving men, women who are aware of the extent of their superiority to and power over men, could acquire complete control over everything within a few weeks, could effect a total submission of males to females.[17]

Moreover, many say that language itself is a tool of male-supremacist oppression, so that even it needs to be transformed, lest one subtly perpetuate male supremacy through the use of categories and concepts it has spawned for the oppression of women.[18] Male supremacy is thus seen as an oppressive, all-encompassing fog that seeps into every area of personal and social relations. Accordingly, in seeking to dispel this, radical feminist ethics takes on the form of an ideology; calling for a radical transformation of the world; explaining virtually all problems—from racism, sexism, and economic injustice to environmental degradation—in terms of male supremacy.

14.6 FEMINIST OBJECTIONS TO TRADITIONAL ETHICS

Given the importance of the representations of traditional ethical theory in much of feminist ethics, we may concentrate on at least some of the claims made against it.

That traditional ethics historically was written largely by males is true and easily documented. That it was written largely by white males is not true unless we screen out all non-Western ethical theory, along with Western but non-European (e.g., African) thought. That it reflects a male bias may also be true. But that would require a careful examination of the full sweep of traditional ethics. It is possible, as Nietzsche seems to believe, that all moral theories promote the ends of those advancing them,[19] which, if true, would tend to support the feminist critique. The question then would be whether those ends are the ends of groups to which those writers belong (such as males)—or are the ends of those particular individuals advancing the theories, as Nietzsche may intend. It might be that some of traditional ethics reflects a male bias and some of it does not, in which case the question would be which theories do and which do not, and if some do to what extent they do. One would also need to consider the possibility that traditional ethics is unintentionally biased.[20] That it tends to be misogynistic may also be true. But, again, that could be justifiably concluded only after a detailed examination of traditional ethics. It might, of course, reflect a male bias without being misogynistic. Misogyny is hatred of women, and an ethical theory might be biased in favor of males without exhibiting hatred of women. And it might be biased without necessarily being part of a systematic attempt by men to subjugate women. Much of discrimination is gradually institutionalized in ways of which both beneficiaries and victims are largely unaware. The point is that there is a plurality of distinguishable claims here, each of which would require close historical, philosophical, and perhaps psychological examination fully to evaluate.

Both standard feminist ethics and radical feminist ethics often cite a supposedly masculine conception of rationality as a feature of traditional ethics. Certainly much of Western ethical thought, from Plato and Aristotle through Kant and Rawls, gives heavy weight to rationality. Whether it is precisely the same sense of rationality in each case might be questioned, of course. Plato, for example, emphasizes reason as the highest of the faculties of humankind, and the life of the reason as the morally best life; whereas Rawls and contractarians emphasize what groups of self-interested persons skilled at choosing means to ends would decide in situations of collective decision making. In any event, another tradition, represented by Augustine and Aquinas, places faith (understood as a virtue), not reason, at the heart of ethics, with a fully moral life not even being fully possible (at least for Augustine) without it. Others, like Hume, as epitomized in his famous saying that "reason is, and ought only to be the slave of the passions," expressly disavows reason as a foundation of morality, appealing not to faith but to sentiment, namely, sympathy. And looking at Eastern thought, Lao Tzu and Chuang Tzu in ancient China decidedly de-emphasized rationality, certainly in anything like a Western sense. Mo Tzu stressed universal love as the basis of ethics, not the pronouncements of abstract reason. Early Buddhist ethics in India not only did not extol reason as the way to enlightenment, it expressly sought to transcend rational, conceptual thought altogether—a more profoundly nonrational (though not for that reason irrational) requirement even than Hume's deflating of reason. In the orthodox, Vedic tradition of India, on the other hand, the *Bhagavad-Gita* counsels disengagement from the consequences of actions in a way that goes against the grain of even the more limited form of rationalism represented, in its preoccupation with the assessment of costs and benefits, by utilitarianism.

Another recurring theme of both standard and radical feminist ethics is that traditional ethics emphasizes principles and rules, which is said to be a distinctively masculine emphasis. Again, moral legalism—the grounding of right and wrong ultimately upon principles or rules—is, as indicated earlier (see section 1.8), a prominent theme in much of Western ethics. But those theories that represent an ethics of virtue rather than an ethics of conduct do not stress principles in this way. This is true of the theories of Plato, Aristotle, Augustine, Hume, and the numerous contemporary writers who see themselves as having revived the insights of those earlier traditions. And even those like Aquinas, who give an important role to the notion of law, do so in the explication of how it is we must live to attain virtue, where virtue is the central concept.[21] Even Kant—often taken to be the paradigm moral legalist—can be read as setting forth principles only as a way of explaining how it is we achieve the one thing good in itself, a good will. Again, Taoism, early Buddhism, and the ethics of the *Bhagavad-Gita,* in various ways subordinate—or seem to dispense altogether with—rules and principles as the guide to a good life. Even in a heavily rule-oriented ethics like Confucianism, Mencius (a follower of Confucius) locates the ground of ethics, not in reason, but in feeling:

> If you let people follow their feelings (original nature), they will be able to do Good. This is what is meant by saying that human nature is good. . . . The feeling of commiseration is found in all men; the feeling of shame and dislike is found in all men; the feeling of respect and reverence is found in all men; and the feeling of right and wrong is found in all men.[22]

This does not mean, once again, that many and even most of the central strands of ethical theory do not emphasize rules and principles, but it does mean that there is much more diversity in the history of ethical theory than such generalizations would suggest.

In any event, both standard feminist ethics and radical feminist ethics often assume that traditional ethics is, at the least, male-biased, and at the worst, misogynistic and part of a systematic attempt to subordinate women. If this could be shown, and if it could be shown further that these considerations establish the need, not only for different moral judgments, but also for a different ethical theory as well, then this would be of momentous importance for ethics. One way in which one might attempt to establish that need would be to maintain, as some feminists seem to, that there are some moral judgments that cannot be made according to traditional ethics.

Let us consider three possible judgments of intrinsic *value*. The first might be taken to be representative of a sexist perspective; the second, of a minimalist feminist ethical perspective; the third, of a radical feminist ethical perspective. These do not by themselves constitute moral judgments, but they are the sorts of judgments that might readily be appealed to in support of moral judgments by those theories (axiological and weak-deontological) that consider value relevant to the determination of rightness.

1. Women are inferior to (i.e., inherently less good than) men.
2. Women are equal to (i.e., inherently as good as) men.
3. Women are superior to (i.e., inherently better than) men.

Perhaps the claim is that judgments like (1) can be (and are) made by traditional ethics, but that judgments like (2) and (3) cannot. If, as we are assuming, these represent judgments of *intrinsic* value, none of them are made by some of the most conspicuous Western theories of value (because of limitations of space, we shall confine ourselves here to Western theories). The prime candidates for possessors of intrinsic value have been such things as pleasure, knowledge, virtue, and happiness. They have not been males and females *per se*, individually or collectively. Nor have alleged differences in the intrinsic values of males and females been cornerstones upon which such theories have been based.

It may be that the claim is not that judgments like (2) and (3) cannot be *made* by traditional ethics, but that they cannot be *justified* by traditional ethics; and that only feminist ethics can justify them. We cannot assess this claim in detail, other than to observe that there is little consensus about how to establish judgments of intrinsic value. Such judgments have sometimes been taken to be incapable of proof, and other times to have been self-evident. There is no readily apparent reason in the *value theories* themselves that would either require or preclude any of these judgments. Many would argue that (1) is, if incapable of proof, at least falsifiable, and would cite the comparative assessment of the qualities of men and women as a way to show its falsity. Others might deny that any of the three is self-evident. Still others, like emotivists, would deny that any of these even has truth value. Since they are but expressions of feelings or attitudes, they are therefore neither true nor false. The point is that it would seem open to virtually anyone from the standpoint of traditional value theory to either affirm or deny any of (1), (2), or (3), and therefore that no new theory is required to enable one to affirm some of them and deny others.

Let us add to them three prescriptive judgments of the sort that often qualify as moral judgments:

4. Men ought to dominate women.
5. Men and women ought to be treated equally.
6. Women ought to dominate men.

Does traditional ethics support judgments like (4) and preclude judgments like (5) and (6)? Again, we should probably take the claim to mean that judgments like (5) and (6) cannot be substantiated by traditional ethics and, for that reason, require feminist ethics.

Let us consider utilitarianism, a theory most would probably regard as typical of traditional ethics. According to utilitarianism, whether any of (4), (5), and (6) could be substantiated would depend upon the central value judgments involved and a correct estimate of consequences. Assuming a hedonistic theory of value, for example (which holds that pleasure alone has intrinsic value), and an account that identifies happiness with a life that maximizes the balance of pleasure over pain, utilitarianism would support judgment (4) only if it could be shown that the domination of women by men maximized happiness. But if, on the other hand, as some radical feminists think, women should dominate men, then (6) could be substantiated if it could be shown that female supremacy would maximize happiness. In each case, which of these judgments would be justified in terms of the theory would depend upon the consequences of the conduct prescribed. *Utilitarianism as a theory doesn't tell us what those consequences are.* Thus the theory, *per se,* neither justifies nor precludes any of these judgments. One could advocate on utilitarian grounds that men should dominate women because that allegedly would have the best consequences. But one could just as easily argue that women should dominate men for the same reason. Advocates of both views could agree on all points of detail on the nature of utilitarian theory, but they would come out with radically different moral judgments if they differed in their estimates of the consequences of different forms of gender discrimination.

If utilitarianism is a reasonably standard traditional axiological theory, W. D. Ross's intuitionism is a reasonably standard deontological theory. According to this theory, there are self-evident *prima facie* duties determined by the various relationships in which we stand to others. On the basis of these we make non-intuitive judgments of actual duties (see section 12.2). It is the relationship in which we stand to a person, not the person's gender, that determines whether we have a *prima facie* duty, say, to benefit or refrain from harming the person. It is hard to find anything in these *prima facie* duties (of loyalty, gratitude, justice, beneficence, non-maleficence that requires that we affirm judgments like (4) and deny judgments like (5). In fact, absent factual judgments about what would promote the intrinsic goods of virtue, knowledge, and happiness, Ross's theory arguably would support (5). If you conjoined the duty of beneficence with a factual claim to the effect that women are less intelligent, less virtuous, and incapable of the same happiness as men, then one might well justify (1) and (4). But nothing in the *theory* of what makes acts right dictates this, and you could just as easily—if you could establish similar factual claims about the comparative deficiencies of men—justify (3) and (6).

If this is correct, it would seem as though various positions on gender relations could be supported by representative traditional ethical theories appealing to different right-making characteristics.

14.7 INTERPRETING FEMINIST ETHICS

There is a further claim that is sometimes made on behalf of feminist ethics, however. It is, in effect, that it is required to promote women's interests. This might mean only that a feminist ethics will defend judgments like (2) and (5), and that setting forth and defending those judgments is part of what will promote a nonsexist society. If so, then, as we have seen above, traditional ethics can do that equally well, provided it can justify the relevant judgments. But the claim in question might be taken in a stronger sense. It might be taken to mean that it is the interests, well-being, and flourishing of women that is the highest good or the end of ethics. This would make of feminist ethics a form of macro ethics (the view, you recall, that it is the interests or well-being of collectivities that is of primary ethical concern—in this case the collectivity being women as a group). Even then, however, it would not mark feminist ethics as different in kind from traditional ethics. In fact, it would make it a form of teleological ethics (see section 2.6), in which the fixed end, or highest good, is defined in terms of the well-being of one gender. Just as some Marxists hold that the end of conduct should be judged as the well-being of a collectivity (the proletariat), and some environmentalists hold that it should be the well-being of the biotic community at large, feminists holding this view would say that the standard of rightness within the theory is the extent to which conduct promotes the interests of women. If, in the process, it also promotes the interests of men (or of animals, or of the environment), that would be fine, for these interests might well coincide. But they might not. And in any event, promotion of their interests would not be the objective. The objective would be the furtherance of women's interests.

There is, finally, one other way this claim might be interpreted. It might be interpreted to mean that ethical theory itself ought not to be neutral; that a criterion of adequacy of *any* ethical theory is whether or not it is designed in such a way as to place women's interests in the forefront. According to this view, the fact that traditional ethics is neutral on this issue (in the sense, as we have seen, that it could support either sexist or feminist moral conclusions when conjoined with the appropriate factual and value judgments) would be a defect. Ethical theory should be partisan.[23] It must be designed from the start in such a way as to showcase women's issues. If the claim were mainly that theory must give equal consideration to women's issues, that would not serve to distinguish feminist ethics from traditional ethics, since, as we have seen, traditional ethics can do that. It must be part of what determines the adequacy of a theory in the first place that it gives a preeminent position to women's issues (and thereby becomes an active part of the campaign to further those interests socially).

This would mark a significant difference between feminist ethics and traditional ethics. For it would reflect a metaethical judgment that ethical theory should be enlisted in a substantive moral cause, the cause of women. The effect would be to absorb ethical theory into substantive ethics. Theorizing about ethics would then be expected to conform to that particular substantive moral judgment. This would preclude there being any vantage point from which to evaluate competing theories (for example, Marxism and environmentalism) if they were designed around different moral judgments. It may be, in the end, that there is no such vantage point. If so, then we seem committed to a thoroughgoing relativism. But that conclusion could confidently be asserted only after a thorough examination of complex epistemological, linguistic, and perhaps metaphysical issues.

Even then, however, there is no substantive judgment that feminist ethics, so designed, could advance that could not also be defended from the standpoint of traditional ethics. Thus, while the importance of feminist ethics (and remember, we are talking only about feminist ethical *theory* and not the many other things that might included under this heading) must not be underestimated, many of its most far-reaching claims are sociological, psychological, and political rather than philosophical; and many of its philosophical claims are epistemological or metaphysical rather than ethical. Many of these claims, if true (and they cannot all be true, of course, because many of them conflict), would require a radical rethinking of the relations between males and females as well as of the most basic institutions of society. In some cases, they would require a rethinking of the international order as well—not to mention the place of both women and men in the broader ecosystem. Such rethinking would be especially important if the claim is true that men and women's moral thinking is different and is reflected in different "moralities." It is no depreciation of the importance of these issues to say that it has not been shown that these claims require any radical reconceptualization of ethical theory itself.[24]

Notes

1. Virginia Held, "Feminism and Moral Theory," in E. F. Kittag and D. Meyers (eds.), *Women and Moral Theory* (Savage, MD: Rowman & Littlefield Publishers, Inc., 1987), p. 126.

2. Annette Baier, "Trust and Antitrust," *Ethics* 96 (January 1986): 259. The reference to Carol Gillian is in light of her influential book, *In a Different Voice: Psychological Theory and Women's Development* (Cambridge, Mass.: Harvard University Press, 1982), in which she documents what she represents as two different themes in moral experience, one (predominantly masculine) that appeals to principles, the other (predominantly feminine) that emphasizes caring and relatedness.

3. I shall speak of what theories "hold" rather than of what they assert, to cover the possibility that certain of the propositions are implied rather than expressly set forth.

4. One might take this possibility to be suggested by the following passage: "Since feminist approaches to morality are suspicious of rather than eager to offer highly abstract theories and simple principles, they are more likely to emphasize methods of moral inquiry and processes of moral improvement than to propound finished, comprehensive theories." See Virginia Held, "Feminist Moral Inquiry and the Feminist Future," in Virginia Held (ed.), *Justice and Care: Essential Readings in Feminist Ethics* (Boulder, CO: Westview Press, 1995), p. 166.

5. *Vindication of the Rights of Woman* (New York: Modern Library, 2001). First published in 1792. Page references will be included in the text.

6. That is, if their rights are not respected; if women's rights are natural rights, then they have them whether they are respected or not.

7. Simone de Beauvoir, *The Ethics of Ambiguity* (New York: Citadel Press, 1962), p. 37.

8. Milton Mayeroff, *On Caring* (New York: Harper & Row, 1971), pp. 75–76.

9. Lao Tzu, *Tao Te Ching*, tr. Stephen Mitchell (New York: Harper & Row), Ch. 10.

10. Nel Noddings, *Caring: A Feminine Approach to Ethics & Moral Education* (Berkeley: University of California Press, 1984), p. 9.

11. Sara Ruddick, *Maternal Thinking: Toward a Politics of Peace* (New York: Ballantine Books, 1989), p. 129. Future page references will be included in the text.

12. Nel Noddings, *Caring*, p. 1.

13. E. Frazer, J. Hornsby & S. Lovibond (eds.), *Ethics: A Feminist Reader* (Oxford: Blackwell, 1992), p. 5.

14. Immanuel Kant, *Observations on the Feeling of the Beautiful and the Sublime,* tr. John T. Goldthwait (Berkeley: University of California Press, 1960), p. 81.

15. "Redstockings Manifesto," 1969, from *Women's Liberation: Major Writings of the Radical Feminists* (New York, 1970), p. 113. Republished in Barbara A. Crow (ed.), *Radical Feminism: A Documentary Reader* (New York: New York University Press, 2000), pp. 223–226.

16. Mary Daly, *Gyn/Ecology: The Metaethics of Radical Feminism* (Boston: Beacon Press, 1990), p. 349.

17. Valerie Solanas, "SCUM (Society for Cutting Up Men) Manifesto," in Barbara A. Crow (ed.), *Radical Feminism*, pp. 216–217. Many feminists reject the idea of domination by women or men.

18. Probably most feminists agree that "sexist" language abounds; not all people, however, see it as playing quite as central a role as some radical feminist ethicists do.

19. See Friedrich Nietzsche, *Beyond Good and Evil*, in Walter Kaufmann (ed.), *Friedrich Nietzsche: Beyond Good and Evil* (New York: Vintage Books, 1966), p. 99.

20. Alison Jaggar writes: "In our present social and intellectual circumstances, it is more than likely that ethics that is not done with an explicitly feminist consciousness will embody at best unintentional forms of male bias." See her "Feminist Ethics: Projects, Problems, Prospects," in Claudia Card (ed.), *Feminist Ethics* (Lawrence: University Press of Kansas, 1991), p. 97.

21. Virtue is the central concept for Aquinas, despite his espousal of the elements of a Divine Command Theory (see section 6.9).

22. From "The Book of Mencius," in Wing-Tsit Chan (ed.), *A Source Book in Chinese Philosophy* (Princeton: Princeton University Press, 1973), p. 54.

23. Theory understood in this way may be considered a part of so-called "critical theory." Regarding the understanding of critical theory as found in feminism and other theories, see Michael Root, *Philosophy of Social Science* (Oxford: Blackwell, 1993), Ch. 10.

24. There may be some recognition of this in the claim that ". . . as feminist ethics has become established as an area in its own right within the study of ethics, there has also been a blurring of the boundaries between feminist ethics and the rest of ethics." See Samantha Brennan, "Recent Work in Feminist Ethics," *Ethics*, Vol. 109, No. 4, July 1999, p. 858.

Discussion Questions

1. Section 14.2 lists forty-eight propositions of a wide variety of sorts in terms of which the distinctions among minimalist, standard, and radical feminist ethical theories are drawn. Which among the propositions do you agree with? Which do you disagree with? How would you support your agreement or disagreement?

2. Wollstonecraft maintains that women can suffer degradation even while (and, indeed, because), they are given special consideration. How? Do you agree? If you are (or were) a woman, and were on the *Titanic*, what would you do when they said, "Women and children first" in loading the lifeboats? Is that a fair question in evaluating Wollstonecraft's point? If so, why? If not, why not?

3. What is an ethics of caring? How does it represent a standard feminist ethics? Do you agree with Sara Ruddick that the experience of mothering provides a basis for ethics?

4. On the basis of what you have studied thus far, how would you evaluate the claim that traditional ethical theory is part of a system for the subjugation of women?

5. Section 14.6 suggests that many (and perhaps most) ethical theories could be used to support a variety of positions on gender relations. Do you find that convincing? If so, might those theories still be part of a system that is oppressive to women? If not, how would you argue that they don't support a variety of positions on gender relations?

6. Given the possibilities discussed in section 14.7, what do you think is the most plausible way to interpret feminist ethics?

> *The most characteristically and peculiarly moral judgments that a man is ever called on to make are in unprecedented cases and lonely emergencies, where no popular rhetorical maxims can avail, and the hidden oracle alone can speak.*[1]
> **William James**

15 CHAPTER | Contextualism: An Ethics of Pragmatism

15.1 A DEWEYAN APPROACH TO ETHICS

In this chapter, I shall sketch the rudiments of a theory that seems to me more promising than those hitherto considered. It is suggested in some measure by the writings of the American pragmatist, John Dewey (1859–1952), though never stated by him in the form in which I shall present it. Its historical antecedents go back to Aristotle, the Stoics, St. Augustine, and Kant, with kindred approaches in the twentieth century in Ross's intuitionism and continental situation ethics. Although it has much in common with moral particularism, it provides an alternative to both particularism and legalism. I consider it an ethics of pragmatism, and following Dewey's orientation shall call it "moral contextualism."

15.2 SUBJECTIVE, ACTUAL, AND ACTIONABLE RIGHTNESS

I observed earlier (section 11.2) that few people seriously doubt that some acts are morally right and others wrong; that is, few people are moral skeptics. Even fewer are moral nihilists and deny outright that there is any such thing as morality. Moreover, almost any ethical theory can distinguish what is right from what is merely thought to be right. Few believe that merely thinking an act right makes it so.[2]

Now let me introduce some distinctions. Let us call what you think is right **subjective rightness** and what *is* right (whether believed to be so or not) **actual rightness**.[3]

Simply doing what you think is right is not particularly meritorious; people sometimes do terrible wrongs convinced they are in the right. Much depends on why you think an act is right and on whether you have good grounds for so thinking (if you flip coins to decide which acts are right, those you choose will be subjectively right, but you will not have good reason for believing them to be right because there is no good reason to believe that flipping coins provides sound moral guidance).

Only acts that are justifiably believed to be right are **actionably right**; that is, justifiably performed.[4] But just as what is subjectively right may differ from what is actually right, so may what is actionably right. You might have good reason to believe that an action is right but be mistaken. Let us see how, using utilitarianism for purposes of illustration.

For most legalist theories, as discussed in section 2.1, actual rightness is what accords with the particular principle the theory espouses.[5] Thus, for act utilitarianism, an act is actually right if and only if it accords with the principle of utility (just as for Kantianism an act is actually right if and only if it accords with the categorical imperative, and so on with other principles). The problem is, we may not know when an act accords with the appropriate principle. We can be mistaken even if we have taken great care in the making of a judgment, and even when we have good reason to believe that we made the right choice.[6]

Suppose you are an act utilitarian. You calculate the consequences of the alternatives in a particular situation and estimate their value in light of all the available information you can gather. If you then choose the act likeliest to maximize value, your choice (from a utilitarian standpoint) will be actionably right. It will be justified because you have made the best judgment you can in that situation.

But you still might be mistaken. Because of unforeseeable circumstances, the act could bring about less good than another. It could even bring about great harm. No matter how careful you are, you may err in such estimates (if only because your knowledge of consequences is always limited).

In this way, an action that is actionably right might nonetheless fail to be actually right. Although it would require a separate examination to show this possibility for each of them, most (though not all) ethical theories allow this possibility (Kant's is a possible exception; he speaks as though with sufficient care in applying the categorical imperative you can accurately determine your actual duty).

So if you want to be moral, you will strive, as consistently as you can, to do what is actually right. That, in turn, will involve trying both to determine what is actionably right and to act in accordance with that assessment.

Although we still might be mistaken, that is the best we can do. We cannot reasonably be held accountable for failing if what we do turns out not to have been actually right (although we can virtually always be held accountable for not trying).[7] This bears importantly on our judgments of people. Our judgments of whether people are praiseworthy or blameworthy depend on more than just whether what they do is actually right. They depend in large measure on whether what they do is actionably right—that is, on whether they justifiably believe what they are doing is right (as well as on their motives and intentions).

This much might be granted by any theory that recognizes a distinction between actionable and actual rightness. It is in the particulars of what enters into the determination of actionable rightness that contextualism diverges from other theories.

15.3 THE CONTEXTUALIST ALTERNATIVE

Contextualism emphasizes the immediate situation in which judgments are made, as does particularism. And like legalism, it gives a role to rules and principles. But whereas legalism and particularism are theories about actual rightness, contextualism is a theory about *actionable* rightness. It contends that you simply cannot know what is actually right much of the time, so you must make the best judgments you can from a perspective of limited knowledge and understanding. And this means judging each situation on its merits.

Let us consider more specifically what this judging involves.

When you act, you try to change the world in certain ways. But as shown in section 6.7, you may distinguish the inner world of your own thoughts and feelings from the outer world of other people, objects, animals, the environment, and the universe as a whole (including God and other supernatural beings, if there be such). In these terms, you are usually trying to change certain aspects of the external world when you act.[8] But if what I said earlier (section 15.2) is correct, all you can be sure of is *trying* to change the external world in desired ways. You have no guarantee of success, even with many simple acts.

If you tell a friend something, you normally want the friend to believe you; that is the desired change. But whether or not that happens is not altogether within your control. If someone else tells him differently, or he thinks you are kidding—or worse yet, thinks you are trying to deceive him—he may not believe you. Or suppose you are intent on getting an "A" on an exam, so you study hard, do extra reading, and work late. Whether you succeed still depends on such things as your having a clear head, which you might not have if you are taken ill or lose sleep because your neighbors partied all night; and it depends, in any event, on the exam's being fair.

So I propose that our obligation in particular situations is not to change the external world; it is rather, *to try* to do so, and to try as carefully and responsibly as possible; and to do so in ways that are morally best. In this, contextualism exists as part of a long tradition that includes, in their various ways, the Stoics, St. Augustine, and Kant—as well as followers of the *Bhagavad-Gita* in Eastern thought.

But there is another dimension to every situation you encounter, the part that is internal. You yourself—your thoughts, feelings, memories, and character—are part of every such situation.

Even if you fail to produce the external consequences you intend (or, before that, fail in the performance of the intended act itself, as sometimes happens), your thoughts, feelings, motives, and intentions can transform the situation. You can try to foster those that tend toward self-absorption, mistrust, selfishness, greed, envy, insensitivity, and violence. Or you can foster those that tend toward respect, consideration, caring, compassion, and nonviolence. This much is within your power. You can *always* do this with regard to yourself, and you can always *try* to encourage the same in others. So you can always make some contribution toward making yourself into one sort of person rather than another; that dimension of every situation is within your control.

15.4 ELEMENTS OF THE MORAL SITUATION

The complexities of moral situations are sometimes so great as to not lend themselves to detailed specification, but we can identify a few of their general features.

In practically every situation we encounter society's rules, practices, and customs. They are, so to speak, part of the external world. As relativists emphasize, they represent the product of centuries of social living, and whatever degree of harmony exists in a society is owed in some measure to them. In addition, other rules, associated responsibilities, and duties often grow out of specific roles you may be playing at the time. You may have various duties as a military officer, or as an elected official, or as a night watchman; you may have various responsibilities as a mother or father or husband or wife. The youth in Sartre's example (section 1.8) felt pulled by both duty to his mother and a responsibility to help liberate his homeland.

There will also often be claims that must be taken into account, including both those you have on others and those others have on you. I have argued (section 13.4) that these claims can always be expressed in terms of the right and wrong ways of treating others, or of being treated by them. Nevertheless, the language of rights is fitting here, and we may say that relevant rights must be taken account of in our moral reckoning.

In addition, there will be what we might call (following Kant) maxims growing out of previous judgments we have made. These arise because of universalizability. Contextualism holds that to judge one act right or obligatory is to commit yourself to judging the same of any other act unless you can show relevant dissimilarities between the two.[9] So in addition to societal rules and rules defining specific duties in the various roles you find yourself playing, there are maxims such as "I am committed to judging all acts of this sort wrong unless I can show relevant dissimilarities among them."

How much weight should you give to these, and what do you do when they conflict, as they often may? There is no final answer to this, and certainly no formula by which to answer it. Specifically, no rule or principle invariably holds the key. Dewey is helpful here on the role of rules and principles in a contextualistic approach:

A moral principle, such as that of chastity, of justice, of the Golden Rule, gives the agent a basis for looking at and examining a particular question that comes up. It holds before him certain possible aspects of the act; it warns him against taking a short or partial view of the act. It economizes his thinking by supplying him with the main heads by reference to which to consider the bearings of his desires and purposes; it guides him in his thinking by suggesting to him the important considerations for which he should be on the lookout.

A moral principle, then, is not a command to act or forbear acting in a given way: *it is a tool for analyzing a special situation,* the right or wrong being determined by the situation in its entirety, not by the rule as such.[10]

Sometimes what you decide is right on balance will involve following a principle, but often it will not. And if it involves following a rule in one context, it may involve following a different rule in another, even if the two contexts are roughly similar.[11] But when it does involve following a rule, that will be because the context is deemed to require it, not because the rule has prior claim on you. *No rule or principle reigns supreme as the final, absolute moral authority.*

Unlike egoism and utilitarianism, contextualism is nonconsequentialist. It does not deny that consequences are relevant; it just says they are not *all* that is relevant. There is, in addition to consequences, the relevance of the goodness of certain acts themselves—such as kindness, fairness, caring, compassion, and love; and of their associated thoughts, motives, and intentions. These represent a goodness we are capable of realizing in practically every situation.

Insofar as unmediated consequences can be known, they should be weighed along with the assessment of the whole situation; they are, after all, properties of the acts we are judging. But as we have seen, we can never know all of an act's unmediated consequences—and sometimes cannot forecast them with much confidence even for the short run.

Mediated consequences, in contrast, are not properties of acts alone, at least they are not properties on a par with unmediated consequences. Rather than being discovered by objective investigation, they are a matter of judgment (see section 9.10). One must decide in any given case whether to weigh them. This itself, I suggest, is a moral decision. Whether or not we count certain mediated consequences among an act's consequences *itself* has consequences—and is an act whose rightness must be assessed in addition to the rightness of the act prompting the initial deliberation. And there is no rule or formula by which to do this.[12]

Most of the considerations emphasized by traditional ethical theories may be relevant in a given situation.[13] But there is no assurance they will always merit the same weight. Sometimes following a particular social rule is called for, sometimes not. Sometimes giving priority to rights or sacrificing one's own good for another's, will seem right. But sometimes not.

15.5 NURTURING GOODS

We cannot make people moral any more than we can make them happy. But we can nurture in them those tendencies that are capable of guiding them to a realization of their moral potential.

Morality, I am proposing, is a creative, cooperative enterprise whose end is to better the world. It is not ultimately a matter of making claims against one another and finding ways to enforce them (although legitimate claims are among the morally relevant aspects of many situations, particularly in social ethics). It is not, in the end, a matter of rights, nor of acquiring for ourselves as much as we can of affective goods such as pleasure. It is, rather, a matter of trying to realize, in ourselves and others, *nurturing goods* such as caring, considerateness, compassion, sympathy, and love. For these traits stand the best chance, I maintain, of issuing into conduct that will actualize the maximum potential good in every situation in which we must decide and act.

To be sure, we cannot know that these goods will in fact be furthered by what we do; that is a matter of consequences, hence largely beyond our control. But we can always transform any situation we are in to the extent of making their realization the governing consideration. Insofar as we do that, it provides a perspective from which to assess the many, varied features of traditional theories as they are deemed relevant. In other words, we often give weight to deontological considerations as the immediate situation demands; but we do so in the faith that it will help us realize what is best for the situation.[14] That choice itself then becomes part of the situation and gives effect to its underlying motivation and intention. That much is under our control.

This account makes the notion of goodness central, which in turn makes contextualism, in its account of conduct, ultimately axiological. The actionably right seeks always to bring good into existence. But it acknowledges the relevance not only of rules and principles, but also of standard deontological considerations such as fairness, consistency, and rights.

I propose, then, that when we deliberate about the morally right thing to do, in the end we choose according to what we judge that particular situation to require. This judgment of what the particular situation requires is basic. It is a function of different contextual features in different situations, which may include any of the standard teleological and deontological considerations. They are appraised from the standpoint of the realization of nurturing goods. When we make a moral choice after making every reasonable effort to understand the situation in all its complexity, our choice is actionably right.

Does this account make contextualism an ethics of virtue or an ethics of conduct?

The pragmatic spirit is relevant here. It is part of that spirit to oppose sharp dualisms, a spirit it shares with much of recent feminist ethics. Approaches that emphasize exclusively either conduct or character can maintain a sharp distinction between the ethics of virtue and the ethics of conduct. But for any theory that gives a place to both, as I believe any complete theory must, the matter is one of emphasis. In the view I am presenting, the emphasis is on character. Behind this lies the conviction that if we become compassionate, caring, and loving people, we will, over the course of a lifetime, engage the world in ways that stand the best chance of enabling us to do what is actually right. This, although it is not its principal aim, will in turn stand the best chance of fostering peace of mind, if not happiness.

So contextualism is an ethics of virtue. It has an ethics of conduct (as, if I am correct, any complete ethics of virtue must), and that ethics is axiological. But its primary emphasis is on excellence of character, which it sees as growing out of actionably right conduct. Such conduct, although valued partly in itself, can in turn then serve as a means to future right conduct.[15]

15.6 A KANTIAN OBJECTION

But doesn't this argument presuppose a principle (such as "Always do what is best" or "Always assess each situation on its merits")? And doesn't that make contextualism a form of legalism after all?

It is the sort of objection a legalist such as Kant has in mind when he says that one could not

> . . . give poorer counsel to morality than to attempt to derive it from examples. For each example of morality which is exhibited to me must itself have been previously judged according to principles of morality to see whether it is worthy to serve as an original example, i.e., as a model.[16]

This objection is serious, and it goes to the heart of many of the most serious issues in contemporary moral philosophy. For that reason, we cannot hope to resolve it conclusively here.

But I want to suggest some reasons for thinking that Kant has things reversed in this passage. These reasons are related to the emphasis on personal decision that we considered in the previous chapter.

15.7 THE IMPORTANCE OF PERSONAL DECISION

Consider again the Kantian example of the murderer who comes to your door asking the whereabouts of a person you are hiding (see section 9.10). What should you do? Kant says one should never lie. The categorical imperative in his view (though not in the view of many of his followers) requires *without exception* that you tell the truth. If, however, you think telling the truth would be wrong in this case, you have three choices. You can

1. Reject the categorical imperative
2. Allow that it has exceptions, of which this is one
3. Try to show that in this case it does not lead to the conclusion Kant thinks it does

Whichever you do, it is you who must decide, and it is you who must decide in the first place whether lying in this particular situation would be justified (if you do not think that, then of course there is no problem).

A principle such as the categorical imperative can only show you that *if* you accept it,[17] you must accept the moral conclusions to which it leads when you apply it. It cannot decide for you what to do.

Recall Sartre's example (section 1.8) of the youth torn between joining the Free French Forces to fight against the Nazis and staying to look after his mother. Sartre says,

> Who could help him choose? Christian doctrine? No. Christian doctrine says, "Be charitable, love your neighbor, take the more rugged path, etc., etc." But which is the more rugged path? Whom should he love as a brother? The fighting man or his mother? Which does the greater good, the vague act of fighting in a group, or the concrete one of helping a particular human being to go on living? Who can decide *a priori*? No book of ethics can tell him.[18]

Take, further, the case of utilitarianism. Even if we assume we know the consequences of following it, we may feel uneasy about accepting some of the conclusions to which it apparently leads. Consider a hypothetical situation set forth by William James. If it were the case that

> . . . millions [are] kept permanently happy on the one simple condition that a certain lost soul on the far-off edge of things should lead a life of lonely torture, what except a specific and independent sort of emotion can it be which would make us immediately feel, even though an impulse arose within us to clutch at the happiness so offered, how hideous a thing would be its enjoyment when deliberately accepted as the fruit of such a bargain.[19]

James is asking us to reflect on whether we could accept such a bargain; permanent happiness in exchange for consigning one person to a "life of lonely torture." This, to be sure, is not a choice anyone will ever have to make; but hypothetical cases of this sort can help us to understand the full implications of a principle.

The point is that even if we know that a principle applies and know what it requires, we still have to decide in the end whether to take what it requires as actionably right. This is true of any principle. In the preceding example, we may feel it unfair that millions should enjoy happiness at the expense of one; utility here seems to conflict with fairness. We could say this shows the principle to be mistaken, and could abandon utilitarianism. Or we could recognize two principles, utility and justice, and say that sometimes they conflict. Still further, we could cling to the principle of utility, but say it admits of exceptions, of which this is one. Or, of course, we could cling to the principle without qualification and say that, yes, it would be right to purchase the happiness of millions at such a dreadful cost. But it is we who must decide—not only what to do, but also what it would be right to do.

This may seem obvious on reflection, but its bearing on the problem at hand may not be so obvious. It means, I suggest, that in the end we inevitably come back to deciding individual cases in all their particularity.[20]

It is we who must decide (1) whether a given principle applies, (2) what the principle requires in this particular case, (3) which takes precedence if it conflicts with another principle, (4) whether this case is an exception to the principle, or (5) whether this case shows that the principle is adequate. To make such a decision is to act. And as with any other act, the decision may be right or wrong. But that determination cannot be made by appeal to a principle, because the situation that creates the need to make such a determination is one in which the relevance of principles is called into question.

I believe, for these reasons, that Kant is mistaken that we need to presuppose principles before judging particular cases (what he calls "examples"). I say this partly because of the difficulty justifying principles, but partly also because I believe that in the end the ultimate justification of our judgments— including those expressing principles—must be moral experience. If we do not just see that certain acts are right and others wrong in *some* situations, no amount of rational argument is likely to convince us of the validity of principles prescribing or prohibiting them.[21]

Indeed, I would suggest that it is the other way around. We can justify principles, in the last analysis, only by looking at what they commit us to in actual and hypothetical cases and then deciding whether that would be right. This justification, while not empirical in the sense of being scientifically testable, is nonetheless *experiential,* in that it directs us to the felt demands of concrete situations. We cannot be surer of any principle, I suggest, than of the rightness of the individual actions it prescribes.

15.8 INTUITION OR EMOTION?

What is the nature of this moral experience? The tendency among particularists has been to say either that it is an intuition of an objective quality or that it is characterized by a feeling or emotion of approval or disapproval occasioned by what one perceives or believes about the situation.[22]

As important as this issue is theoretically, I believe it is undecidable. It represents, as pragmatists might say, a difference that does not make a difference. Let me explain by means of an example.

William James once described a dispute that arose on a camping trip.[23] It concerned a man trying to get a look at a squirrel on the far side of the trunk of a tree. As the man moved around the tree, the squirrel moved also, always keeping to the opposite side. The controversy was over whether the man was going around the squirrel. Clearly he is not, James says, if by that you mean that first he is in front of the squirrel, then to the side of it, then behind it, and finally in front again; for the squirrel sees to it that the man never gets behind it. But clearly he is going around the squirrel if we mean that he is first to the north of the squirrel, then to the east, then to the south, and then to the west, because that much follows from the fact that he is going around the tree and the squirrel is on the tree. Once we clarify what is meant by "going around," there is no more to be said. Continuing disputation is pointless. According to pragmatism, many philosophical disputes are like this.

I suggest this is also true of the issue at hand. What one person reports as an intuition of rightness may be precisely what another reports as an emotion of approval.

An awareness of the difficulty of distinguishing one from the other is acknowledged by the intuitionist Richard Price in the eighteenth century:

> Some emotion or other accompanies, perhaps, all our perceptions; but more remarkably our perceptions of right and wrong. And this . . . is what has led to the mistake of making them to signify nothing but impressions, which error some have extended to all objects of knowledge; and thus have been led into an extravagant and monstrous skepticism.[24]

And in the twentieth century this awareness has been acknowledged even more charitably by the emotivist[25] A. J. Ayer, who believes that our moral judgments express feelings and emotions:

> What of those who claim that they do observe ethical properties . . . not indeed through their senses, but by means of intellectual intuition? . . . I am surely not entitled to assume that all these honest and intelligent persons do not have the

experiences that they say they do. It may be, indeed, that the differences between us lie not so much in the nature of our respective experiences as in our fashion of describing them. I do in fact suspect that the experiences which some philosophers want to describe as intuitions, or as quasi-sensory apprehensions, of good are not significantly different from those that I want to describe as feelings of approval.[26]

This suggests that these experiences are describable in either cognitive or emotive terms, perhaps with equal plausibility. But it may not be decidable once and for all which description is correct. And it may not matter, other than for purely theoretical purposes. Of greatest practical importance is to consistently make sound moral judgments, not to decide whether what is experienced when one does is an intuited quality or an emotion.

15.9 CONSCIENCE AND HUMAN NATURE

What is important is not so much how we describe such experiences as that we recognize that we are so constituted as to experience morality in the direct way common to both intuitionist and emotivist accounts. This thought was captured by Bishop Butler when he said,

> . . . we naturally and unavoidably approve some actions, under the peculiar view of their being virtuous and of good desert; and disapprove others as vicious and of ill desert. That we have this moral approving and disapproving faculty is certain from our experiencing it in ourselves, and recognizing it in each other. . . . It is manifest [that the] great part of common language, and of common behaviour over the world, is formed upon supposition of such a moral faculty; whether called conscience, moral reason, moral sense, or Divine reason; whether considered as a sentiment of the understanding, or as a perception of the heart, or, which seems the truth, as including both.[27]

Butler here describes part of what he takes to be our moral constitution (our nature as moral beings). He seems to want to have it both ways, of course, in his tantalizing reference to a "sentiment of the understanding" and "perception of the heart," which would appear to give equal recognition to both cognitive and emotive elements. But the central point is that something in us just experiences some things as right and others as wrong.

Rather than speak of either intuition or emotion, however, I would speak here, as Butler does, of **moral discernment**.[28] Although it is generally neglected by contemporary moral philosophers, I find the notion of **conscience** appropriate for this capacity for moral discernment.[29]

If we are all so constituted as to have a conscience—if, as Butler puts it, we "naturally and unavoidably" approve of some actions and disapprove of others—then conscience provides a universal ground of morality. This does not make morality absolutistic because it does not affirm an eternal and unchanging moral principle. Contextualism denies that any principle, absolutistic or relativistic, invariably determines actionable rightness even within the same culture. It does not even affirm anything about the origins of conscience, which may very well have evolved in humans over the centuries, along with the idea of morality. But it does mean there is a foundation for morality in human nature. This is the element of truth in natural law ethics.

15.10 CONTEXTUALISM AND RELATIVISM

Does this universal ground of morality lead to uniformity in basic moral judgments of actionable rightness? This we cannot know without extensive and
sophisticated study of the moral experience of people generally, both in our own
society and in others. To undertake such a study would require winnowing out ill-
considered, unreflective, and biased judgments to see whether there is an identifi-
able core of well-founded judgments on which all people agree. If there should be,
as I suspect there might well be, it would not be their being agreed on that makes
them actionably right (as the relativist might maintain). It would be the verdict of
reflective, critical conscience in the many situations in which people make moral
assessments that makes them actionably right. But there might not in fact be such
agreement. Contextualism concedes the possibility that not all individuals or
groups will find the same actions actionably right. Various individuals and
groups may be so situated as to have different access to facts, or to have their perception of facts understandably, and perhaps even justifiably, influenced by
different—and perhaps equally plausible (or implausible)—cultural conditions.
In other words, it concedes that what is actionably right can vary from person to
person or society to society. It has this much in common with relativism.

But this does not make contextualism relativistic. There can be such variation even on absolutist theories. If there is a God and God's commands determine what is right, then different individuals and groups nonetheless arrive at
conflicting—and yet perhaps equally well-founded—judgments about what
that is. In any event, relativism, we recall, is a theory about actual rightness
(see section 11.2). It, no less than universalism, presumes that what is actually
right can be widely known—or, at least, that enough can be known *about* actual rightness to be certain that it varies from person to person or culture to
culture in the way relativism contends. To establish that contextualism is relativistic would require showing that, according to it, differing judgments about
the actual rightness of the same acts or practices can both be correct.

Relativism insists that different moral judgments about the same conduct
may be equally true (or correct or valid). A kind of action could at one and the
same time correctly be judged to be right (because, for example, practiced by
one society) and wrong (because prohibited by another society). The same is
true in the case of extreme relativism for an act approved by one person and
disapproved by another. This possibility violates universalizability, and one
might, indeed, take such violation to be necessary and sufficient for a theory's
being relativistic.[30]

According to contextualism, however, when we judge an act right or obligatory we must be prepared to judge the same of any other act if we cannot
point to relevant dissimilarities between the two. Often there are many acts of
which this is true, and we judge them all the same way. But sometimes—in
those "unprecedented cases and lonely emergencies" of which William James
speaks in this chapter's epigraph—there are none. The situation may be so
unique that we never encounter another like it. That does not matter. Universalizability commits us only to judging cases similarly *if* there are no relevant
dissimilarities between them. It gives no indication of whether there are in fact
any such dissimilarities in any given case.

Often there are conspicuous dissimilarities between situations. But sometimes there are not, and yet subtle differences may warrant differing moral judgments—just as such differences may often warrant different aesthetic judgments in our assessment of works of art.[31] Indeed, W. D. Ross, a particularist with respect to actual (though not with regard to *prima facie*) obligations, says in this regard that "the judgment as to the rightness of a particular act is just like the judgment as to the beauty of a particular natural object or work of art."[32]

To be sure, there is no guarantee that any two people will judge the same act to be actionably right. But there is no such guarantee in any theory, relativistic or universalistic.

There remains much to be done in filling out this brief sketch of contextualism; in particular, more needs to be said about what it means, in a contextualist account, for actions to be justifiably believed to be right, because it is this that renders them actionably right, and that justification is not provided by principles. It also remains to explain the operation of conscience more fully, and how it reflects human nature in such a way as to constitute a universal ground of morality. But we have the outline—the program, if you like—of an alternative to the standard traditional theories. I conclude, however, with one final thought that may help to provide the larger perspective of which contextualism is a part.

15.11 UNIVERSALISM AND A MORAL POSTULATE

Contextualism recognizes, as I have said, the diversity of moral beliefs and practices. It believes we would do well to try to understand other cultures in the event they have achieved a deeper insight into morality than our own. We must be open to the possibility, not only that we may be enriched by such broadening, but also that it may prove morally enlightening as well.

Suppose all peoples do this. Is there any assurance it will bring them closer together? There is no assurance, but I believe it will.

Another pragmatist, Charles Sanders Peirce, characterized truth as that opinion that is fated to be eventually agreed on if inquiry is carried on long enough by competent inquirers. The object of that opinion, he said, would be the real.[33]

Although Peirce was speaking mainly about scientific truth, I propose something similar here, except I call it a **moral postulate.** It is that if humankind strives to understand the human situation in all its complexity, and to follow the guidance of morality as steadfastly as it does science, moral judgments will eventually converge. The resultant moral beliefs and practices will be actionably right; not for all *conceivable* rational beings, as Kant held, but for humans living in this world, interacting with one another and with other living things and the environment. We cannot say for certain that those beliefs will also constitute what is actually right. If we cannot derive an "ought" from an "is," we cannot say conclusively that even what is agreed on by all people is right. But it is the best we can do. And we may, with as much confidence as we can achieve in this matter, postulate that it constitutes the actually right.

What will those moral beliefs be? We must wait and see, of course, toward what assessments moral judgments tend to converge. But my guess is that at the heart of those beliefs will be found to be something close to William James's conviction that, "There is but one unconditional commandment, which is that we should seek incessantly, with fear and trembling, so to vote and to act as to bring about the very largest total universe of good which we can see."[34]

Notes

1. William James, *The Principles of Psychology,* vol. 2 (New York: Dover, 1950), p. 642. Originally published 1890.

2. An exception would be any radically subjectivistic theory contending that right and wrong simply represent feelings of approval or disapproval, and that *any* such feelings represent what is actually right or wrong.

3. Subjective and actual rightness, as here characterized, should be distinguished from subject*ivism* and object*ivism*. Subjectivism and objectivism are theories about the nature of actual rightness. To call an act subjectively right, on the other hand, says something about the speaker; that he or she believes the act is right. To call an act actually right, says, in effect, that the act is right, and warrants the designation "right" for some reason beyond (or instead of) the fact that it is thought to be right. But it says nothing of what that warrant is. The final account of the nature of actual rightness might be objectivistic, but it might not.

4. As I conceive the notion of actionable rightness, it is not enough that *someone* might be able to produce a justification for believing the act in question is right; the agent who contemplates performing the act must justifiably hold that belief. This does not mean that each and every time we act we must think through all the possible moral ramifications of what we do. Sometimes (as when we get out of the right-hand side of bed, as we may have done for years), it is enough that we have no reason to believe the act is wrong.

5. The matter is more complicated with legalist theories that advance several rules or principles, no one of which invariably takes precedence over the others. See the discussion of Ross's theory in section 12.2.

6. What I am saying applies particularly to our assessment of proposed acts of our own. When we are judging previous acts of our own, or those of others, there arguably may be cases in which the chances of our being mistaken are minimal.

7. I say "virtually" always, because trying to do something is itself doing something, although that "something" is something different from actually doing the thing that one is trying to do. (Trying to lift a boulder, or to play Chopin's Minute Waltz in less than a minute—is different from actually doing either of these things.) Even successfully trying to do something depends on some conditions beyond our control, such as that we do not die first.

8. Sometimes, through acts of omission, we may try to keep the world from *being* changed in certain ways. In either case, our concern is to try to bring about a world that is different from what it otherwise would have been had we not acted.

9. R. M. Hare speaks of these as decisions of principle, but I think the notion of maxim is more appropriate.

10. *John Dewey: The Later Works, 1925–1953,* vol. 7: 1932, *Ethics,* ed. Jo Ann Boydston (Carbondale: Southern Illinois University Press, 1985), p. 280.

11. This does not, however, mean that it violates the principle of universalizability, because two situations can be relevantly dissimilar even though generally similar.

12. Insofar as those consequences may be both mediated and unmediated, as they conceivably might be, the problem is replicated, showing further the difficulties in rendering plausible any purely consequentialist ethical theory.

13. Meaning considerations such as self-interest, the happiness of others, consistency, and fairness; if there is a God, and God is known to issue certain commands, those will always be relevant, providing he gives reasons for them.

14. There is a parallel here with Butler's view that while humans are deontologists, God is a utilitarian—in that he has ordered things in such a way that it is for the best that humans are so constituted as to sometimes act on deontological considerations. I am suggesting that we sometimes act on deontological considerations, not because God has ordained that we do (though if there is a God, that may be so, though what I am saying does not rest on that assumption), but because we feel that so doing is what will be best for that situation—where that is not a deduction from a principle but an assessment of what the situation demands.

15. Thus there is a directive, of the sort I spoke of in section 3.11, to be virtuous; but it does not antecede judgments of rightness in particular cases; it springs rather from the hypothesis, rooted in moral experience, that cultivating excellence of character is the best route to consistent moral living.

16. Immanuel Kant, *Critique of Practical Reason and Other Writings in Moral Philosophy,* tr. Lewis White Beck (Chicago: University of Chicago Press, 1949), p. 68.

17. And, of course, are sincere in your acceptance, and attempt to follow it in your judgments and actions.

18. Jean-Paul Sartre, *Existentialism and Human Emotions* (New York: Philosophical Library, 1957), p. 25.

19. William James, "The Moral Philosopher and the Moral Life," in *William James: The Essential Writings,* ed. Bruce Wilshire (New York: Harper Torchbooks, 1971), p. 297. Originally published 1891.

20. Unless, of course, there is an infinite regress of principles.

21. We may sometimes conclude subsequently that we were mistaken in what we took to be right. Whether we can always be mistaken, or whether there are in morality certain indubitable basic judgments (analogous to basic propositions in epistemology) that invariably reflect what is actually right, I have not here tried to resolve.

22. Intuitionists of this sort are saying that we intuit a property of the situation or possible act in question, rather than the truth of a proposition, as in the case of philosophical intuitionism considered in Chapter 12.

23. William James, *Essays in Pragmatism* (New York: Hafner, 1954), p. 141. From *Pragmatism. A New Name for Some Old Ways of Thinking,* 1907.

24. Richard Price, *A Review of the Principle Questions of Morals,* in L. A. Selby-Bigge, ed., *British Moralists,* vol. 4 (Indianapolis: Bobbs-Merrill, 1964), Ch.1, Sect. III, p. 124.

25. Emotivists hold that moral judgments express feelings or emotions of approval or disapproval and that this is their distinctive feature *qua* moral judgments.

26. A. J. Ayer, *Philosophical Essays* (London: Macmillan, 1963), p. 239.

27. Joseph Butler, *The Analogy of Religion, Natural and Revealed, to the Constitution and Course of Nature* (London: Society for Promotion of Christian Knowledge), pp. 325–326.

28. It may very well be that just as our sense organs respond to the outer world in sense perception, our emotions similarly respond to certain kinds of conduct in ourselves

and others; and that just as the former are necessary for adapting to physical surroundings, the latter are necessary for harmonizing with others in the moral dimension of our existence. This, I suspect, points out the direction to a proper analysis of the concept of conscience.

29. If, that is, it is broadened to include our capacity for moral discernment in general, and not only with regard to our own conduct, as conscience is often popularly understood.

30. Relativism is often understood to violate the principle of universalizability. See William K. Frankena's suggestion in *Ethics*, 2d ed. (Englewood Cliffs, N.J.: Prentice-Hall, 1973), p. 109. Relativists could, however, though implausibly (in my judgment), adhere to universalizability by insisting that being approved by a speaker or society is a relevant aspect of an action, so that any time apparently conflicting judgments are made, there will always be relevant dissimilarities between the two cases.

31. Imagine a painting identical to the "Mona Lisa" except that the eyes are a quarter of an inch closer together. A small difference, to be sure, but it would almost certainly affect our aesthetic valuation.

32. W. D. Ross, *The Right and the Good*, p. 31.

33. *Collected Papers of Charles Sanders Peirce*, vol. 5: *Pragmatism and Pragmaticism*, ed. Charles Hartshorne and Paul Weiss (Cambridge, Mass.: Belnap Press of Harvard University Press, 1960), p. 268.

34. William James, "The Moral Philosopher and the Moral Life," in *William James: the Essential Writings*, ed. Bruce Wilshire (New York: Harper Torchbooks, 1971), p. 297. Although this quotation could be taken to express a principle from which we then derive what is right in particular cases, it can also be taken, as I intend here, to refer to what we find required of us in particular cases, before recognition of a principle and underivatively from any such principle. This is a particularist as opposed to a legalist understanding of it.

Discussion Questions

1. What is the distinction among subjective, actual, and actionable rightness?

2. Do you agree with section 15.3 that our obligation in particular situations is not to change the external world but to try to do so? If this should be true, would it make any difference to our moral judgments and conduct?

3. What do you make of Dewey's claim that a moral principle is "*a tool for analyzing a special situation?*" How does this differ from the way in which moral legalism seems to understand principles (as discussed in Part III)? Which approach seems to you most plausible (note: you should guard against thinking a view is correct just because it is the last one discussed in this book!).

4. Do you think personal decision has the importance attributed to it in section 15.7? Or do you think that view vests too much power in personal decision? Do you think your answer to either of these questions represents a personal decision?

5. Do you think it can be settled whether moral judgments represent intuitions or are simply expressions of emotion? If so, where do you think the truth lies? If not, what implications does that have for standard metaethical theories of the sort considered in Chapter 13?

6. Do you find the moral postulate described in section 15.11 plausible? Why, or why not?

Appendix

We may summarize what we covered in Chapter 2. The activities of evaluating and directing presuppose the concepts of goodness and rightness respectively and the associated notions of value judgments and prescriptive judgments. Each of these, in turn, may be either moral or nonmoral.

Theories maintaining that moral rightness (expressed in prescriptive moral judgments) depend solely on goodness (expressed in value judgments) may be defined as follows:

    I. *Axiological:* An act is right if and only if it actualizes at least as great a balance of good over bad (in the act itself, or its consequences, or in the combination of the two as any other alternative available to the agent).

Deontological theories can then be defined as follows:

    II. *Deontological:* Any theory about moral rightness that is not axiological.

        A. *Strong:* Goodness is relevant to the determination of moral rightness.
        B. *Weak:* Goodness is relevant to the determination of moral rightness but not decisive.

Similarly, theories about the role of consequences in determining moral rightness can be defined as follows:

    III. *Consequentialist:* Moral rightness is determined solely by the consequences of actions.

    IV. *Nonconsequentialist:* Any theory of morally right conduct that is not consequentialist.

        A. *Strong:* The consequences of acts are irrelevant to the determination of moral rightness.
        B. *Weak:* The consequences of acts are relevant to the determination of moral rightness but not decisive.

The most prominent axiological theories appeal to the goodness of the consequences of action, and can be defined as follows:

    V. *Teleological:* An act is right if and only if it produces at least as great a balance of good over bad in its consequences as any other act available to the agent.

The principal forms of teleological theory are

    A. *Micro ethics:* Rightness is determined by the value of consequences for individual persons.

1. *Ethical egoism:* An act is right if and only if it produces at least as great a balance of good over bad *for the agent* as any other act available to the agent.
2. *Utilitarianism:* An act is right if and only if it produces at least as great a balance of good over bad in its consequences *for all people (and perhaps sentient beings) affected* as any other act available to the agent.

B. *Macro ethics:* Rightness is determined by the value of consequences for the relevant *collectivity* or *superentity* (considered as an organic unity).

Teleological theories of all types define obligatory actions as acts that produce a *greater* balance of good over bad for the relevant entities than any other alternative.

Again, the axiological theories that have received most attention in recent moral philosophy have been consequentialist. But there may be important non-consequentialist axiological theories as well, particularly some forms of the ethics of virtue.

Most deontological theories are nonconsequentialist. In fact, deontological theories are sometimes contrasted with consequentialism, as though all deontological theories were nonconsequentialist. But they need not be. Many theories of justice are consequentialist, for example, in maintaining that the consequences of acts and policies determine what is just. But what is relevant about the consequences is not solely their goodness, but the way that goodness is distributed—a deontological consideration.

The interrelations among these can be seen in the following diagram:

	Axiological	Deontological
Consequentialist	Teleological Ethical egoism Utilitarianism Macro ethics	"Utilitarianism" of rights Some theories of justice
Nonconsequentialist	Contextualism Some forms of virtue ethics	Kantianism Divine command theory Some rights-based theories Ethical intuitionism

Index

Abortion, 58–59, 155–156, 197–198
Abraham, 66, 78
Absolutism, 152, 160
Acquired qualities, 25
Act utilitarianism (AU), 124–125, 127–128
Actionable rightness, 225–226
Actual rightness, 225, 236n3
Actual rule utilitarianism (ARU), 125–127
Adam, 48
Altruism, 60, 63
Analytic statements, 80
Anthony, Susan B., 159
Anti-realism, 188
Applied ethics, 10
Aquinas, Saint Thomas, 63, 66, 168, 217, 218
  divine command theory, 73–75
  natural law ethics, 91–93
  virtues, 48
Aristotle, 218
  Aquinas and, 91
  deontologism, 37–38, 182
  happiness, 45
  human nature, 67
  justice, 136
  moral perceptions, 35–36
  and nonconsequentialism, 18
  and particularism, 14
  virtue, 33–35, 45
Assertorical imperatives, 105
Augustine, Saint, 84, 217, 218
  divine command theory, 72–73, 79
  virtue and, 46–48
Autonomy
  of ethics, 185
  Kantian principle of, 112–113
  reductionism and, 186–187
Axiological theories
  consequentialist versus nonconsequentialist, 18
  defined, 17, 239
Ayer, A. J., 232–233

Baier, Annette, 206
Beauvoir, Simone de, 211
Benedict, Ruth, 50
Bentham, Jeremy, 121, 129, 182
Bhagavad-Gita, 31, 32, 217, 218
Britain, 157–158
British New Guinea, 158
Buddha, 213
Buddhism, 217, 218
Butler, Joseph, 51, 62–64, 233

Cardinal virtues, 92
Caring, ethics of, 212–215
Caste system, 32
Categorial definitions, 181
Categorical imperatives, 106–113
Catholicism, 85
Character
  qualities of, 25
  virtue and, 22–23

Christianity
  commandments, 67–68
  God and nature, 85, 90
  human nature, 67
  love, 46–48, 71–73
  natural law ethics, 90–91
  war, 72–73
Chuang Tzu, 217
Cicero, 85
Cognitivism, 189–190, 200–202
Collectivities, 20–21
Commandments of God. *See also* Divine command theory
  perspectives on, 67–68
  rightness and, 79–80
Commutative justice, 137
Compassion, 213
Complete moral realism, 188
Conduct
  character and, 22–23
  ethics of, 22–23, 30, 39–41
  guiding and directing, 4
  language as guide for, 200–202
  virtue and, 29–31, 39
Confucianism, 218
Conscience, 233, 238n28, 238n29
Consequences
  balance of good and bad, 19
  calculation of, 123
  foreknowledge of, 128–130
  mediated versus unmediated, 130–131, 228
Consequentialism
  attraction of, 117–118
  axiological, 18
  defined, 18, 239
  deontological, 118
  Kantianism versus, 113–114
  problems with, 128–132
  utilitarianism, 119, 126
Consistency
  justice, 138–139
  Kantianism, 100, 103, 106–107, 109–111, 113
Contextualism
  conscience and human nature, 233
  Deweyan approach, 224
  explained, 226–227
  Kantian objection, 230
  moral experience, 230–233
  moral situation, 227–228
  nurturing goods, 228–229
  relativism versus, 234–235
  universalism and, 235–236
Contractarianism, 171–174
Cooper, John, 37
Corrective justice, 136
Courage, 28
Creation, 90, 93
Cross-categorial definitions, 181
Cultural diversity, 149–150, 157–158, 163n4
Cultural relativism, 151, 155–157, 163n4, 164n8

Darwall, Stephen, 196–197
Declaration of Independence, 15
Definitional naturalism, 189, 193–195
Definitions
  categorial and cross-categorial, 181–182
  indefinability, 186–188
  noncognitivism and, 198–199
  philosophical, 181
Deontic terms, 180, 182–184
Deontological theories
  Aristotle, 37–38
  consequentialist, 118
  defined, 17, 239
  strong versus weak, 17–18
Dependency thesis, 150, 160
Descriptive statements, 5–6
Desert, justice based on, 141
Desire
  for happiness, 45–48
  justice based on, 141, 143
  satisfaction of, 62–64
  Stoic view of, 87–89
  for virtue, 87–89
Dewey, John, 14, 224–225, 227–228
Dharma, 32
Diderot, Denis, 57–58
Distributive justice
  consistency, 138–139
  defined, 137
  deontological consequentialism, 118
  egalitarian, 139–140
  explained, 137–138
  pure procedural justice, 143–145
  selective, 140–143
  three conceptions, 139–143
Divine command theory (DCT)
  explained, 69
  goodness of God, 76–79
  human judgment, 72–76
  idealism, 71–72
  as moral legalism, 13, 69
  problems for, 70–71, 176–177
  rightness, 79–80
Divine permission theory (DPT), 68–69
Divine will theory (DWT), 82n18
Dogmatical intuitionism, 36
Duty
  Kantianism, 102–103, 110
  prima facie, 169
  Stoicism, 89–90
  virtue and, 40

Economic justice, 140
Economics, 7
Egalitarian justice, 139–140
Egoism. *See* Ethical egoism; Psychological egoism
Eliot, George, 130
Emotion, 232–233, 237n28
Emotivism, 198
Empiricism, 86

241

Entitlement terms, 180, 183–184
Epicureans, 21
Epicurus, 55, 60, 182
Equalitarian principle, 142–143
Error theory, 196–197
Eskimos, 158
Ethical absolutism, 152, 160
Ethical conditionalism, 150
Ethical egoism
    defined, 20, 55, 240
    explained, 55–56
    as moral legalism, 13
    objections, 56–58
    paradoxical nature, 58–60
Ethical intuitionism, 168–169,
    187–192, 232–233
Ethical naturalism, 170–171, 185,
    189–192
Ethical relativism
    absolutism versus, 152, 160
    abuse of women, 154
    basic beliefs, 157–160
    contextualism versus, 234–235
    cultural diversity, 149–150,
        157–160
    explained, 150–151
    logic and truth, 161–162
    moral disagreements, 154–157
    moral tolerance, 162
    multiculturalism, 153–154
    universalism versus, 151–153,
        160–161
Ethical universalism, 151–153,
    160–161, 235–236
Ethics
    autonomy of, 185
    of caring, 212–215
    of conduct, 22–23, 30, 39–41
    of love, 13
    micro versus macro, 21–22
    of nonviolence, 13
    normative versus applied, 10
    as study of moral philosophy, 1
    theological, 190
    of virtue, 18, 22–23, 26, 29–31,
        38–41, 229
Euthyphro (Plato), 70
Evaluation
    activity of, 3–4
    prescription in relation to,
        17–18
Eve, 48
Evil, 73, 84
Ewing, A. C., 185
Existentialism, 14
Experience, role of, 230–233
Extra-categorial definitions,
    182, 184
Extreme relativism, 151, 155–157
Extrinsic goodness, 77
Extrinsic value, 119–121, 191

Fact/value distinction, 193
Fascism, 7, 20
Feminist ethics
    as advocacy, 220–222
    caring, ethics of, 212–215
    minimalist, 208, 209–212
    overview, 207–209
    radical, 209, 215–216
    standard, 208, 212–215
    versus traditional ethics, 206,
        215–220
    Wollstonecraft and, 209–212
Foot, Philippa, 117
Formal principle of justice (FJ), 139
Fortitude, 92

Francis, Saint, 47
Frank, Anne, 44

Gandhi, Mohandas, 52, 159
Gilligan, Carol, 206
God. See also Commandments
    of God; Divine command
    theory
    as creator, 90
    goodness of, 76–79
    as highest good, 46–48
    Kantianism, 112
    as loving, 78–79
    natural law, 85
    natural law ethics, 96–97
    omnipotence of, 77
    omniscience of, 77
    Stoic view, 86, 89
    will of, 68–70, 82n18
Golden mean, 35
Golden Rule, 118
Goldman, Emma, 159
Good will
    intrinsic value of, 120
    Kantianism, 101–102
    as virtue, 40
Goodness. See also Highest good
    balance of, with harm, 19
    of collectivity, 20–21
    concept of, 2–3
    definability of, 187–188
    ethical naturalism, 190–191
    extrinsic, 77
    of God, 76–79
    idea of, 27–28
    intrinsic, 76–77, 191
    nurturing goods, 228–229
    rightness and, 15–17
    virtues and, 25–26
Gorgias (Plato), 136, 192–193
Greek view of human nature, 67
Grotius, Hugo, 97

Happiness
    contingency of, 101
    goodness as, 38
    as highest good, 120
    Kantianism and, 100–101
    satisfaction of desire, 63–64
    supernatural, Aquinas on, 91
    virtue and, 43–45
Hedonism, 120
Held, Virginia, 206
Highest good
    perfectionism and, 45–46
    permanence of, 46–48
Hindu ethics, 31–33
Hitler, Adolf, 20, 129, 142
Hobbes, Thomas, 60
Homosexuality, 94–95
Human condition, 150
Human nature
    conscience and, 233
    ethical relativism, 150
    Greek versus Christian views, 67
    Stoic view, 87–89
Human rights, 96
Humanity, principle of, 111–112
Hume, David, 115, 192, 213, 217,
    218
Hypothetical imperatives, 104–105

Ideal rule utilitarianism (IRU),
    125–127, 127–128
Imperatives, 104–106
Imperfect procedural justice,
    144, 173

Incas, 158
Indifference, 87–88
Individual relativism. See Extreme
    relativism
Individualism, 33
Infanticide, 158
Intellectual virtues, 34, 92
Intrinsic goodness, 76–77, 191
Intrinsic value, 119–121, 191
Intuitionism. See Ethical
    intuitionism
Iran-Iraq war, 67
"Is" versus "ought," 94–95,
    192–193
Isaac, 66, 78
Islam, 67–68

Jägerstätter, Franz, 26
James, William, 224, 231, 232,
    234, 235–236
Jesus, 71–72, 159, 213
Job, 44
Judaism, 67
Judgments
    cognitivism and, 189–190,
        200–202
    criteria for, 9–10
    divine command theory and,
        72–76
    moral, 6–7, 9–10
    noncognitivism and, 197,
        200–201
    nonmoral, 6–7
    normative, 5–6
    prescriptive, 5
    value, 4–5
Justice. See also Distributive justice
    as cardinal virtue, 92
    consistency, 138–139
    corrective, 136
    economic, 140
    egalitarian, 139–140
    formal principle of, 139
    as harmony, 28
    idea of, 135–137
    legal, 141
    moral legalism and, 13
    natural, 136
    political, 141
    procedural, 137, 143–145
    retributive, 141
    utilitarianism and, 122

Kant, Immanuel, 97–98, 100,
    147n9, 182, 215, 218, 230
Kantianism
    categorical imperatives, 106–113
    consequentialism versus,
        113–114
    duty, 102–103, 110
    foundation of morality, 100–101
    good will, 40, 101–102
    happiness, 100–101
    hypothetical imperatives,
        104–105
    imperatives, 104–106
    as moral legalism, 13
    objective principles, 103–106
    principle of autonomy, 112–113
    principle of humanity, 111–112
    problems with, 114–115
    rationality, 103, 107–110,
        114–115
    subjective principles or maxims,
        106–107
Khomeni, Ayatollah, 67
Kierkegaard, Søren, 68

King, Martin Luther, Jr., 47, 160
Knowledge
    intrinsic value of, 120
    wisdom compared to, 1
Koran, 67

Language
    categorical and cross-categorical
        definitions, 181–184
    categories of terms, 180–181
    conduct guided by, 200–202
    definability of "good," 187–188
    ethical and non-ethical terms,
        184, 186–188
    extra-categorial definitions, 182,
        184
    male oppression through, 216
    meaning of terms, 179–180
    moral versus descriptive,
        200–201
    use versus meaning, 199
Lao Tzu, 212, 217
Law, 7, 96
Lawrence, D. H., 48
Legal justice, 141
Lewis, C. I., 118
Logic, and relativism, 161–162
Lorenz, Konrad, 94
Love
    ethics of, 13
    of God, 46–48
    God's, 78–79
    idealism and, 71–73
    self-, 60
    virtues of, 47

MacIntyre, Alasdair, 25
Macro ethics, 21–22, 240
Maimonides, 47
Marcus Aurelius, 89
Marxism
    distributive justice, 140–141
    as frame of reference, 7
Masai, 154
Master morality, 49, 136
Maternal Thinking (Ruddick),
    213–214
Maximin rule, 173
Maxims, 106–107, 114
Mean, Aristotelian, 35
Meaning, of language, 199
Mediated consequences,
    130–132, 228
Mein Kampf (Hitler), 142
Mencius, 218
Meno (Plato), 179
Merit, justice based on, 141–142
Metaethical relativism, 164n16
Metaethics, 146
Metaphysical naturalism, 185
Micro ethics, 21–22, 239
Mill, John Stuart, 12, 15, 121,
    123–125, 168, 182, 183
The Mill on the Floss (Eliot), 130
Milton, John, 48
Minimal moral realism, 188
Minimalist feminist ethics, 208,
    209–212
Misandry, 216
Misogyny, 217
Mo Tzu, 217
Moore, G. E., 18, 80, 125, 129,
    168, 179, 191–192
Moral coherentism, 174–175
Moral contextualism. *See*
    Contextualism
Moral discernment, 233

Moral epistemology, 146
Moral experience, 230–233
Moral judgments, 6–7, 9–10
Moral knowledge, 197
Moral legalism, 12–14, 69, 85,
    145–146, 177, 218
Moral particularism, 14
Moral perceptions, 35–36
Moral philosophy, reasons for
    studying, 1–2
Moral postulate, 235
Moral principles
    coherentism, 174–175
    contextualism, 227–228
    contractarianism, 171–174
    diversity of, 167
    ethical naturalism, 170–171
    in ethical thought, overview
        of, 218
    intuitionism, 168–169
    original position, 171–174
    problems in applying rules and,
        175–177
Moral problems
    examples, 7–10
Moral realism, 97, 188–189
Moral rightness. *See* Rightness
Moral situation, elements of,
    227–228
Moral tolerance, 162
Moral virtue. *See also* Virtue
    Aquinas on, 92
    desirability of, 51–53
    good will and, 40
    habituation of, 34
    right conduct and, 39
Morality
    ground of, 160–161
    master versus slave,
        49–51, 136
    nature and, 84–85
    origins, 2
    rights, 183
    situation for, 227–228
Mothering, 214
Motives, 101–102
Multiculturalism, 153–154
Mussolini, Benito, 20

Nagel, Thomas, 167
Natural justice, 136
Natural law ethics
    Christianity, 90–91
    duty, 89–90
    explained, 84–85
    God's role, 96–97
    homosexuality, 94–95
    as moral legalism, 13, 85
    nature in, 85
    outline of theories, 86
    problems for, 93–95
    sexual harassment, 95
    social, political, and legal
        philosophy, 96
    Stoicism, 86–90
Natural qualities, 25
Naturalism, 170–171, 185
Naturalistic fallacy, 186,
    192–193
Nature, 84–85
Nazi Germany, 20, 26
Needs, justice based on, 141
New Testament, 67, 72
Nietzsche, Friedrich, 49–51,
    136, 217
Noddings, Nel, 70, 213, 214
Noncognitivism, 197–201

Nonconsequentialism, 18, 239
Nonmoral judgments, 6–7
Non-natural property, 187–188
Non-naturalism, 187–188
Nonviolence, 13
Normative ethics, 10
Normative judgments, 5–6
Nurturing goods, 228–229

Objective principles, 103–106
Objectivism, 155, 236n3
Obscenity, 149
Oedipus, 176
Old Testament, 67, 68, 74
Omnipotence, of God, 77
Omniscience, of God, 77
Ontological naturalism, 189, 195
Open-question argument (OQA),
    194–196
Oppression, of women, 215–216
Organic unity, 21
Original position, 171–174
"Ought" versus "is," 94–95,
    192–193

Pantheism, 86
Particularism, 14
Peirce, Charles Sanders, 235
Perceptional intuitionism, 36
Perceptions, moral, 35–36
Perfect procedural justice, 144, 173
Perfectionism, 45–46
Perry, R. B., 190–193
Personal decision, role of, 230–232
Phaedo (Plato), 138
Philosophy, etymology of, 1
Piaget, Jean, 135
Plato, 217, 218
    on collective good, 20
    consistency, 138
    divine command theory, 70
    goodness, 3
    happiness, 43–45
    Hindu ethics compared to,
        31–33
    human nature, 67
    Idea of Good, 27–28
    justice, 135–136
    naturalistic fallacy, 192–193
    and nonconsequentialism, 18
    right conduct, 9, 29–31
    soul's function, 27–28
    virtue, 26–27, 29–31, 43–45
Pleasure
    happiness and, 63–64
    intrinsic value of, 120
    virtue and, 87–88
Political justice, 141
Practical reason, 200
Practical syllogism, 36
Practical wisdom, 33–34, 38
Pragmatism. *See* Contextualism
Prescriptive judgments, 5
Price, Richard, 232
Prichard, H. A., 14
Pride, 48
Prima facie duties, 169
Principle of autonomy, 112–113
Principle of humanity, 111–112
Procedural justice, 137, 143–145,
    173–174
Promise keeping, 108–110,
    121–124
Protagoras (Plato), 135
Prudence
    as cardinal virtue, 92
    imperatives of, 105

Psychological egoism
  Butler on, 62–64
  critique of, 61–62
  explained, 60
Punishment, 136, 141, 143, 147n7
Pure procedural justice, 144–145,
  173–174

Racism, 7
Radical feminist ethics, 209,
  215–216
Rationality. *See also* Reason
  in ethical thought, overview
    of, 217
  as foundation of ethics, 97
  gender and, 147n9, 215, 217
  justice, 138–139
  Kantianism, 103, 107–110,
    114–115
  natural law ethics, 86
  Plato, 33
  Stoicism, 89
Rawls, John, 135, 144,
  171–175, 217
Reason. *See also* Rationality
  Christian natural law ethics, 91,
    93
  functions, 33–34
  as part of soul, 28
Reductionism, and autonomy,
  186–187
Reflective equilibrium, 175
Relativism. *See* Ethical relativism
Religion. *See also specific religions*;
  Divine command theory; God
  as frame of reference, 7
  personal qualities, 25
Retributive justice, 136, 141,
  143, 147n7
Revelation, 91
Rightness
  actionable, 225–226
  actual, 225, 236n3
  commandments and, 79–80
  God's will and, 68–70
  goodness and, 15–17
  subjective, 225, 236n3
Rights
  deontic and value terms,
    183–184
  deontological consequentialism,
    118
  entitlement terms, 180, 183–184
  morality and, 183
  natural law and, 96
  utilitarianism and, 15, 118, 122
Rights-based theories, 15, 209–212
"Ripples in the pond"
  postulate, 130
Ross, W. D., 14, 36, 97, 123,
  168–169, 220, 235
Ruddick, Sara, 213–214
Rule utilitarianism (RU), 124–125
Rules
  contextualism, 227–228
  in ethical thought, overview
    of, 218
  problems in applying, 13–14,
    175–177
  utilitarianism, 123–128

Santayana, George, 1
Sartre, Jean-Paul, 8, 230
Schopenhauer, Arthur, 213
Schweitzer, Albert, 52

Selective principles of justice,
  140–143
Self-interest, 7
Self-love, 60
Seneca, 88
Sermon on the Mount, 67
Sexism, 7
Sexual harassment, 95
Shiite Moslems, 67–68
Sidgwick, Henry, 36, 37
Slave morality, 49
Slavery, 159, 211
Smith, Adam, 56
Social relativism. *See* Cultural
  relativism
Socrates
  on collective good, 20
  and ethical relativism, 159
  trial of, 21–22
  on virtue and happiness, 44
Sons and Lovers (Lawrence), 48
Sophists, 26, 159
Soul
  Aristotelian view, 33–34
  Christian view, 67
  Platonic view, 27–28
Spencer, Herbert, 135–136
Stalin, Joseph, 122
Standard feminist ethics, 208,
  212–215
Standpoint, 213–214
Stoicism, 40, 85, 182
  duty, 89–90
  natural law ethics, 86–89
Sturgeon, Nicholas, 202
Suárez, Francisco, 97
Subjective principles, 106–107
Subjective rightness, 225, 236n3
Subjectivism, 155, 236n3
Supernaturalism, 187
Survival of the fittest, 136
Sympathy, 151, 213

Tahiti, 158
Taoism, 218
Teleological theories, 18, 37, 91,
  119, 239
Temperament, qualities of, 25
Temperance, 28, 92
Ten Commandments, 67
Teresa, Mother, 47
Terminology. *See* Language
Theological ethics, 190
Theological virtues, 91
Theoretical reason, 200
Theoretical wisdom, 33, 38
Theory of Justice (Rawls), 171
Thoreau, Henry David, 51, 159
Tolerance, 162
Torture, 77–79
Toulmin, Stephen, 125
Truth, and relativism, 161–162
Truth telling, 121–122

United States
  human rights and founding
    of, 96
  traffic laws, 157–158
Universalism
  contextualism and, 235–236
  ethical relativism versus,
    151–153
  and ground of morality,
    160–161
Universalizability, 138–139

Unmediated consequences,
  130–132, 228
Use, of language, 199
Utilitarianism
  act, 124–125, 127–128
  actual rule, 125–127
  consequentialism, 119, 126
  defined, 20, 119, 240
  hedonistic versus ideal, 121
  ideal rule, 125–127, 127–128
  intrinsic and extrinsic value,
    119–121
  justice and, 122
  as moral legalism, 13
  problems for, 121–124
  rights and, 15, 118, 122
  rule, 124–125
  types of, 127

Value
  concept of, 2–4
  fact/value distinction, 193
Value judgments
  explained, 3
  prescriptive judgments and, 4–5
Value terms, 180, 182–184
Vedic tradition, 31, 32, 217
Veil of ignorance, 172
*Vindication of the Rights of
  Women* (Wollstonecraft), 209
Virtue
  Aquinas on, 91–93
  character and, 22–23
  conduct and, 29–31, 39
  happiness and, 43–45
  Hindu ethics, 31–33
  human versus theological, 91–93
  intrinsic value of, 120
  kinds of, 25–26
  love and, 47
  mean and, 35
  moral perceptions, 35–36
  Plato on, 26–27, 29–31
  pleasure and, 87–88
  practical syllogism, 36
  Stoic view of, 87–89
Virtue ethics, 22–23, 26, 29–31,
  38–41, 229
Vocabulary. *See* Language

Wants, justice based on, 141
War, 72–73
West Victoria, Australia, 158
Westermarck, Edward, 149
Western culture, 153–154, 164n12
Will. *See also* Good will
  God's, 68–70, 82n18
  as universal lawgiver,
    112–113
Will to power, 49
Wisdom
  knowledge compared to, 1
  theoretical versus practical,
    33–34, 38
  as virtue of leaders, 28
Wolf, Susan, 52
Wollstonecraft, Mary, 209–212
Women. *See also* Feminist ethics
  ethical relativism and abuse
    of, 154
  morality from perspective
    of, 206
  and rationality, 147n9,
    215, 217
Worth, justice based on, 142